BUILDING THE KINGDOM
from the Inside Out

Jean Andrews, PhD

Cover Design by Kirstin Salazar

Interior Design by Kirstin Salazar and Melisha Morris

Illustrations by Margreet Visser 't Hooft, Melisha Morris and Jean Andrews

Interior Layout by Kevin Johns, Chalitphakorn "Tatae" Phrommin and Agnello Vieira

Editors Claire Berninger and Tina VanYzendoorn

Photography by Rami Cherolis

Idea for a community creed credited to Dr. Darius Williams (www.theWordCenterMinistries.net)

Publishing consultant Tom Carroll (www.tomcarrolldesign.com)

ISBN: 979-8-9996905-0-0

This book and our entire lives are joyfully dedicated to
Father God, Jesus Christ, and our dearest Holy Spirit

The team committed to research, test and produce this book and use it for the Glory of God:

Jean Andrews, author and visionary

Mimi Allred, strategies for children

Margaret Barrett, legal advisor and board member

Alexis Brand, strategies for children

Josh Brand, core team leader

Kelley Brink, strategies for children

Scott Brink, financial advisor and board member

Carol Chawla, school resources

JoAnn Daniels, our intercessor

Ursula Delgado, business advisor and troubleshooter

Ashley Gunn, strategies for children

Kalen Lee, strategies for children

Margreet Visser 't Hooft, illustrator

Melisha Morris, designer and illustrator

David Turner, our intercessor

Tina VanYzendoorn, editor

Lucie Veselka, strategies for children

We are deeply grateful for the legacies of Arthur Burk, Randy Clark and John L. Sandford

Table of Contents

My Story

From the first time I felt the atmosphere of love in the heavenly realm, I've dreamed of building communities that were able to bring this culture and fragrance of heaven to earth. At first, I wanted this for myself, then for God, and then for others. Not a good priority list I know, but it's where I started.

When I moved to a new city, I spoke with a pastor about joining his church. He asked me what I wanted from the church. Coming right out of the deepest intent of my heart at the time, I responded that I wanted to be loved for who I am even if I'm not perfect. I could tell by his expression I would probably not fit in his church and he turned out to be right. Seems like I could never measure up or down to expectations in community, no matter how authentic or measured I tried to be.

So went my life for decades until I connected with Sapphire Leadership Group, LLC, (TheSLG.com) and Arthur Burk. As many of the tribe have, I came to SLG bearing trophies earned and junk in my trunk. After tons of hard work, lies renounced, wisdom gained, and critters evicted, I finally began to thrive in community.

Life has not been easy for me. Nothing has been easy, it seems, especially being in community. So perhaps I'm the perfect person to write about how to thrive and build in community. Like a former paraplegic who was healed and learned to walk late in life, who best to teach other adults how to walk? Defying all logic, God chose one of the least in community to teach others about community. And that, my friend, is one of the joys and principles of living in a healthy community. The least has an important role to play for all.

We define a servant or slave as someone who, in their heart, sees themselves as an orphan who cannot trust or expect fathering or mothering and is satisfied with mere survival, dependent on others for their needs to be met. A son, on the other hand, knows he or she has a rich inheritance, secure in the Love of God, mature enough to fight for what is right and empowered to build big and build well.

Goals for This Book

Many of us grew up in homes that did not teach us how to grow our inside character and build our lives using skills and tools based on principles of Wisdom. In the Book of Numbers, we can see the process that Father God led Moses to take the people of Israel through transforming spirits and hearts from slaves in Egypt into sons who knew how to build. *The overarching goal of this book is to resource you, the reader, to establish a culture to grow yourself and others from slaves to sons who can provide a community where God can rest and His Kingdom flourish.*

For an overview of what it's like to mature from a slave to a son of God, see Growth Project 1.1 at the end of Chapter 1. We accomplish this goal to grow and build by:

1. Applying the seven foundational principles of Wisdom from God's Word to our lives. Arthur Burk defines a principle as a universal, non-optional, cause and effect relationship.

2. Working on the missing links in the seven stages of growth to adulthood

3. Solving problems and doing projects we are likely to encounter in family life, careers, and business as we continue to grow and build.

How to Use This Textbook

The seven chapters of this book are organized according to the seven principles of Wisdom and stages of growth, as shown in Table I-1.

Scripture refers to Wisdom as both a person (Proverbs 8) and a concept. When used as a person, we capitalize Wisdom, and when used as a concept, we use lower case.

Chapter	1	2	3	4	5	6	7
Principle of Wisdom	Design	Authority	Truth	Reality	Stewardship	Freedom	Fulfillment
Stage of Growth	Belongingness	Know myself	Right and wrong	Peer relationships	Self-development	Building and standing for right	Be my own person

Table I-1 Seven chapters cover the seven principles of Wisdom and seven stages of growth

How long will it take you to work your way through all seven stages? It took me almost two years to write this book because I had to grow myself at several stages along the way. The time it will take you depends on how much of your growth was skipped. For those not as chewed up as I was, I'd allow about nine to 12 months, assuming you are working with a partner. If you're working alone, it might take longer.

To use the book, start anywhere that makes sense to you. I suggest you first graze through the book to get familiar with how it's organized and what it offers. Then find your current felt need. Keep drilling down until you find the keys you need to grow yourself through this problem. Of course, you can always start with Chapter 1!

Problems usually present themselves when we are trying to build something and hit an obstacle that won't budge. Figure I-1 shows that process, which can lead us to recognize that our inside character needs to grow in some area, which leads to a search for a principle or value to help us get there.

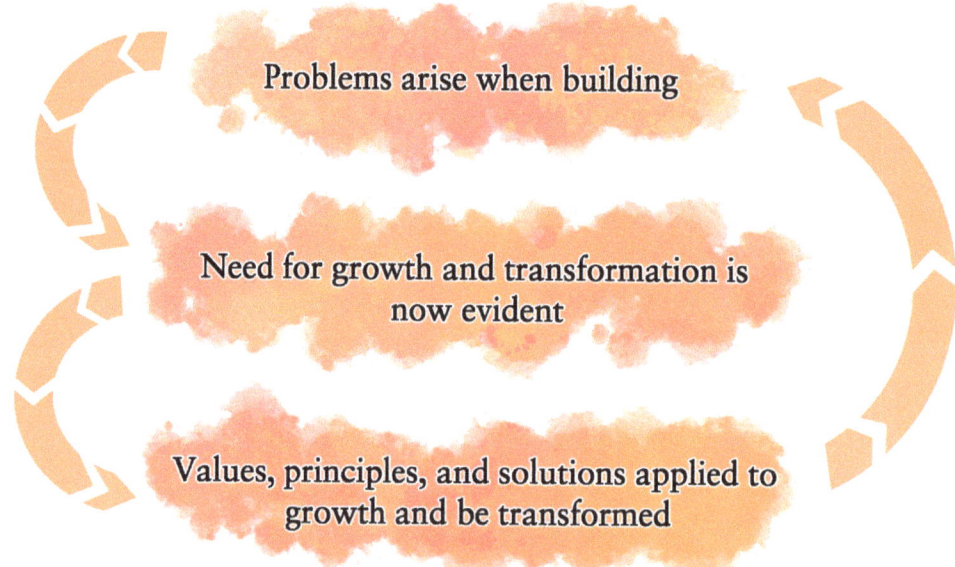

Problems arise when building

Need for growth and transformation is now evident

Values, principles, and solutions applied to growth and be transformed

Figure I-1 Problems can be opportunities to grow and to transform inside character.

One caution. ***Don't just read the content.*** Answering the questions and discussing your answers with God and others will not only reinforce the concepts but help you internalize the content so that you are changed from the inside out. Each chapter has more work to do than you'll probably want to do. Why don't you set a goal to keep doing the projects until you feel you have internalized the content? Then you're ready to move on to the next concept.

This book is best studied in community. To get the most out of it, work through each story, problem and project with a partner or in a small group. For best results, keep a workbook or journal of your progress. Many problems and projects build throughout the book, and you will find it valuable to refer back to previous work.

Introducing Fractals of Seven

Fractals are repeating patterns of numbers that align in some way. For example, God created the world in seven days, which align to the seven redemptive gifts and the seven letters to the seven churches in Revelation. In this book, we use many repeating patterns of seven to learn about principles, growth, redemptive gifts, blessings, curses, and many other concepts.

The table on the following pages can be used as a reference to the big picture of fractals of seven in the entire book and how they work together to build a culture for builders who deeply love Father God and represent Him well in community.

THE BIG PICTURE							
	1	**2**	**3**	**4**	**5**	**6**	**7**
Principles	**Design** God's design works	**Authority** Secure boundaries	**Truth** Rights and responsibilities	**Reality** Cause & effect	**Stewardship** God owns everything; we are stewards	**Freedom** To be and do what God has called us to	**Fulfillment** Alignment and joy
Stages of Growth to Adulthood	I belong to community and trust my needs will be met	I know what I like and I'm beginning to know myself as a person	I have a good sense of right and wrong, and I can reconcile in community	I thrive in peer relationships without supervision	I see talents I have and I'm developing myself	I can fight for what is right and build something bigger than myself	I have made the passage to adulthood. I choose my own life
Redemptive Gift	Prophet	Servant	Teacher	Exhorter	Giver	Ruler	Mercy
Purpose of Gift	Reveal light, build authority based on intimacy and legitimacy	Release authority, reveal resources.	Enthrone Jesus in the land through principles and values	Catalyst for transformation via new view of God, model purpose	Access to God, authenticity, integrity, steward resources	City builder and fathering leader	Alignment in the culture
Essential Virtue	See beyond to what is possible, pointing the way	Legitimate boundaries and delegated authority	Sanctify others in reconciliation to God	Embracing challenges that bring life to communities	Walking by faith, using resources to provide access for others	Provide life-giving structures for others to thrive	Worship and rest in community with God
Demonic Stronghold	Fractured relationships	Victim spirit	Religious spirit	Comfort and selfishness	Ownership	Predator spirit	Self-gratification
Root Iniquity	Rights of individuals	Peace at any cost	Selective responsibility	Denial of reality	Control	Exploitation	Stubbornness

THE BIG PICTURE

	1	2	3	4	5	6	7
Curses on birthright	Aramean: Can't get justice	Moabite: No help getting started	Philistine: Lack key resources	Canaanite: Oppressive workload	Midianite: Seasonal devouring of money and relationships	Jotham: Betrayal from within	Ammonite: Barrenness, trade-based relationship with God
Blessings needed for effectiveness	Blessing of Hosea: Favor and second chances	Blessing of Esther: Secure borders	Blessing of Daniel: Supernatural strategies	Blessing of Moses: Time to develop partnership with God	Blessing of Job: Accruing capital	Blessing of Nehemiah: Synergistically life-giving communities	Blessing of John: Possessing your birthright
Legitimacy Lie	When I fix your problem	When I use my authority to benefit man	When I know more than you	When I have a following	When I can resource you	When I have an institution	When I have earned God's favor
Leviathan righteous head	Light in me and in my family. As I seek God's light, He gives light to solve problems.	The atmosphere and weather cooperate with us when we use our authority to honor God and empower others	Life of God in me; enjoy life. I accept the right and responsibility to develop the life of God in me. I am unpacking me.	Reality: Every effect has a cause and can be seen and solutions embraced. Able to release a new experience with Father.	People hear my heart, my true motives. Communication flows.	Favor. Win-win for many to one and one to many. Able to father and raise up next gen of leaders.	Radically serve and seek God because of love.

Leviathan unrighteous head	Hard to hear God. Dark people are attracted to me. I am not seen.	Weather patterns bring destruction	Death; little life. Rights and responsibilities are out of balance.	Denial. Does not see the reality that others around me see. Cannot see cause and effect.	Poor communication. People can't hear my heart. I cannot govern or unpack my blessings. I choose when and how I give time/resources.	No flow or flow is choppy. Little momentum. Loose-win Win-lose Lose-Lose	Never enough or settling for little. Affects all of community.
Stages of building	Personal authority based on essence, identity and legitimacy	I am resourced for success and confident these resources match my design and calling	I know my core values, and they are built on the principles of God	I know my core passion and I'm modeling my core ability, based on my design	Authenticity is birthed from stewarding what God has entrusted to me	Structures work to impart life and freedom to people I lead	Building culture that represents Father God well
Social RG of business	New ideas and paradigm shifts (R&D companies)	Raise up leaders (UPS produces leaders)	Perfection with massive degree of excellence.	Catalyst to release new truth that can transform culture	Access to resources (McDonalds sells access)	Strong and effective structures. High level of fathering.	Atmosphere (Starbucks not selling coffee but ambience)
Seven mountains of culture	Media	Religion	Education	Family	Celebration	Government	Economy and ecosystem

Notes about the Flow of the Book

Each chapter has these six sections and some stories to inspire:

PRINCIPLE

Read the Principle sections through all chapters to gain insights and wisdom about the seven principles of Wisdom, which lay the foundations for each chapter.

HERE WE GROW

Use the Here We Grow sections in each chapter to understand the seven stages of growth and build a growth plan.

CONCEPTS

The Concepts sections of each chapter explain how to apply the principles to our lives so that we can know God better, grow and build.

SOLVING PROBLEMS

The Solving Problems sections teach how to solve problems that might occur at each stage of growth and building in community.

GROWTH PROJECT

The Growth Projects help us mature and grow into bigger people.

SPIRIT PROJECT

The Spirit Projects are designed to normalize working with our human spirits and building up our spirits so they can give life to our souls and bodies and bring the treasures of heaven to earth.

Sprinkled throughout the book, look for stories that inspire. We hope that you can absorb the heart of the book through these stories. The questions in each story are designed to help us become bigger people.

Feedback and Blogs

Would love to hear from you about this textbook.
You can reach me at Jean@FromHisTable.com.

For some lively discussions about the topics introduced here and how they can apply to spirit and soul growth, families, schools, businesses, communities and nations, find our blogs at FromHisTable.com. Come check out our online communities!

CHAPTER 01 GROWING IN THE AWE OF GOD

"I am in awe of Father God and His essence in me."

The Principle of Design

We start each chapter by looking at one of the seven foundational principles of Wisdom. The first principle is the **principle of design**, which is foundational to all other principles.

PRINCIPLE

A principle is a universal, non-optional, cause and effect relationship. Principles apply in our relationships with the spirit realm, with other people, and with creation.

God designed you and me and our physical and spiritual worlds out of His perfect and loving nature and essence as an exquisite expression of Himself. To know God is to be totally in awe of you and me and His essence in us. If we see ourselves as poor, broken and inadequate, there is no way we are going to trust our Maker. How could He have created me like THIS and still be a good God! When our relationships, families, finances, churches, businesses and health don't work, how can we trust that God is the awesome Maker of it all? Until these attitudes toward God, ourselves and our worlds are resolved, we can never trust Him enough to be intimate with Him or love Him. And we certainly would not find any joy in building a Kingdom for Him when He is such a flawed Designer and Creator.

Before the fall, all of creation worked as it should. Man and woman lived in beautiful harmony with their Maker and all of creation. After the fall, mankind and all of creation was immersed in death, separation, destruction, and brokenness.

The good news (Gospel) is that Jesus Christ came to restore all things and reconcile all creation back to God's original design.

For it pleased the Father that in him should all fullness dwell; and, having made peace through the blood of his cross, by him to reconcile all things unto himself; by him, I say, whether they be things in earth, or things in heaven.
Colossians 1:19-20

When we receive Jesus Christ as Lord and Savior, we are a new creation. We are returned to the original design before the fall. Actually, if you can conceive it, we are better than before the fall because when God redeems something, He makes it better than the original.

For in Christ Jesus you are all sons of God through faith, for as many of you as were baptized into Christ have put on Christ. There is neither Jew nor Greek, neither slave nor free, there is no male and female, for you are all one in Christ Jesus. And if you are Christ's, then you are Abraham's offspring, and heirs according to promise.
Galatians 3:26-29

No one rejects the one true God. People, can, however, reject who they think God is. To know Him is to love Him and move toward Him. The better we know Him, the more awe we have for Him.

Son or Orphan?

In your heart, are you an orphan or a son? When we have the heart of an orphan, we cannot believe we have a good Father who created us in His perfect image and qualified us to inherit all things. When the Israelites first came out of Egypt, they had hearts of orphans and slaves. Those with slave or orphan hearts tend to believe they lack resources that God and others are withholding from them and can feel powerless that their needs will not be met.

So the people grumbled against Moses, saying, 'What are we to drink?'
Exodus 15:24

On the other hand, when we are sons in our hearts, we have a foundational groundedness that our basic needs will always be met by our good Father. Even though we are aware there might be tough spots, in general, we expect that life will go well for us.

In this book, we use the term sons to describe both male and female children of God, and we primarily use the term to describe a condition of the heart. Sons are commissioned to build their Father's Kingdom. The Kingdom includes all things that are submitted to and governed by Jesus, our King.

The redemption of all things was made possible by the finished work of the Lord Jesus Christ and the Blood covenant He attained with you and me. The rest of this chapter is focused on understanding what He did for us in this Blood Covenant. It's all done for us! Our part is to receive it and walk it out.

HERE WE GROW

In this textbook, each chapter covers one of the seven stages of growth from conception to adulthood.

Growth Stage 1: I Belong to God and His Community

You and I were sent to earth to grow in intimacy with God into sons of God who can build our Father's Kingdom. We grow because we are nurtured by Him with all things we need, including His presence, His love, wisdom, family, home and many other resources He provides as our good Father.

We begin growing the moment our earthly father's sperm fertilizes our mother's egg. Our growth to mature adults follow the seven stages of growth outlined in Figure 1-1. These seven stages align with the seven chapters in this book and all the other groups of seven outlined in the Big Picture table at the beginning of the book. The first stage of growth addressed in this chapter is to know that we belong to God and His community.

Womb/Infant	Toddler	Elementary	Middle	Preteen	Teen	Adult
I belong in community and I trust my needs will be met	I know what I like and I'm beginning to know myself	I have a good sense of right and wrong, I know how to reconcile with others when problems arise	I can thrive in peer relationships without supervision from leaders	I see talents I have, and I'm developing myself	I can fight for what is right and I can build something beyond myself	I have made the passage to adulthood, I choose my own life, I am legitimate in community

Figure 1-1 Seven stages of growth from childhood to adulthood

We all grew up in imperfect families and some of us missed chunks of what we needed to mature. But it's never too late to fill in what we missed as children. It's never too late to grow up!

Belongingness

Belongingness is an emotion we experience when we are consistently loved and cared for in the womb and during infancy and lasts a lifetime. Because we started out experiencing a stable, grounded and loving environment, we generally feel that:

- I have rights in a community that my basic needs will be met, for example, the right to feel safe.

- My security in community comes from within and not from outside me.

- I am grounded inside and can recover quickly when rattled.

- In a crisis, I stay calm and handle myself well.

Many of us did not experience this consistent loving care at the beginning and we tend to see life differently:

- In a crisis or under stress, I get anxious and can react without thinking. I might panic, get emotionally wobbly or cannot be counted on to stay engaged. I might try to escape, shut down, fight, or be unreasonably compliant. (Psychologists call these reactions flee, freeze, fight, or fawn.)

- My groundedness (emotional stability) depends on external factors, such as how others treat me or what needs I perceive as being met or not met.

- Generally, I often feel uncomfortable and out of place in community. I might withdraw, control, or be a people pleaser, hoping to get my needs met. I struggle with feeling insecure and not valued by others.

> We all need to feel at an emotional level that we belong to a loving God who consistently takes good care of us. In the womb, a loved and nurtured baby bonds to the mom. As an infant, they don't yet know where they end and mom begins because they are one. Later they can develop a healthy otherness. It's difficult to understand otherness until you first attach to someone.

Growing into Belongingness

I grew up without this emotional belongingness and was constantly striving for what seemed like never enough love. As I was able to come to Father God to receive His love, He rooted, grounded and filled me with Himself and I was able to grow into a deep sense of belongingness.

> *For this reason I bow my knees to the Father of our Lord Jesus Christ, from whom the whole family in heaven and earth is named, that He would grant you, according to the riches of His glory, to be strengthened with might through His Spirit in the inner man, that Christ may dwell in your hearts through faith; that you, being rooted and grounded in love, may be able to comprehend with all the saints what is the width and length and depth and height -- to know the love of Christ which passes knowledge; that you may be filled with all the fullness of God.*
>
> Ephesians 3:14-19

People can help us to feel belongingness in community by:

- Creating an atmosphere or culture of "I'm glad to see you!" We can all help people feel welcomed, wanted, desirable, valued, celebrated, and cared for.

- We can take the time to get to know the treasure someone is and express from the heart, "I see you. I believe in who you are and who you will become. I see God is in you and with you. The world is a better place because you are here."

Belongingness with God is possible because of the finished work of the Lord Jesus Christ who made a way for us to be reconciled with (reattached to) God. In this chapter, we discuss two steps toward belongingness:

1. **Legitimate with God.** When we are born of the Spirit of God into the family of God as a new creation, we have His **essence,** His divine nature. When we come to Him, we learn that He is glad to see us and He can be counted on to meet our every need. That's our Daddy! See Figure 1-2.

2. **Legitimate with people.** As we grow in confidence in our relationship with Him, we become more and more confident of **our legitimacy in various communities and situations.** We don't need to rely on what people think about us, our reputation, or even our own confidence in our abilities. Just as growth happens little by little over time, legitimacy is seldom a one-time event. Over time, we grow in our legitimacy with people as we grow in our legitimacy with God.

Figure 1-2 We are comfortable in the presence of Father God because we came from Him and we are like Him

CONCEPTS

Most of our work for the first two chapters is about how we see God and ourselves and our relationship with God. All this is founded on the finished work of the Lord Jesus Christ. In Him, we start at the finish line!

Concept 1.1 Starting at the Finish Line

I once asked Jesus, "What is the greatest compliment You ever received?" He took me to the Scripture, "For God so loved the world that He gave His only begotten Son..." Jesus was deeply honored that God chose Him as God's very best gift He could give to us, His creation!

With a heart of infinite love for us, Jesus walked out life here on earth perfectly, with no sin, and then allowed Himself to be hung on a tree. On the cross, He took to Himself all our sickness, sin, iniquity, rebellion, defilement, defeat, law, poverty, enemies, curses, and death, making it possible for Him to reconcile all things in heaven and earth to the Father. In Christ, we are able to express the fullness of God! Glory!

For in Christ all the fullness of the Deity lives in bodily form, and in Christ you have been brought to fullness. Colossians 2:9–10

We will be forever learning what all He did for us and in us. A good place to start is the diagram in Figure 1-3 and Scriptures in Table 1-1.

Figure 1-3 The finished work of the Lord Jesus Christ

Surrender to Jesus as my Savior, Lord and King	Water Baptism by Faith into the Lord Jesus Christ			Of His Essence and Seated with Him	START HERE
	Old Me Crucified with Him	Old Me Buried with Him	New Me Resurrected in His Body		
Ephesians 5:8 I once was darkness with a nature to sin. Romans 10:10 With my heart and mouth, I am saved.	Romans 6:1-11 I died with Him. Death was my way out of sin, slavery and past covenants with evil.	Colossians 2:9-12 As with circumcision, the cutting away of the old me.	John 3:5-8 I am light, born of water and the Spirit. I was conceived as Jesus was conceived.	Ephesians 2:6 I am ascended in Him and seated with Him.	The Finish Line

Table 1-1 When we surrender our lives to Jesus, we start a new life at the finish line of what He completed

Jesus completed all the requirements of the Blood covenant before you and I were aware of His work. When we surrender our lives to Jesus, we enter into the Blood covenant already available to us. It's our job to receive it.

When you enter into a covenant with someone, you become one with them. As impossible as it seems, consider what it might look like to be **one with God!** We must start with our very essence.

Concept 1.2 Born of the Spirit of God in His Essence

When we surrender our lives to Jesus, we are born a second time, this time born of the Spirit and born of water. As diagrammed in Figure 1-3, we receive forgiveness at the cross. We enter into His body and our dark selves are crucified with Jesus in the waters of baptism. In the waters of baptism, we die with Him and are buried with Him. As we come up out of the water, we are raised up with Him in His resurrected body. As He is seated with Father, so our relationship with the Father is restored.

We are a new creation! 2 Corinthians 5. As God is light, so we are light. As we share in this divine nature, we are fully acceptable and pure in the eyes of the Father.

> *For ye were once darkness, but now are ye light in the Lord: walk as children of light.* Ephesians 5:8

> *Whereby are given unto us exceeding great and precious promises: that by these ye might be partakers of the divine nature, having escaped the corruption that is in the world through lust.*
>
> 2 Peter 1:4

Because we are like Him, of His essence, the relationship with Him can be restored and reconciled. Because we are of Him, we are His. We belong to Him.

Once the truth that we are of His essence settles into the core of our being, we no longer fear that Father God will reject us when we come to Him. We know He receives His own, and even in our deepest guilt, failures, and disappointments, we can run to Father and receive His love as any small child would run and jump into her Daddy's arms.

> Think of an immense inheritance of money left to you. Until you know about it and step forward to receive it, you might never actually benefit from it.

> Whoever tells the best story wins agreement! Following is the first of many stories you'll see in this book. A well-told story with punch and passion can inspire and change the course of our lives.

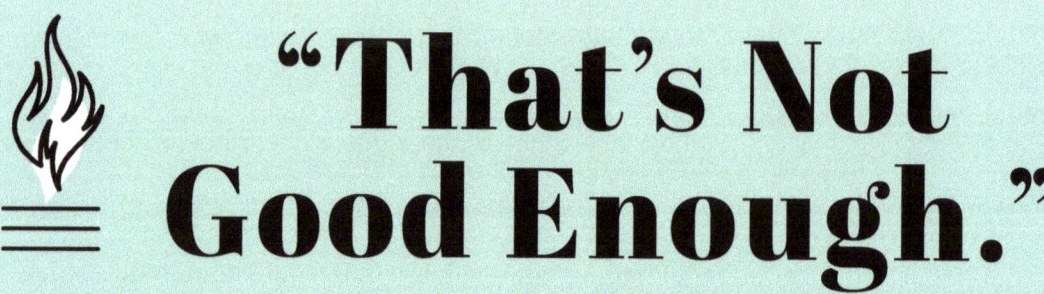

"That's Not Good Enough."

In deep depression, I once said to God, "God, I give You my poor broken life. I give You my mess." As I prayed that, I sensed a little pride as I thought I had prayed a pretty nice little prayer. It certainly was an improvement over other recent prayers about putting me out of my misery. But when I heard Him say, "That's not good enough," I was stunned. I couldn't imagine that giving Him my broken life was not good enough for Him.

I asked with some indignation, "Lord, what do you *mean*, it's not good enough?"

Immediately, He directed me to these verses in Malachi:

> *"But you profane [my name] by saying of the Lord's table, 'It is defiled,' and of its food, 'It is contemptible.' And you say, 'What a burden!' and you sniff at it contemptuously," says the Lord Almighty. "When you bring injured, crippled or diseased animals and offer them as sacrifices, should I accept them from your hands?" says the Lord. "Cursed is the cheat who has an acceptable male in his flock and vows to give it, but then sacrifices a blemished animal to the Lord. For I am a great king," says the Lord Almighty, "and my name is to be feared among the nations."* Malachi 1:12–14

I was appalled! Not only did He call me a cheat, but He said I had accused Him of offering me contemptible food! At first, I didn't know what to think, I was too shocked. But then I settled down and recognized my mistake. I had so undervalued the finished work of Jesus Christ at the cross that I saw the only offering I had to make to Father God was me, a blemished and wounded sacrifice. But Jesus had done it all. I am one with Jesus, the acceptable male in the flock. I had a perfect sacrifice to offer Him – my redeemed self!

Months earlier, I had vowed to give Jesus everything I was and had. I told Him my life was no longer my own; it belonged to Him. I knew He had made me the righteousness of God. All that Jesus is, He put into me, re-creating me in His likeness and image. God had spared nothing for my sake. He had given me everything He had, and I had given Him everything I had. And yet, in the moment, I thought all I had to offer Him was brokenness, and forgot that I had His redeemed me to offer Him!

I kneeled down and asked God to forgive me for belittling all that Jesus is in me. I told Him that night I would never, ever come to Him with only the problem. When He gave me Jesus, He gave me everything.

For thought and discussion:

1. When you think of coming to speak with Father God, what feelings or expectations come to mind? Can you use this story of being the acceptable sheep in the flock to change the way you approach Him?

2. Some people see themselves as merely legally adopted by God rather than being born again into God. A legal adoption does give us our identity as sons of God but does not change our essence. Describe the difference between the position of legally adopted son and born again son of God using the words "essence" and "identity."

Concept 1.3 Spirit, Soul and Body Made Whole

We began as a spirit, created by our Father God in heaven, created in His image, of His likeness, from His essence. God is light, but not just any light. He is divine light. Our spirits are made of the substance of His divine light (Ephesians 5, II Peter 1), and that light is the same light that created the universe with the spoken Word.

> Father God reached into Himself, pulled out of Himself some of His very essence, the substance of light, and formed you and me!

God wrote a book about each of us (Psalm 139) and in it, He recorded all the good works we are designed to do as sons of God in the earth (Ephesians 2). He sent us to earth to represent Him on the earth, fully equipped with His divine design, to fulfill His purposes on the earth as creative beings of light. He sent us from His heart into the fertilized egg in our mother's womb (see Figure 1-4). At that time, He knitted us together, spirit, soul and body, into the bloodline of humanity.

Figure 1-4 We were sent from Father God into the fertilized egg in our mother's womb

As sons of Father God, our spirits carried to earth the DNA of God, His divine nature, character and design. When our spirits entered the fertilized egg, our spirits began the process of giving us life, which will continue until the day we die (2 Corinthians 3:6, James 2:26). Our spirits can exist, think, feel, speak, listen and make decisions. Some moms report they can communicate with the spirit of their babies just hours after conception. Our spirit, soul and body also inherited the generational blessings and curses of our earthly family lines.

As spirit beings, created in God's image and likeness, the spirit is designed by God to sustain, nurture and interact with the soul and body (see Figure 1-5). We as spirit, soul and body are designed to represent God in the earth, to rule and reign as God instructed Adam. However, having entered into a disobedient and fallen humanity, we eventually sin and our brilliant spirits grow dark. With our spirits dark and separated from God and our souls and bodies hurting in the pain of fallen humanity, we need a Savior. We need a rebirth.

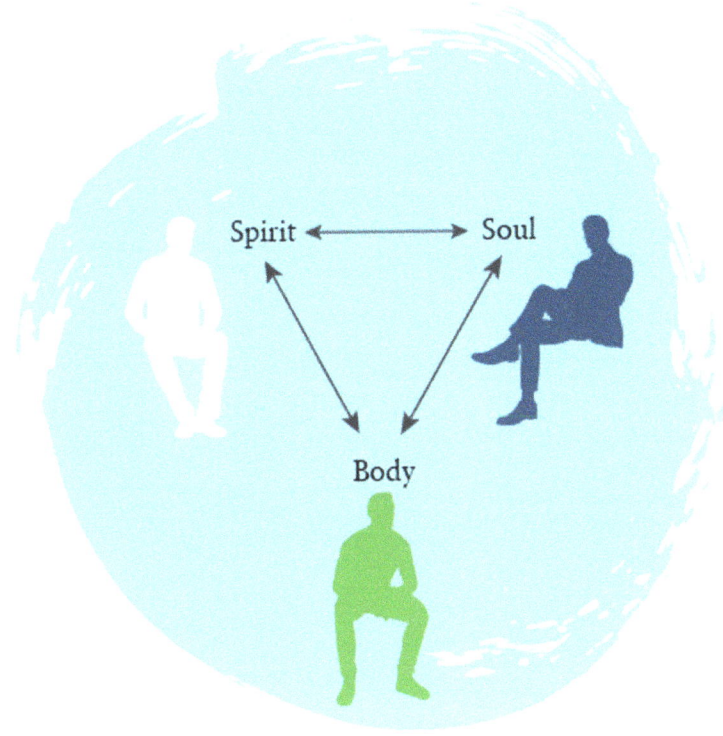

Figure 1-5 **We are created in God's image as spirit, soul and body**

What part of us is saved? Spirit, soul and/or body? Even though we don't all experience complete freedom and wholeness in spirit, soul and body at salvation, I believe God has given this all-encompassing and complete salvation to us:

For in Christ all the fullness of the Deity lives in bodily form, and in Christ you have been brought to fullness. He is the head over every power and authority. In him you were also circumcised with a circumcision not performed by human hands. Your whole self ruled by the flesh was put off when you were circumcised by Christ, *having been buried with him in baptism, in which you were also raised with him through your faith in the working of God, who raised him from the dead.*

When you were dead in your sins and in the uncircumcision of your flesh, God made you alive with Christ. *He forgave us all our sins, having canceled the charge of our legal indebtedness, which stood against us and condemned us; he has taken it away, nailing it to the cross.*

Colossians 2:9-14

I've heard testimonies and witnessed people having powerful encounters with God in the act of water baptism where Father spoke to a person their new name and spiritual destiny, covenants with evil were broken, terrorized demons fled, hearts were transformed, addictions were broken, tattoos of evil covenants disappeared off the body, and many other miracles. Our spirits, souls and bodies are created by Him in His image, and Father God wants all parts of us made holy and set apart for Him.

May God himself, the God of peace, sanctify you through and through. May your whole spirit, soul and body be kept blameless at the coming of our Lord Jesus Christ.

I Thessalonians 5:23

Concept 1.4 No Lack Because of the Blood Covenant

When we enter into Blood covenant with Jesus, an exchange takes place. He gives you all that He has, and, ideally, you give Him all you have. Now, as with a marriage covenant, you and He have all things in common. You and He are becoming one.

No Lack in the Core of Who We Are

Remember that Jesus even gives us His essence when we are born again. Knowing we have the essence of God in us can heal our shame. Shame is rooted in the lie that "at the core of my being, I am not enough." Believing this lie causes us to feel unworthy in the presence of God or community. Experiencing the truth that we are made in His essence allows us to be with Him and in community secure in who we are. We are like Him.

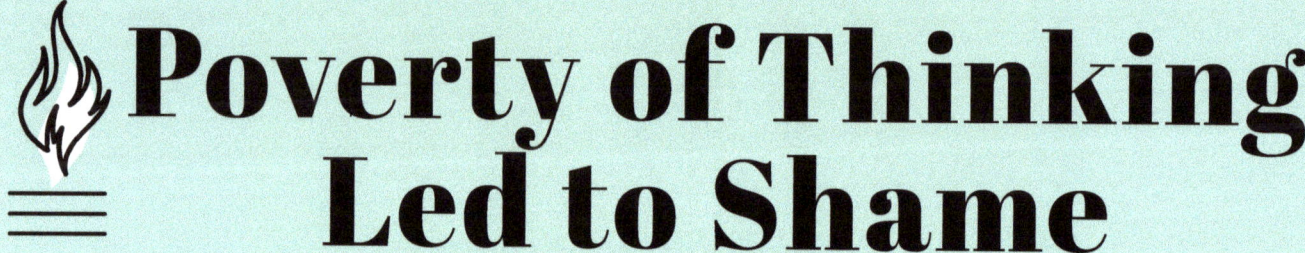

Poverty of Thinking Led to Shame

In Genesis 3, we learn how the enemy set up Eve to create a sense of false lack. She lacked for nothing but when she believed she was in lack, she acted on it and that led to the Fall. We can all fall into this same trap whenever we begin to entertain thoughts that we are not enough or God is withholding from us.

Let's follow the drama as it unfolds:

1. The enemy said to the woman, "Did God really say, 'You must not eat from any tree in the garden'?"

2. The woman answered they could eat from any tree except the one in the middle of the garden and they also should not touch it. When we read the Scriptures carefully, we see she was already a little confused because God had said nothing about not touching the tree. But more importantly, we see the lie deceptively implied that God was withholding good from her.

3. When Eve considered the thought that God might be withholding good from her, she positioned herself for the bigger lie. The enemy then said, "God knows that when you eat from it your eyes will be opened, and you will be like God, knowing good and evil."

4. Just as the first lie, this one is implied and not clearly stated. The premise of the statement is that she was not already made in the image of God, even though God had made it clear that she was indeed created in His image. How was she deceived that she was not already like Him? I believe it was because the enemy had positioned her to think, if God is withholding good from her, He might also be withholding Himself. So perhaps she was not truly as like Him as she *thought* she was and needed to *do something* to better herself.

5. And so she ate. When we begin to see ourselves as less than enough, it's easy to see others in the same light. She turned to her husband and basically said, "Hey, you don't look so good yourself. *Do something* to better yourself." And so he ate.

6. But even with all that happened and the immense consequences, God still believed enough in Eve that He stated that one day her offspring will defeat this enemy.

7. In Matthew 4:3, we see Jesus tempted in the same way as Eve was tempted when the enemy said, "*If* you are the Son of God, tell these stones to become bread." The question on the table was are you really who God says you are? If so, prove it.

8. But Jesus answered, "It is written: 'Man shall not live on bread alone, but on every word that comes from the mouth of God.'" Eve failed the test when her identity and essence as a child of God was questioned, but Jesus passed the test for us all!

9. The last recorded word that God had spoken over Jesus before the temptation is in Matthew 3:16, "This is my Son, whom I love; with him I am well pleased." Jesus stood on what God had said about Him and chose not to *do anything* to prove He is who God says He is.

For thought and discussion:

1. Can you think of a situation where you attempted to prove to someone that you were worthy to be in their community?

2. What could you have said or done differently to establish your worth in community based solely on the fact that God sent you as His son into the community?

His Covenant Grace Makes Up for Our Weaknesses

You might be thinking about your own genuine shortcomings that make you feel unworthy to be with God or community. The shortcomings might be real, but God's Grace is more than enough to make up the difference (see Figure 1-6). Grace is available for us when we are in covenant relationship with the Lord Jesus Christ, one with Him, sharing in all things. Suppose Jesus is so tall and we are so short. Grace lifts us up to be as tall as Jesus is. Where we are weak, He is strong. In Christ, all things are possible.

Figure 1-6 By His Covenant Grace, Jesus lifts us up to His level and we have no lack

Suppose you have a weakness that is difficult to overcome. You can pray, "Jesus, I need you to strengthen my will so that I can overcome this weakness. We call this self-control. You and He together are strong in the Blood covenant.

> *"The LORD is my shepherd, I lack nothing."* Psalm 23:1

Concept 1.5 We have Intimacy with Him in the Blood Covenant

And he took bread, gave thanks and broke it, and gave it to them, saying, "This is my body given for you; do this in remembrance of me." In the same way, after the supper he took the cup, saying, "This cup is the new covenant in my blood, which is poured out for you.
Luke 22:19–20

At the heart of the Blood covenant with Jesus is sharing our essence. When we eat His body and drink His Blood, we enter into the most intimate of moments with Him. The Word became flesh and dwelt among us. When we eat His flesh, we eat the Word, and that Word does it work in us. Life is in the Blood, and when we drink His Blood, we can ask Him to cleanse our DNA, intermingling it with His DNA, and give us a Blood transfusion of life. Out of these intimate moments with Him, we grow and are transformed. In these moments, we can ask Him to bring us into the presence of Father in the most childlike and innocent way.

Concept 1.6
Building the Kingdom on the Blood Covenant as Sons of God

Up until Jesus revealed Himself as the Son of God, no one as a part of fallen humanity had claimed that status. When Jesus claimed to be one with the Father and the Son of God, the Jews tried to stone him.

For this reason they tried all the more to kill him; not only was he breaking the Sabbath, but he was even calling God his own Father, making himself equal with God.

John 5:18

What about the one whom the Father set apart as his very own and sent into the world? Why then do you accuse me of blasphemy because I said, 'I am God's Son'?

John 10:36

King David, Isaiah and Daniel wrote about the eternal Kingdom of God and looked forward to its coming. In Luke 22:16, Jesus explained that the Blood covenant will find its fulfillment in the Kingdom of God. David, Isaiah and Daniel looked forward to the sons of God bringing His Kingdom. Jesus explained in Luke 17 that the Kingdom is within us. As mature sons of God, we are the ones chosen by God to bring forth the Kingdom from within us to all of creation. This is possible only by the Blood covenant He has with each of us.

Concept 1.7 Do You Love Me?

In 2003, when I was in my fifties, Jesus took me, as a five-year-old girl, to the Father and placed me in His arms. As I gazed into His face, I *knew* I was loved. The look in His eyes changed me. In that moment, I saw I was His cherished daughter, and He was so delighted I had come to Him. It astounded me to realize that He was more hungry for me than I was for Him! I began a journey that day from having the heart of an orphan to that of a beloved and legitimate daughter. Love is a feeling expressed by what we do, and I was feeling His love for me as *His emotions toward me.*

For teachings on each of these four keys to knowing God's love, listen to the "Am I Loved?" audios at **FromHisTable.com**.

Love is not a theology; it's a feeling, an emotion expressed by what we do.

Just a few months before, I had changed my prayers to God from, "Why don't You use me?" to "What I really need to know is do You love me?" I had finally asked the right question! Over the next few months, He slowly showed me lies I had believed and mindsets I had accepted that had kept me from knowing His love. Four key issues emerged:

1. **Forgiveness.** I needed to forgive from my heart my earthly father. As long as we hold our parents accountable for our problems, we tie God's hands from fixing them. My father was never loved himself, so how could he love me?

2. **Judgements.** I needed to repent of judging my earthly father. I had judged my father for being distant from me. In fact, he was distant but when I judged him for that, I reaped that judgement in my own life that I would also see Father God as distant.

3. **Shame.** I was covered in shame. I saw myself as flawed and inadequate and not deserving unconditional, relentless love from God.

4. **God's goodness.** I had always thought I was chasing hard after God. In a powerful encounter with Jesus, I discovered the truth that He had been chasing hard after me and I was finally allowing Him the joy of experiencing me.

Once these four issues were resolved, I was ready to allow Jesus to bring me to Father. Feeling Father's love for me as I looked in His eyes, changed me from the inside out. Knowing His love first hand allowed me to start the maturing process from a servant of God who obeys Him to a son of God who can inherit His Kingdom. My identity (the way God and man know and see us and the way we see ourselves) as a child of God had to be rooted and grounded in His love for me at an emotional level.

Concept 1.8 Maturing as a Son of God

As we mature, our identity needs to grow into what we do and the fruit we produce. Jesus compared us to trees and said:

Jamie Winship, author of the book "Living Fearless" and former police officer and CIA operative, has boiled down his identity statement to, "I am a militant peacemaker."

"By their fruits you shall know (identify) them."
Matthew 7:20

And Paul reminds us that creation is waiting to know us:

For the creation waits with eager longing for the revealing of the sons of God. Romans 8:19

The fruit that identifies us as sons of God is love, joy, peace, patience, kindness, goodness, faithfulness, gentleness and self-control (Galatians 5). The reflection of the image of God in our essence must equally reflect the images of the Father, Son, and Holy Spirit. The cyclic and ongoing process of growing to mature sons of God who are rooted in love and bear good fruit is outlined in Figure 1-7. The figure ties together many of the concepts in this book.

Figure 1-7 We are rooted in love and by our fruit, we will be known (identified) as sons of God

Our identity is rooted in who God is, how He designed us, and how He wants us to see ourselves. As we mature, our identity grows to include the birthrights He wants to give us and how He wants to partner with us so that we can possess our birthrights. Think of Abraham, whom God called or identified as the father of many nations. Who God decided Abraham would become and do was His identity. God partnered with Abraham to secure his identity and birthright.

Building Belongingness, Worth and Competence

God intended for the feelings of belongingness, worth and competence to be established in us as children, as shown in Figure 1-8.

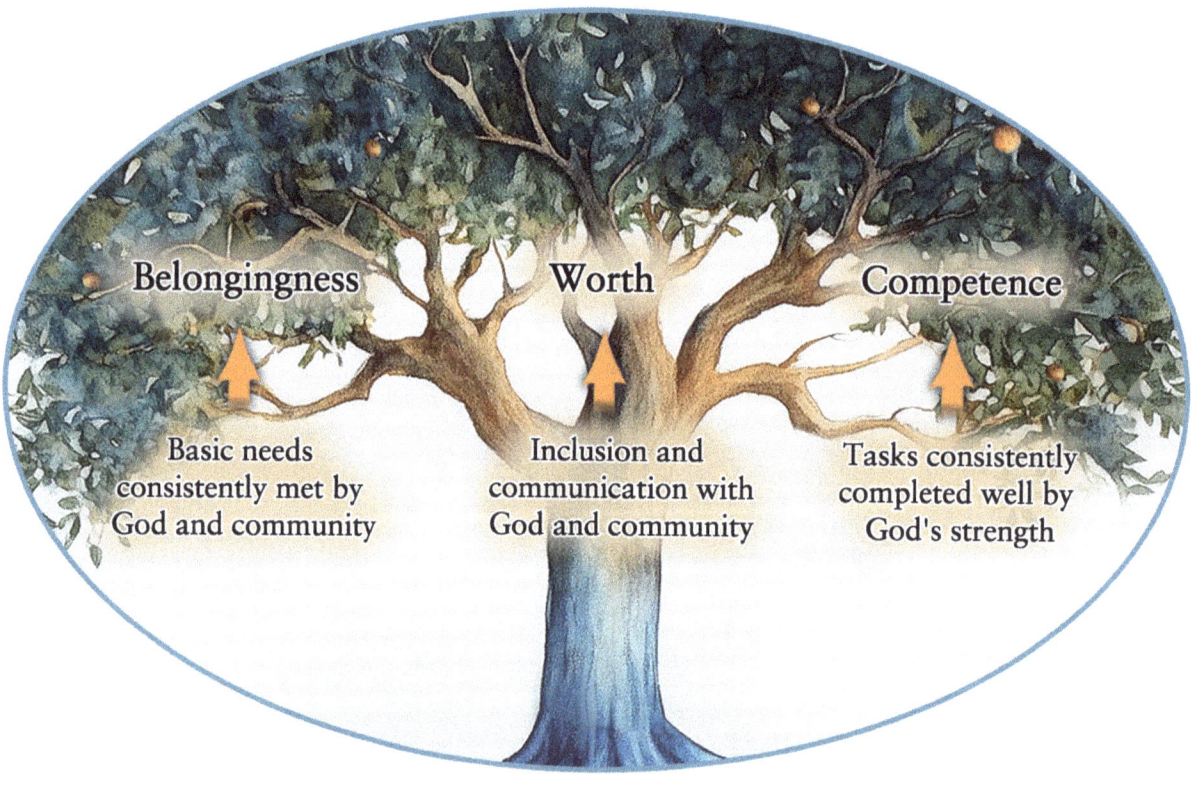

Figure 1-8 Personhood and legitimacy are built on belongingness, worth and competence

Here is God's plan for building belongingness, worth and competence in us as children in healthy families:

- **Belongingness.** The emotion of belonging comes when we feel loved and our needs are consistently met. Baby cries and someone consistently responds with love to meet the current need (for example, comfort, food or sleep).

Later, as adults, we have a groundedness and stability about us that no matter what crisis or current need, we feel a deep sense of expectation that we will find a way through.

- **Worth.** A sense of worth happens with inclusion. It has been said that with children, love is spelled T-I-M-E. When parents spend time with children, watching them play, playing with them, talking with them, listening to their stories, and generally enjoying the joy their children are experiencing, children feel inclusion and develop a healthy sense of worth.

Worth is developed in a child based on the degree of loving inclusion by parents and the surrounding community.

- **Competence.** When our parents gave us tasks to do that we were able to do with some appropriate stretching, we felt confident that we can handle the demands of life.

Because none of us grew up in perfect families, no one has fully experienced this ideal process as children. With God, it's never too late! God wants to accept responsibility for our growth to maturity as sons of God and will gladly do so as we submit to Him and His ways. Some general ways He accomplishes this are:

- **Father God builds our belongingness.** When belongingness did not happen as children, we can ask Father God to help us grow in these areas.

  1. Father God, as our loving provider, builds into us a sense of belongingness by expressing His love to us and consistently meeting our every need.

  2. When we intentionally engage with God, expecting Him to be our loving provider, we learn over time that He is who He says He is.

  3. In a healthy community, we learn that we are loved and cared for by others who actively engage with us in appropriate ways. We learn that "right or wrong, we belong."

  4. We learn it is safe to ask for and expect appropriate love and help when needed.

- **Jesus Christ builds our worth.** When inclusion did not happen, we feel unworthy and not valuable. Rather than seeking value through symbols such as popular brands and the best clothes or through our hard work, we can ask Jesus for help:

  1. Jesus Christ embraced the crucifixion so that we can be included and reconciled to our Father. Jesus consistently includes us in His communications with us as His friends and members of His family.

  2. When we ask God to show us the value He places on us, He will likely do that with inclusion. He will speak with us, share His authority with us, and include us in what He is doing, demonstrating how much of Himself He desires to share with us. And He loves it when we include Him in what we are doing.

  3. In a healthy community, a sense of worth is established in us by two-way inclusion:

      - I include you in my life.

      - I am interested in being included in your life.

- **Holy Spirit builds our competence.** Holy Spirit builds competence in us as we learn to take on tasks that He directs us to do and learn that He can be trusted to resource us with whatever is needed to complete these tasks. We learn that nothing is impossible when He partners with us.

No, Not a Commodity!

Belongingness and worth must be given to us by others, but we can build feelings of competence in ourselves by our own efforts. When belongingness and worth were not given to us as children, to develop an identity, we can resort to becoming highly competent by working hard to excel in school, sports, or other activities. When we build our belongingness and worth on competence, we become a commodity. See Figure 1-9.

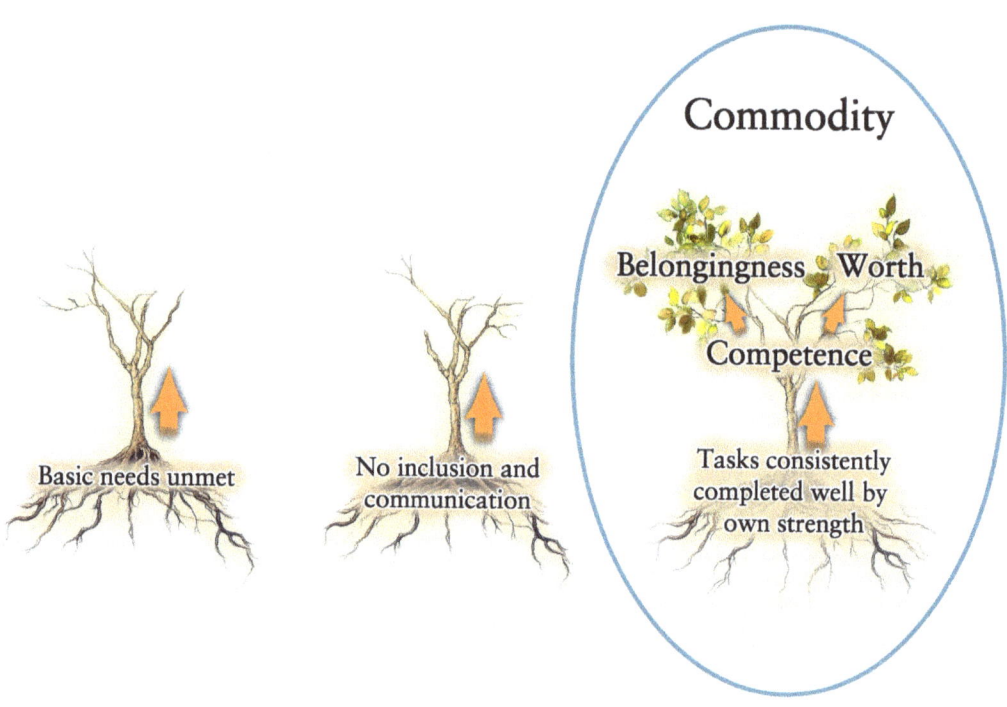

Figure 1-9 When we must build our identity without the help of others, we can become a commodity

A commodity, such as coal, sugar or gasoline, is a basic good or service in commerce where one unit is of the same value as another unit. (All coal is as good as any coal.)

As a commodity, our belongingness and worth never feel solid nor bear good fruit because they are built on a wrong foundation. We repeatedly need to prove that we are legitimately valuable to God and others.

Person or Commodity?

Our ultimate goal in pursuing a healthy identity is to more accurately reflect each Member of the Trinity. See Figure 1-10.

To stand in the office and authority of person (personhood), I must know that I am loved and uniquely me. But as a commodity, one human being is as good as another regarding what we can contribute to God and community. We must not settle for just competence. We must build our identities on seeing our unique designs and value as God sees us.

I am growing into an accurate reflection of the Trinity, Father, Son, and Holy Spirit

Belongingness   Competence

Worth

Figure 1-10 A three-legged tripod of belongingness, worth and competence can support an accurate reflection of the Trinity

What's in a name? A commodity (such as coal or sugar) needs no name. When God gives us a name, He embeds in the name our birthrights. To know the name God has given you helps to establish you in the office of person with His personal authority to be present in community with a commissioning from Him to bring His Kingdom to earth in a specific way that only you can accomplish. If you don't know the name God has given you, ask Him. Sometimes, He gives different names for different seasons of our lives.

A Boy Learns About His Worth

A mom recognized her 10-year-old son, Dennis, did not value himself and wondered whether that was why he struggled with unforgiveness and poor behavior. They attend a church where he does not speak the language. One Sunday, his mom decided to be more inclusive with Dennis, so she drew her son to her and quietly translated the sermon for him. That afternoon, Dennis told his mom he had decided to forgive several people in his life, including forgiving her. The conversation ended with reconciliation and tender hugs.

For thought and discussion:

1. How did Dennis' mom build up the feelings of worth in her son?

2. It's hard to forgive when we don't feel that we have worth or value because forgiving is giving. Read Luke 6:37-38. Explain how forgiving is a type or form of giving. We cannot give unless we have first received. According to Luke 6, what happens when we give?

3. Why do you think Dennis found the strength to forgive after feeling more worth or value?

4. Is there someone you need to forgive? Perhaps you can find His strength or Grace to do so by asking Him to show you how valuable and worthy you are to Him.

To learn more about belongingness, worth and competence as a foundation for legitimacy, listen to the album "The New Spiritual Authority: Intimacy" by Arthur Burk at **theSLG.com.**

Gangs often provide counterfeit legitimacy built on belongingness, worth and competency. They are perceived as meeting every need, highly inclusive, and will train people to fight well. It is my hope and dream that many righteous communities rise up to meet these three basic needs for true legitimacy based on unconditional love.

Legitimacy in Community

Building a strong and intimate relationship with God can take time and requires that we be reconciled with Him at many levels:

- My spirit must know at an emotional level that I am always loved and received by God

- My soul and body must also know at an emotional level and I am loved and received by God

- I must be reconciled to my spirit, soul and body, as His beautiful and perfect creation

- I must be reconciled to my past, present and future, securely rooted in His love

When this reconciliation happens, we find a legitimacy with God, an emotional confidence that I have a right to be with God, receive all He wants to give me and do whatever He has called me to do.

Once we know this legitimacy with God, we can experience that same legitimacy with people. We don't have to earn or prove our value to others or edit ourselves to fit the expectations of others. We are comfortable in our own skin and we rest securely in our **personal authority** to be in any community and for any purpose that God sends us.

Lord, you alone are my portion and my cup; you make my lot secure. The boundary lines have fallen for me in pleasant places; surely I have a delightful inheritance. I will praise the Lord, who counsels me; even at night my heart [kidneys] instructs me. I keep my eyes always on the Lord. With him at my right hand, I will not be shaken. Therefore, my heart is glad and my tongue rejoices; my body also will rest secure... Psalm 16:5-9

> A **legitimacy lie** says that we are legitimate when we can do something or have something another cannot do or have.

Counterfeit Legitimacies

A counterfeit legitimacy is any feeling of legitimacy that does not come directly from God. When we depend on legitimacy from sources other than God, we are not free to follow wherever God is leading when He directs us to step outside what others consider legitimate. In fact, we will never grow to complete maturity as sons of God able to build the Kingdom when we don't have permission to grow past others who legitimize us or our own beliefs in what makes us legitimate.

As we explore what makes us feel legitimate, know that our legitimacy in one area of our lives (for example, I am legitimate in my family when I take care of people) might be based on a totally different foundation than in another area of our lives (for example, I am legitimate at work when my boss brags on me). Father God sometimes will remove a counterfeit legitimacy (we cannot meet the needs of our family or our boss berates us) so that we can see the need to build a better, more righteous legitimacy in Christ alone.

Leah Discovered Her True Source of Legitimacy in Community

Jacob had two wives, Leah and Rachel (Genesis 29-30), and Jacob loved Rachel but not Leah. Leah passionately struggled to gain legitimacy in community by gaining her husband's love. Her legitimacy lie was, "I am legitimate when my husband loves me." When God saw that Leah was not loved, He opened her womb so she could have children, and Rachel was barren. Notice the names Leah gave her first three sons:

- Reuben means misery. Leah said the Lord had seen her misery and maybe now her husband would love her.

- Simeon means one who hears. She said the Lord heard she was not loved.

- Levi means attached. She said maybe now my husband will attach to me.

But with the fourth son, she turned from looking for legitimacy from her husband's love, and she said, "This time I will praise the Lord!" She named her son Judah, which means praise!

Leah finally realized that she might never have her husband's love, no matter what she did to earn it. She *did* realize that God Himself was favoring her! She had His love and His attention! She took her eyes off her husband to meet her need for legitimacy and put her eyes on God. She began to praise Him for what she did have, laying aside what she didn't have.

There's no indication her husband ever learned to love her. But we can see her true legitimacy growing by looking at what she named her later children:

- Gad means good fortune.

- Asher means happy.

- Issachar means reward.

- Zebulun means honor.

- Dinah means justice.

For thought and discussion:

1. The power of this story is how God favored her with children even before she decided to root her legitimacy in God alone. God always has a way of compensating us for deep loss. As Leah responded to His favor in a righteous way, He chose Judah as the son of Jacob and Leah in the bloodline of His own Son, the Lord Jesus Christ. As Christ followers, you and I are part of the Tribe of Judah, the Lion of Judah! How does this fact affect our understanding of true legitimacy?

2. Leah sought after her husband's love. What counterfeit legitimacies might you have sought after in the past?

3. The principle of compensation assures us that when we are weak, He is strong. Who do you know who has a significant personal weakness, such as a mental or physical handicap? What treasure has God put in them to compensate for this weakness?

4. This entire book is a work in growing in true legitimacy. Based on what you've learned in this chapter, describe a personal strategy to help you grow into true legitimacy. Expect to add to and revise your strategy throughout the book.

C. S. Lewis in "The Weight of Glory" writes about our struggle for legitimacy as our passion to be in the innermost circle. He said, "As long as you are governed by that desire you will never get what you want. You are trying to peel an onion; if you succeed there will be nothing left. Until you conquer the fear of being an outsider, an outsider you will remain." May we all conquer the fear of being an outsider!

Concept 1.9 We Must Choose to Grow and Build

Why are we here? As we begin to seek God and find His truths in the Word, we realize we have a purpose in life (also called our birthright) and we want to get there. To possess our birthrights, we must both grow and build. By God's design, we must receive *from* Him before we build *with* Him. We cannot give what we've not first received. The process of cyclic receiving and giving is shown by the pink arrows in Figure 1-11.

Figure 1-11 As we move through repeated cycles of finding truth in God's word, we grow through intimacy with God and are able to build His Kingdom

Many of us don't realize our need to grow through intimacy with Him until we try to build His Kingdom and fall short of our expectations (see Figure 1-12). When we fail to build all the magnificent Kingdom of God we envision, we realize a need to grow. Our felt need to build motivates us to embrace the productive pain to seek a deeper relationship with Him, where we lean more deeply into His truths and grow through knowing Him better.

"Trials and obstacles in life are inevitable, but growing and maturing through them is optional." Author unknown

Growing and building are choices, and some choose not to grow or build. Two situations that can stop our growth and stop our being more and more effective as builders of the Kingdom are:

- We don't know how to grow or we decide growth is too painful or difficult and we stop growing. We might even stop trying to build the Kingdom.

- We are able to accomplish something in the Kingdom and settle for that even though it is not all we dream of.

Earned Trust and Earned Authority

To continue to grow through intimacy with Him and build His Kingdom, we need more dominion as sons of God. Jesus teaches us that His trust in us is earned, and earned trust leads to earned authority. Here is one of many examples in the Gospels:

Growth through Intimacy with God

Building God's Kingdom

Truth in God's Word

Figure 1-12 **When we are not yet mature, what we build is small compared to what we envision**

Who then is the faithful and wise servant, whom his master has set over his household, to give them their food at the proper time? Blessed is that servant whom his master will find so doing when he comes. Truly, I say to you, he will set him over all his possessions. Matthew 24:45-47

As children of God and human beings, we all have some innate authority in our lives. In addition, as we grow and mature, we earn more authority to help others.

==We earn God's trust and resulting authority when we make right responses to pain.== Two types of earned authority are:

- **Moral authority.** Our personal experiences of trusting God that we can share with others to help them see what is possible in their own similar situations.

- **Spiritual authority.** The standing we have before God that moves His heart to intervene for others as we celebrate with Him what He has done for us. We also gain authority to displace evil in a person's life. It has been said that spiritual authority is:

  - When God listens to us and responds.

  - When the devil listens to us and responds.

> Building the Kingdom is expressing our dominion as sons of God. As we grow through intimacy, we are able to express more of His dominion.

> Anne Hamilton defines authority as the delegated right to uphold the Word and will of God.

An example of earned trust and authority is when someone has learned to rely on God for supernatural help to stop smoking. That person is in a much better position to encourage a friend to rely on God and embrace the pain needed to stop smoking than a person who has never smoked. Through their own victory over smoking, they know God better and have earned God's trust and authority to pray for their addicted friends.

A Pastor Is Honest with God About His Legitimacy

Kent Mattox was led by God to open a new church. In brutal honesty, he told God, "I'm probably the most insecure pastor You've got. But I know You want to deliver me. I ask You to pour out Your people and provisions until I don't care and until You can deliver me." As the church grew to several hundred in only a few short months, Kent realized his insecurity had most likely caused God to make the church explode. When he heard about a church that closed its doors for the month of July as a seventh month Sabbath rest, God said, "I want to show you that you don't need money to build a church."

Kent admitted he was scared that, at the end of July, there would be no people and no money. But, as he obeyed God, he told the church:

1. If you came from another church and did not leave in good standing, go back and clean that up. Come back with a clean slate.

2. God might tell you to take what you've received here and go bless another church. Be free to do that.

3. Some need to take a break and enjoy family, coffee and the Sunday paper.

Near the end of July, money was running quite low when a lady dropped off a big check that paid all the bills for the month. At the first service in August, all the people returned plus an extra 140!

For every Sabbath July since then, God was faithful to perform many financial and spiritual miracles. The momentum and excitement when people returned in August after a month of rest was enough to propel them through the entire year.

For thought and discussion:

1. How did God respond to Kent's brutal honesty about his legitimacy issues?

2. Describe the legitimacy with God and community that Kent was able to develop by closing his church for a month.

3. What earned authority did Kent achieve by closing the church?

SOLVING PROBLEMS

Throughout this book, you learn to solve problems by identifying and applying the principles of God. In this section, we demonstrate the process of problem solving in four steps, which we apply many times in this book.

The four steps to solve a problem:

1. Collect data.

2. Analyze the data looking for repeating patterns.

3. Identify one or more principles from the patterns. Recall that a principle is a universal, non-optional, cause and effect relationship.

4. Apply the principle to the problem at hand and then to other problems in the future.

Let's take a very simple example to see how the four steps work:

1. Here's the data: Red, blue, chair, sofa, yellow, green, lamp, table, purple…

2. What is the pattern? Two colors are listed, followed by two pieces of furniture.

3. What is the principle? Alternating lists of two colors and two pieces of furniture.

4. Applying the principle, what will be the next item listed? A color.

Problem 1.1 Build Legitimacy in Those You Lead

A leader or mentor needs to be able to recognize that someone they lead (a child or adult) has not matured in one or more of the stages of growth and know how to help this person mature through the missing stage. The first stage of growth is belongingness, which builds in a person a deep sense of legitimacy or personal authority to be here.

In this team activity, you learn how Jesus interacted with His apostles to build legitimacy by establishing in them feelings of belongingness, worth and competence. You learn how to solve the problem of someone not feeling legitimate before God and in community by exploring how Jesus did it:

1. **Form a team of three or four people.**

2. **Collect data.** Each team member selects one of the four Gospels. Don't use the same Gospel as does another team member. Read or search through and make a list of each time Jesus interacted with His twelve disciples. Fill in the first two columns with a reference and state the interaction.

Reference	Interaction	Purpose
John 1:38	Jesus invites Andrew to spend the day with Him in His home.	Worth
John 1:42	Jesus gives Simon his new name, Peter.	Worth
...	...	...

3. **Analyze the data.** Working as a team, go through each of your lists and identify the purpose of each interaction, filling in the last column of the table:
   - Consistently meeting needs: **Belongingness**
   - Inclusion, often through communication: **Worth**
   - Command a task that stretches the person: **Competence**

   Make sure you all three agree on the purpose of each interaction. If you see more than one purpose for an interaction, pick the one you think was His primary purpose.

4. **Identify the principles.** Working as a team, examine the data and your analysis looking for consistent patterns that we can use to identify a principle that Jesus used to build belongingness, worth and competence. Collect as many observations of principles as you can. For example:
   - The data: Jesus built competence in His apostles by giving them tasks.
   - The pattern: All tasks Jesus assigned required supernatural resources.
   - The principle: God always provides the resources needed to complete a task He assigns us.

5. **Scripture to support the principle.** Find a Scripture that supports each principle. For example, one Scripture to support the above principle that God supplies resources to do His tasks is Philippians 4:19-20.

6. **Apply a principle to a new situation.** In the problems that follow, apply the principles you have just identified. You might need to return to your data and analysis to look for principles you might have overlooked.

Problem 1.2 Legitimacy Lies and Counterfeit Legitimacy

Dorothy works as an administrative assistant to the CEO of a construction firm. No matter how hard she works, she can never seem to please her boss. He criticizes her performance and reminds her daily of what she did not do, rarely praising her for what she did well. Rather than recognizing the boss is a blamer and predator and she needs to fire him (look for a new job), Dorothy beats herself up each day for not performing well.

Here are some legitimacy lies we can believe that lead to a counterfeit legitimacy:

- I am legitimate when people praise and acknowledge me.
- I am legitimate when I can solve your problems.
- I am legitimate when God answers my prayers.
- I am legitimate when I have friends who love me and care for me.
- I am legitimate when I know things or do things that you don't know or can't do.
- I am legitimate when I have more stuff or have a better life than you have.
- I am legitimate when God speaks to me more than He speaks to you.
- I am legitimate when I'm a leader and others look to me for their legitimacy.
- I am legitimate when I have an impressive title or degree.
- I am legitimate when I'm associated with the right people.

Questions and activities:

1. Of these legitimacy lies, which lies cause us to see ourselves as a commodity?

2. Of these legitimacy lies or others you can identify, which lies is Dorothy agreeing with to establish her legitimacy?

3. Do you think Dorothy's boss wants to be the one to legitimize her? Why or why not?

4. How can counterfeit legitimacies keep us from growing past people who try to legitimize us?

5. Self-blame can keep us from facing the real core problem and solving it at its root. State the core problem in her boss as best you can.

6. State the core problem in Dorothy as best you can.

7. Using the principles Jesus used to establish legitimacy in His apostles, propose a solution to each of the two core problems.

8. List three things Dorothy can do to reject a counterfeit legitimacy and embrace her true legitimacy based on the love of God.

9. Dorothy has come to you for help. You don't want to overwhelm her with your solutions. What are five questions you can ask her to steer her in the direction of uncovering the root of her problems and finding solutions?

Problem 1.3 Counterfeit Legitimacy by Title and Association

Read in 1 Kings 13 the story of the man of God sent from Judah to Israel who lost his life on that assignment.

Questions and activities:

1. What did the man of God do that was in disobedience to God?

2. Why do you think the man of God was deceived by the old prophet?

3. Fundamentally, which feeling did the man of God lack, belongingness, worth or competence, that led him to be deceived?

4. What statement or title of legitimacy was the man of God seeking?

5. What association do you think the man of God might have been seeking, which led him to be deceived?

6. What could the man of God have said to the old prophet when the prophet invited him to dinner that would have pleased God?

7. What counterfeit legitimacy would he have had to deny to please God in this situation?

8. If you were discipling this man of God, what strategy would you use to build in him the legitimacy he craved? Model your strategy after a strategy Jesus used to disciple His apostles.

9. Search deep into your own life for something you have done or said to attain legitimacy from a person or group that you admire. What is the legitimacy lie that you believed caused you to do that? (I would be legitimate if...)

10. Ask Holy Spirit for a story or character in the Bible where this same legitimacy lie was believed. Can you relate to the character in the story?

11. What heart-felt changes can you make to move your heart toward more genuine legitimacy before God and man?

12. What can you ask God to do for you to help you build more legitimacy with Him?

Problem 1.4 Embracing Productive Pain

Servants and slaves want to avoid all pain and tend to look for the fast and easy fixes in life or simply decide to live with their nonproductive pain. True sons of God know that productive pain is necessary for growth and transformation and are willing to pay the price.

For example, we can put up with a dripping faucet running up our water bill for months or years because we don't want to pay a plumber to fix the problem. Paying a high water bill is nonproductive pain. Paying the plumber to fix the problem is productive pain.

01

Questions and activities:

1. Is feeling illegitimate in community a source of nonproductive pain or productive pain? Explain your answer.

2. Are facing and renouncing the legitimacy lies we have believed a source of nonproductive pain or productive pain? Explain your answer.

3. Suppose a leader you admire de-legitimizes you because you failed to meet their expectations. Describe how this source of pain can be nonproductive or productive.

Problem 1.5 Building Belongingness in Community

You've just started a new job as assistant manager in an ice cream shop. After a few days, you realize that the staff is struggling to do community well and you're beginning to feel you do not belong. Rather than giving up on this job and starting a new job search, you decide to take this opportunity to learn the skill of building belongingness in community. To get started, you consider these six principles and activities that can help build belongingness:

- **Enjoy my joy.** People grow in belongingness when they can identify what gives them joy and learn to enjoy and savor what gives joy.

- **Celebrate.** Celebrating past and current achievements, both individually and corporately, helps bring a community together and builds belongingness. Celebrating essence, not based on what we do, is the foundation of belongingness.

- **Anchor truths.** We all need to have identified a few truths that we can always count on as anchors when life is not going well. For example, "God has a plan for my life."

- **"I'm glad to see you."** We all want to feel welcomed when we first walk into a room. Faces, words and behavior can make us feel welcomed or unwanted.

- **Physical stability.** Furniture, schedules and food can all be used in moderation to create an atmosphere of stability, which can help us feel that we belong.

- **Heritage.** Belongingness can be established in the generations by sharing the backstories and history of our family, school, or business. New family members, student or employees feel more a part of an organization when they know and celebrate its heritage.

Questions and activities:

Jesus often taught by asking questions. Because you don't know the staff well and have not yet gained enough respect to make major changes in how the ice cream shop is run, you decide to teach and build by asking questions:

1. What questions can you ask an employee when they are within ten minutes of finishing their shift?

2. Anne is the store manager and you know her birthday is coming up next week. What questions can you ask her best friend at the store to encourage her to celebrate Anne on her birthday?

3. John, the store owner, stops by a couple times a month to check on the store. What three questions can you ask John to help discover the heritage of the store? How can you best use the answers to these questions?

4. What anchor truth might you embrace about your job that you can share with other staff members? How can you share it with a question?

5. When it's your turn to lead a shift, what can you do or questions you can ask to help staff realize that you are glad to see them?

6. What simple things can you do during your shift to help staff members feel celebrated and valued?

7. You notice that schedules are not consistent from week to week, and this often creates stress with the staff because they don't know the hours they will work until Saturday for the following week. How can you approach the problem with Anne and John? What suggestions might you make? What reason might you give to convince them that stable schedules are good for business?

8. How can you celebrate essence and a person's right to belong to community regardless of their performance?

Problem 1.6
Renounce Legitimacy Lies and Build True Legitimacy

Legitimacy in community comes from knowing and experiencing God as a loving Father. Only then can He build into us the emotions of belongingness, worth, and competence which satisfy our feelings of being legitimate in a community.

> *His divine power has given us everything we need for a godly life through our knowledge of him who called us by his own glory and goodness. Through these he has given us his very great and precious promises, so that through them you may participate in the divine nature, having escaped the corruption in the world caused by evil desires.* 2 Peter 1:3-4

> For we are his workmanship, created in Christ Jesus for good works, which God prepared beforehand, that we should walk in them. Ephesians 2:10

We have the dignity of knowing we are chosen by God and these good works were all written in the book our Father wrote about us. Here is our true legitimacy in community that no one can take from us.

> *Your eyes saw me when I was formless; all [my] days were written in Your book and planned before a single one of them began.* Psalm 139:16 CSB

This verse does not indicate a few major good works, but rather speaks of *all* the days of our lives. Every day we walk with God in true legitimacy as His son or daughter.

Questions and activities:

1. What *everyday* activities might be written by your Father in your book that you are now doing or plan to do?

2. What *major* activities that you are now doing or hope or expect to do might be written in your book?

3. What preparations are you working on now to prepare for these good works?

4. What legitimacy lies have you been tempted to believe about yourself that oppose what you believe is written in your book?

Many of us have never given much thought to the good works God designed for us to do. In the next chapter, we lay a foundation for discovering these assignments by looking at how our Father uniquely designed us. Our design perfectly matches the good works He has assigned to us.

Problem 1.7 Build Belongingness for a New Family Member

You and your family have decided to take Susan into your home. Susan turned 18 the fall of her senior year in high school, and her parents decided they no longer needed to provide a home for her because she is legally an adult. She plans to graduate from high school, work full-time during the summer months, and go to college in the fall with plans to become a physician. She is an excellent student, stays out of trouble, smokes to calm her nerves, and works at a local restaurant on evenings and weekends. You want Susan to feel like she belongs to your family and can thrive in the family.

Christway Counseling Center *(www.christwaycounseling.com)* has identified 12 basic needs in a family. You can access the list on the Forms and Resources page on their website. Here is a brief description of the 12 needs:

1. **Acceptance.** The most basic need in a family is to know we are willingly accepted by another even when we mess up. We are accepted because God put us here.

2. **Admonition.** To know that we can count on a family member to gently warn us about potential problems helps build our confidence that we can be competent as a member of the family.

3. **Affection.** Physical touch, even a gentle tap on the shoulder, says someone cares about us and wants a close relationship.

4. **Appreciation.** Simple expressions of appreciation and thankfulness help us know that we are welcomed and wanted as a family member. We need to feel celebrated.

5. **Affirmation.** We all need to know that someone has a favorable opinion of us and is willing to say so.

6. **Attention.** We each need to feel that someone in the family is interested in our projects and goals.

7. **Comfort.** When we hurt, it's important another person in the family tenderly acknowledges that we are in pain.

8. **Encouragement.** We need family members to believe in us and our goals enough to urge us to keep going when the going is tough.

9. **Instruction.** We all need someone to model and train us in how to thrive in community.

10. **Respect.** We each need to be treated as though we are valuable and important to the family, even when we mess up.

11. **Security.** To rest and be at peace in the family, we cannot live on high alert or fear that we might be physically or emotionally harmed or kicked out at any time.

12. **Support.** A family member sometimes needs another to help carry the load, assisting as appropriate for the situation.

Do the following:

1. In the list of 12, categorize each need in one of three groups that build legitimacy through belongingness, worth or competence.

2. Look at your family and how you do life together. Describe how well you think your family meets each of the 12 family needs.

3. Of the 12 needs, list three needs that you believe your family does best.

4. Of the 12 needs, list three needs you believe the family should work on the most.

5. Based on the 12 needs, describe how successful you think your family would be at welcoming Susan into the family and meeting her needs.

6. To admonish Susan, what might you say to warn her to avoid causing potential problems in the family? Do you need to make a list of what she should avoid?

7. To encourage Susan, what instructions might you give her to help her fit into the family with joy and grace?

8. A written social contract can help establish some ground rules to help Susan fit into the family without too much stress on everyone. Write a social contract for every family member and Susan to sign. For example, one item in the social contract might be "No smoking inside the house." (An admonition to avoid problems.) Another might be "Everyone takes turns washing the dishes and taking out the garbage." (An instruction for success.)

9. Make a plan as to how your family might better meet one of the needs in the list and discuss your plan with your family. You might want to adjust the plan based on the family discussion.

10. What if anything did the family decide to do to implement the plan?

Problem 1.8 A Problem You Want to Solve

What is a minor or major problem in your life that you want to solve? You might begin this process of identifying a problem by asking God what is a problem He would like you to solve. State the problem as accurately as can. What data do you need to collect to help you solve the problem? What patterns can you observe from the data? What principles are involved? Can you solve the problem by applying these principles? Be sure to ask God for help and guidance as you work.

If you cannot solve the problem, perhaps the tools gained in later chapters will give you the skills and wisdom you need. Keep a record in your journal of progress made toward a solution.

GROWTH PROJECT

These projects are designed to help us grow ourselves and unpack our spirits so that we are better able to grow those we lead.

Growth Project 1.1 Evaluate Yourself as a Servant or Son of God

In the book of Exodus, God told Moses how he intended to bring the nation of Israel into their birthright with His seven "I will's":

> "Therefore, say to the Israelites: 'I am the Lord, and I will bring you out from under the yoke of the Egyptians. I will free you from being slaves to them, and I will redeem you with an outstretched arm and with mighty acts of judgement. I will take you as my own people, and I will be your God. Then you will know that I am the Lord your God, who brought you out from under the yoke of the Egyptians. And I will bring you to the land I swore with uplifted hand to give to Abraham, to Isaac and to Jacob. I will give it to you as a possession. I am the Lord.'" Exodus 6:6–8

But when Moses told the people what God had promised, they would not listen because of their small spirits and cruel oppression. In response, God devotes the entire book of Numbers to tell the stories of how He grew a nation of slaves and servants raised in Egypt into a nation of sons able to possess their land birthright in Canaan. Some of the characteristics of slaves and sons are listed in Table 1-2.

Table 1-2 Slaves consume what they can and sons build beyond themselves

Slaves, Servants or Consumers	Sons or Builders
I work to earn God's love and belong in community.	I know I belong to God and community based solely on His unconditional love for me, and I know my needs will be met.
I see myself as a commodity. What I like is not that important.	I see myself as a person. I know what I like and how I am designed with purpose and joy.
I obey when it is required. Tell me what to do. I reserve the right to sync or not sync to others.	I value the blessing of obedience. I take initiative. I do well even when my supervisor is not looking because I know it's right. I sync to my leaders, and I expect my followers to sync to me.
I avoid pain whenever I can. I want a free ride. I deserve it. The consequences of my wrongdoing are not that big a deal. I hope to get by with it.	I voluntarily embrace productive pain. Cause and effect: I recognize that every effect has a cause.
The end justifies the means. In general, I will go along with what others wants to do. I don't have the resources I need to be successful. Others have these resources and won't give them to me.	I will stand up for what is right even when I am put out of community. I don't generally look outside myself for solutions to my problems. I know the solutions are inside me to be unpacked.
I expect to be paid well for my skills, and I will do as I am told.	I see my value in an organization is more in my potential I can unpack than in the skills I currently possess. I look at myself and other people and see many resources we are not yet using. I want to unpack them in me and in others.
I see myself as a standalone. I often see myself as a loser and follower.	I see myself as a life-giving part of this tribe. I usually see myself as a winner and leader.

The book of Exodus describes the heart of God's people as slaves when they first came out of Egypt, and this book is about growing us from slaves to sons. At the beginning of each chapter, in the Principle section, is a Scripture from Exodus to help us understand the heart of a slave being transformed to the heart of a son.

Do the following:

1. In a table similar to the one started in Table 1-3, collect the seven Scriptures from the book of Exodus found in the Principles section of each of the seven chapters. Also list the corresponding characteristics of a slave and the "I will" of God that overcomes.

Table 1-3 The nature of slaves as described in seven verses in the Book of Exodus

Book chapter	Scripture	Nature of a slave	God promises "I will"	Do you need to grow in this area?
1	"So the people grumbled against Moses, saying, 'What are we to drink?'" Exodus 15:24	I lack resources. I don't expect my needs will be met.	"I will bring you out from under the yoke of the Egyptians."	
2...	...	...	...	...

2. In the last column in Table 1-3, evaluate yourself in this stage of growth.

3. Which stages of growth will you work on as you work your way through this book? Try to identify exactly what you expect to learn about God and His ways that will grow you to this level of maturity as a son of God. How do you expect your relationship with God will change?

Fundamentally, the yoke of the Egyptians is a poverty mindset that God is not enough and I am not enough. This up-side-down thinking causes us to see Jesus as weak and less than the real Jesus we need and causes us to work hard to make up for our intrinsic lack or give up trying because of our powerlessness.

To learn more about how to identify the stages of growth that are missing in our lives, see the Growth Project 5.3 near the end of Chapter 5 "Assessing Stages of Growth."

Growth Project 1.2
A Treasure Hunt for Resources

In the book of Numbers, the first thing God told Moses to do was to take a census of all the men in Israel able to serve in Isarel's army. A slave doesn't see the resources they have, and God as a good Father wanted His children to see how well equipped they were.

Suppose you have a friend who is having difficulty identifying the internal resources and assets they have available. This problem-solving activity guides you through a treasure hunt to find these resources. God puts inside us resources and assets through two ways: (1) our innate design and (2) the moral and spiritual authority we earn throughout our journey of life.

> It's not so much the favor or anointing on our lives that allows us to possess our birthright, but the authority we earn through overcoming the struggles of the journey.

Do the following:

1. Choose a partner. Ask your partner to tell you their life story as you take notes. Ask probing questions looking for the choices or voluntary actions your partner made throughout their life.

2. Create a table with four columns and collect your data into the first two columns, like this:

Situation or time range	Choice or action	Good/Bad/Both	Design (yes or no)
Went on first date and realized the girl did not have high moral standards	Did not ask her for another date		
Entered high school	Signed up for football		
Entered college	Played in a jazz band on weekends		

3. To begin analyzing the data, fill in the third column. Did your partner consider the choice a good one, bad one, or both good and bad, considering what they knew at the time?

4. Looking just at the good choices, what principles has your partner embraced? When we make good choices that affect how we live (cause and effect), we build earned authority to apply the underlying principles in our lives. With this earned authority, we can influence others for good. For example:

"My partner made a choice to play football, a tough team sport that teaches multiple principles of perseverance and teamwork."

5. Make up three stories where your partner can use their earned authority for good. For example:

    "Sally is struggling to keep up her schoolwork. My partner can describe to Sally how difficult it was to practice football in the sweltering August heat and how wonderful it felt when all that hard work paid off and the team won their first game."

6. Go back through all your partner's choices, good or bad, and fill in the fourth column. Did the choice uncover part of your partner's design? Yes or no.

7. Summarize what you have uncovered about your partner's design. For example

    "My partner has a love and talent for music and spontaneous performance."

Growth Project 1.3
Celebrate God with Thankfulness and Gratitude

We all need to see our good Father God as a good provider. This project is designed to build belongingness and heal our brains by applying the strategy given in the book of Romans:

For although they knew God, they neither glorified him as God nor gave thanks to him, but their thinking became futile, and their foolish hearts were darkened. Romans 1:21

Paul teaches here that people who do not express gratitude and thankfulness toward God will think empty thoughts and their hearts will become unintelligent. To prevent this brain rot and a dark heart that has little understanding, we must develop a lifestyle of gratitude and thankfulness toward God for all the good things He gives us and does for us. When we do so, we can expect not only a healthy brain and heart, but also to know His will for us:

Do not conform to the pattern of this world but be transformed by the renewing of your mind. Then you will be able to test and approve what God's will is—his good, pleasing and perfect will. Romans 12:2

When God gives us His plans or directions and our minds and hearts can only think empty (barren or unproductive) thoughts, we cannot hear His will, test it, or approve it. The thoughts from God never land, or if they do land, we dismiss them as being too wonderful for us with our rotting brains and small thinking and lack of understanding.

Design a plan to express thankfulness and gratitude each day. Decide where, how and with whom you intend to say thank you to God and tell Him and others how grateful you are for what He has done that day. Share your plan with your discussion group, class, spouse or family. Then work the plan.

Growth Project 1.4 Create a Creed for Your Organization

A creed is a formal statement of your core values or beliefs. In an organization, it can serve as a written social contract of how the organization does life together. In Figure 1-13, you see a creed based on the seven stages of growth, written for a school. The children recite the creed at the beginning of each school day and work toward following the expectations in the creed they have all agreed to.

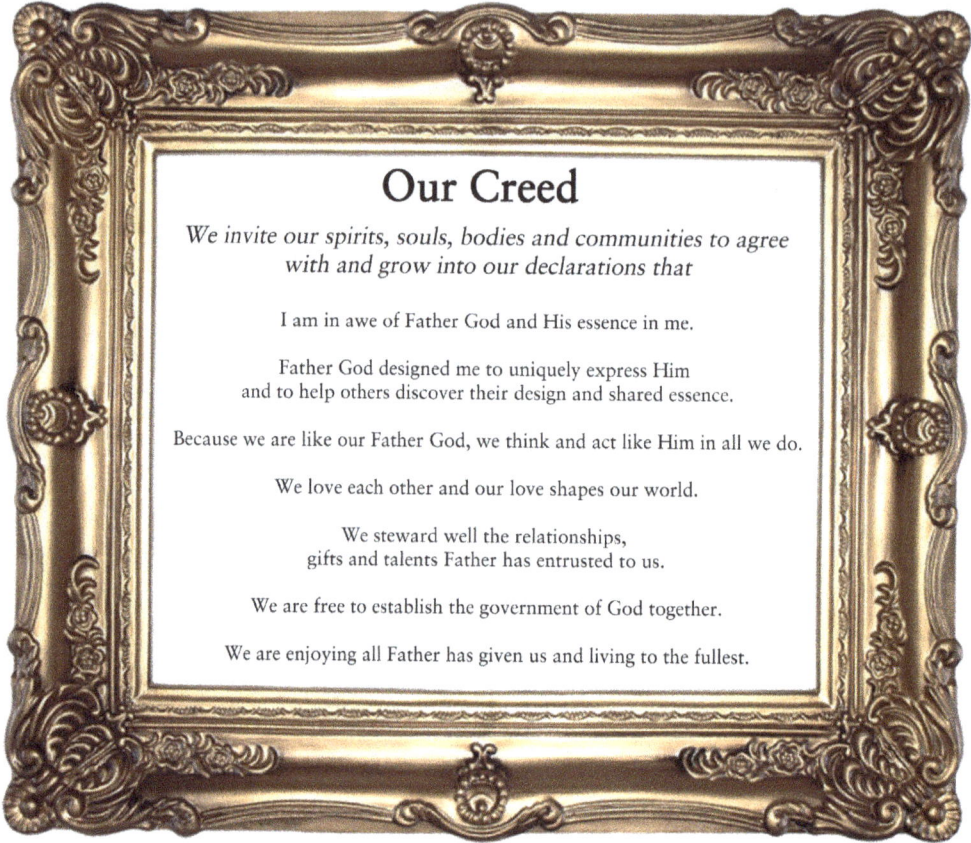

Our Creed

We invite our spirits, souls, bodies and communities to agree with and grow into our declarations that

I am in awe of Father God and His essence in me.

Father God designed me to uniquely express Him
and to help others discover their design and shared essence.

Because we are like our Father God, we think and act like Him in all we do.

We love each other and our love shapes our world.

We steward well the relationships,
gifts and talents Father has entrusted to us.

We are free to establish the government of God together.

We are enjoying all Father has given us and living to the fullest.

Figure 1-13 A sample creed based on the seven stages of growth and principles of Wisdom

Using this creed as a beginning point, do the following:

1. Read the "Here We Grow" sections near the beginning of each chapter to understand the seven stages of growth. Discuss with your organization (family, school or business) how you want to do life together to create an atmosphere of growth and transformation.

2. Write your own creed so that everyone can agree on it and commit to it.

3. Reciting the creed each day can set the atmosphere for the organization and change the culture.

SPIRIT PROJECT

The spirit projects at the end of each chapter are designed to enlarge your spirit, help you unpack the design of your spirit and learn to dialog with your spirit so that you can better know and synchronize with God.

Spirit Project 1.1 Is There a Spirit World?

Read Psalm 18 and Psalm 23. David is spirit aware and writes about this awareness in many of the Psalms. How would you describe his spirit world in Psalm 18? In Psalm 23? Can you describe or draw a picture of his spirit world at one point in these Scriptures?

In Luke 22:29, Jesus said, "I confer on you a kingdom, just as my Father conferred one on me." In John 18:36, Jesus said, "My kingdom is not of this world." The Kingdom of God is in the spirit realm and so are our kingdoms. As profound as it might sound, we are expected to rule and reign in the spirit world. As you work your way through these Spirit Projects in the book, my hope is you will be able to see and experience your spirit world and learn to rule and reign in it. Can you describe or draw a picture of what you see when you ask Jesus to show you this realm?

Spirit Project 1.2 Blessing the Spirits of Those You Lead

Throughout this course, you will get to know your spirit better and learn to talk with your spirit and the spirits of others, be led by your spirit, and learn from your spirit. In this chapter, we begin the process by blessing your spirit and the spirits of others.

Do the following:

1. Go to Arthur Burk's website at **theSLG.com** and search under Free Stuff, Audio, where you will find several albums on blessing your spirit. Download and listen to one of these albums, inviting your spirit to come to the front and receive these blessings.

2. Invite your spirit to come to the front and, in your own words, bless your spirit. As you speak your blessings, consider what you know that God wants your spirit to know and do. Develop the habit of blessing your spirit each day. A good time to bless your spirit is right before you go to sleep or wake up.

3. Write a blessing for the spirits of all those you lead. If you lead a family, business or classroom, write the blessings based on goals you have for your organization. Read the blessings aloud each morning. If the people in your organization are not ready to hear you bless their spirits, you can bless them in private.

4. Watch and record the changes you see that reflect your blessings.

To learn to bless your spirit, listen to "Blessing Your Spirit: Precious Daughter" or "Blessing Your Spirit: Beloved Son" at **theSLG.com**

Spirit Project 1.3 Receiving Father's Love

Hebrews 12 refers to Father God as the Father of our spirits. When we realize that God is spirit and we are spirits made by Him and like Him and coming from Him, it's easier for us to receive His love. Father hungers to receive us into His arms and love on us as His dear children of light. If you have never experienced the emotions of being received into the arms of your loving Father God, ask Jesus to help you.

Settle yourself down in a calm place and fix your eyes on Jesus. In this place of quietness with Him, ask Jesus to take you to the Father to receive His love. The feeling of experiencing this unconditional love is beyond any love the earth can offer and is sufficient to heal an orphan heart. Take the time to soak in this love often.

Spirit Project 1.4 My Essence

When I first became a Christ follower, I saw Jesus reach His hands into God expressed as the eternal River of God flowing as liquid light. Then He brought up a large double-handful of this essence of God and formed me as solid and finite light that shone with divine brilliance. I knew then I was from God, of God. Ask God to show you the essence of your spirit. How do you see your spirit? What is your spirit made of?

Where to Go from Here?

With Chapter 1 as your foundation, I suggest, rather than reading the book sequentially from cover to cover, you search the book, looking for the content that best helps meet your current needs. Figure 1-14 can get you started, and so can the Table of Contents. And don't forget the forums at *FromHisTable.com* where you can meet up with others to ask questions and process solutions.

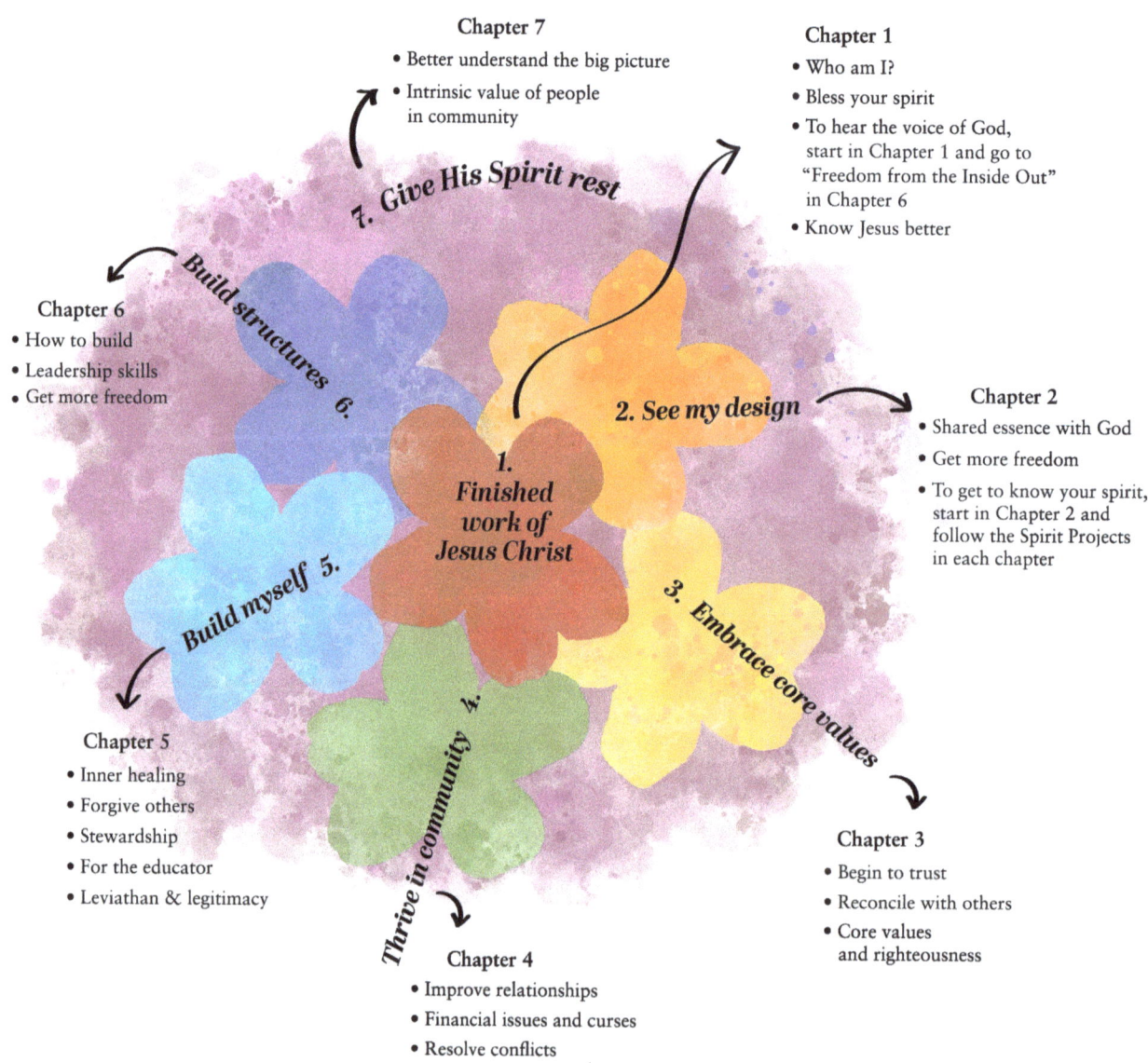

Chapter 7
- Better understand the big picture
- Intrinsic value of people in community

7. Give His Spirit rest

Chapter 1
- Who am I?
- Bless your spirit
- To hear the voice of God, start in Chapter 1 and go to "Freedom from the Inside Out" in Chapter 6
- Know Jesus better

Build structures 6.

Chapter 6
- How to build
- Leadership skills
- Get more freedom

2. See my design

1. Finished work of Jesus Christ

Chapter 2
- Shared essence with God
- Get more freedom
- To get to know your spirit, start in Chapter 2 and follow the Spirit Projects in each chapter

Build myself 5.

3. Embrace core values

Chapter 5
- Inner healing
- Forgive others
- Stewardship
- For the educator
- Leviathan & legitimacy

Thrive in community 4.

Chapter 3
- Begin to trust
- Reconcile with others
- Core values and righteousness

Chapter 4
- Improve relationships
- Financial issues and curses
- Resolve conflicts

Figure 1-14 Explore the book for what you need next

"I am in awe of the God who patiently waits for my question"

"*My sheep hear my voice, and I know them, and they follow me.*" John 10:27

CHAPTER 02 GROWING IN OUR GOD-GIVEN DESIGNS

"I am in awe of God who designed me and sent me to carry His light and likeness into the earth."

02

PRINCIPLE

The Greek word for authority in Matthew 8:9 is "exousia" and means "power of choice." When we are under the authority of God or a righteous leader, their authority empowers our choices. We can do something we could not have done without their authority. To have this power of choice is to have freedom. A key to understanding dominion and authority is to know that when we submit to God, the result is freedom to do, not oppression.

The Principle of Dominion or Authority

With the **principle of dominion**, God designed us with His expectation that you and I love and care for His creation by ruling over it. He gives us His authority over our own lives, our physical world, and evil in the spirit realm. He intends us to love and empower those we lead to also walk in dominion. If we don't exercise our dominion or empower others to have dominion, we can become victims.

Sons Trust Their Leaders and Release Authority to Others

Jesus taught that we cannot effectivity rule over creation without trusting God.

The centurion replied, "Lord, I do not deserve to have you come under my roof. But just say the word, and my servant will be healed. For I myself am a man under authority, with soldiers under me. I tell this one, 'Go,' and he goes; and that one, 'Come,' and he comes. I say to my servant, 'Do this,' and he does it."

When Jesus heard this, he was amazed and said to those following him, "Truly I tell you, I have not found anyone in Israel with such great faith.

Matthew 8:8–10

The centurion understood that to have authority, we must be under the authority of someone who can do what we cannot do. In this situation, he trusted Jesus that He was indeed submitted to the God who could heal. He also understood that God had given this authority to heal to Jesus. Jesus called his understanding and confidence to act on this authority "faith."

The centurion also understood that to have authority is to give authority to those we lead. Part of God's nature and essence is authority, and His desire is to give that authority to His sons and daughters. We understand that God expects us to not hold that authority selfishly but to release it to others. God gave authority to Adam and Eve and expected them to give that same divine authority to their sons and daughters who would give it to their sons and daughters. Thus, the garden of Eden would grow to encompass the entire earth. In doing so, the essence and authority of God would cover the earth, as expressed in all His sons and daughters.

Slaves Don't Trust Authority and Can Disobey to Get Their Needs Met

Slaves see authority differently. Because they find it difficult to trust God and their leaders, they also cannot trust authority. When we don't trust authority, we can believe we must disobey authority to get our needs met:

In the desert the whole community grumbled against Moses and Aaron. The Israelites said to them, "If only we had died by the Lord's hand in Egypt! There we sat around pots of meat and ate all the food we wanted, but you have brought us out into this desert to starve this entire assembly to death."

Then the Lord said to Moses, "I will rain down bread from heaven for you. The people are to go out each day and gather enough for that day. In this way I will test them and see whether they will follow my instructions."

Exodus 16:2–4

Trusting God with His Authority and Our Design

When we can trust God that He gave us all we need for godliness and good works, we see no value or need for disobedience and find delight in following God and His ways. To willfully disobey Him is to not know Him. To know Him, is to joyfully accept His authority as our authority and to use that authority to give authority to others.

> *"I am in awe of the God who is passionate about our walking in dominion."*
> Arthur Burk

How do we build authority in ourselves and others? The first step is to discover what God has put in us of His divine nature and essence, which gives us everything we need to live a godly life.

His divine power has given us everything we need for a godly life through our knowledge of him who called us by his own glory and goodness. Through these he has given us his very great and precious promises, so that through them you may participate in the divine nature, having escaped the corruption in the world caused by evil desires.

2 Peter 1:3–4

HERE WE GROW

In stage 2 of growth, we are free to discover what we like and don't like and to begin the process of knowing ourselves.

Growth Stage 2: I'm Discovering Myself, and I Like What I See

Discovering who we are generally happens at the toddler or preschool age. Ever watch a two-year old step into the ocean or taste a new food for the first time? They instantly know, yes, I love this or no, I hate that and are quite free to allow their preferences to be known loud and clear! Even before the age of five, God designed us to discover our likes and dislikes. He wants us to get to know ourselves at this early age and to know what we love and what feels good and right to us. See Figure 2-1.

Figure 2-1. Preschool children need time and encouragement to discover what they like and don't like.

As we discover ourselves, we discover His design within us.

- What of Himself did He put in me?
- How am I like my Father God?
- What are my innate talents, likes, dislikes, and creativity that He wants me to enjoy and express?

My unique design matches up perfectly with His plans for my life. To know this helps me to like myself and also helps me to discover what I want in life – that which will ultimately bring me true happiness and fulfillment. In so doing, I keep discovering my Father, what He is like and what brings Him joy.

Building Intuition

When I know something of what is inside me and some of what I want in life, I begin to trust **my intuition** because I know what feels good and right to me. As I settle into knowing and liking me and my sense of what is good and right for me, I gain confidence in making decisions. Often, decisions are based on feelings of pleasure and intuition. The progressions are shown in Figure 2-2.

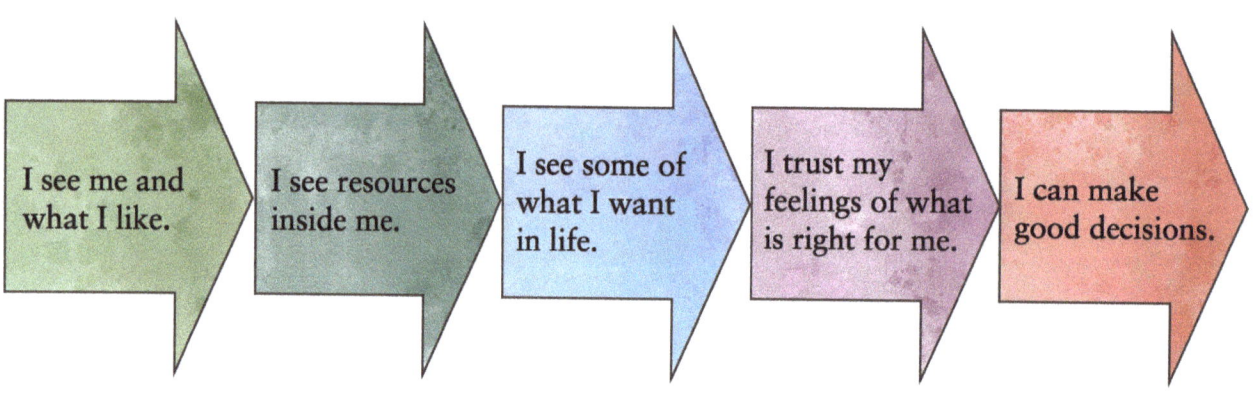

Figure 2-2. By discovering myself and what I want in life, I begin to trust my intuition when making decisions.

When this stage of growth does not happen or is not complete, we might:

1. Not know what we want.

2. Not make decisions easily or will make decisions from the head and not the heart.

3. Have little intuition, which can make us blind followers of others. We can take the attitude, "Whatever you like is fine with me."

4. Be a people pleaser, always thinking about what the other wants or needs without ever taking care of our own needs. We might not even be in touch with our own needs.

5. Be a poor leader, unable to make bold decisions and inspire others to follow even when it hurts. Or we might lead based on what others want or the consensus of the group.

6. Not take risks because we don't trust what we want or what is inside us.

02

When We Missed This Stage of Growth

Children who lived with abuse, trauma, sickness, extreme poverty, homelessness or other crises during their first five years might not have had the opportunity to discover themselves or their likes and dislikes. But remember, it's never too late to grow up.

To grow into this stage of discovering ourselves and liking what we see, we can:

- **Intentionally pay attention to what we like and don't like.** Because of severe trauma during my early years, I largely missed this stage of growth. Later in life, when I understood its importance, I kept a notebook of all the things I liked to do or eat or see. As I did this, I began to discover myself and what I loved. Why was this so important? Because I needed to discover my design. I needed to know what of Himself my Father God had put in me that would take me to a deeper bond with Him and a greater capacity to have a fulfilling and powerful life.

- **Discover our design**. God designed each of us in unique ways by putting some of His own essence in each of us. In this chapter, you learn about your Trinitarian design and your redemptive gift. He wrote all the pages of our book with assignments unique to our design, and we will spend a lifetime discovering it.

- **Discover our talents.** Talents might include music, art, athletic abilities, intellect, leadership, discernment, and so many others. When we discover a talent we have, the next question is if and how we develop that talent.

- **Discover our core passions.** In later chapters, we explore our core passions in detail. We all have core passions that can help us identify what really matters to us and what God has called us do.

- **Discover our birthrights.** Paying attention to what we like, our designs, our talents and passions can help us discover our callings or birthrights. However, many times the biggest clue to our birthrights is the greatest problems or obstacles we face in life.

For more on how to discover who we are and what God has put in each of us, listen to the audio album "Office of Personhood" by Arthur at **theSLG.com.**

CONCEPTS

In this part of the chapter, we explore some categories of design, and how we each uniquely express God in our design.

As we discover our unique design, keep in mind:

- It can be difficult to see our own design because it's so natural for us that we can easily miss it. For this reason, we often need others to point it out to us. Our design is like free money to us. No one taught us or showed us how to operate out of our design, and yet it comes so easily because it's just who we are.

- Woundedness can mask our design. The enemy knows our design and attacks us in that area to shut us down and destroy our greatest strengths before we can be a threat.

> Think of Jesus sent to earth to rescue us from death and slavery, defeat the enemy, and reconcile us to the Father and yet, because of His birth, all the baby boys in the region were murdered. His design and birthright were attacked even at His birth.

Concept 2.1 Our Trinitarian Design

By design, God created each of us to express one Member of the Trinity more prominently than the others. Each Member of the Trinity has a specific domain of greatest influence:

- **Father God** is all about family and our being reconciled back into His **community**.
- **Jesus Christ** is intensely committed to our walking in **dominion**.
- **Holy Spirit** passionately desires that we steward well His **creation**.

We are created to relate well with each Member of the Trinity and to engage in community, dominion and creation. However, our design and destiny are tied primarily to one over the others (see Figure 2-3).

Community   Dominion   Creation

Figure 2-3 Where is our passion and intense fire?

We're all on a journey. At different stages in life, we might express one Member of the Trinity more than the other two. God knows we must get to know each Member of the Trinity at different stages of our journey. Consider these situations:

- Jessica, a dominion person, was often abused by her father. Jesus has her on a journey to become a magnificent expression of Himself as Dominion. She must, however, learn to do community first; otherwise, she might become a predator with little compassion for others. During one season of her life, Father God showed Himself to be her tender and gentle Father who loves her deeply and taught her to live in a healthy community with trustworthy men. Then Jesus began to move toward her to heal the powerlessness and teach her to walk in His dominion from a place of tenderness rather than toughness.

- Joe was created for community, but early in life, because of a learning disability, he was shamed and rejected by his peers and teachers. For comfort, he turned to alone time in nature and everyone pegged him as a creation boy where he learned to meet with Holy Spirit, even learning to care for wounded wild animals in his free time. As an adult, he found his love and passion for Father God and community when he chose psychotherapy as his profession. In his role helping others get free, he learned to partner with Jesus in His dominion role of setting the captive free.

As God heals us and shows us our birthrights, we can expect it to become clear which playing field (community, dominion, or creation) burns hottest in our hearts. The main point now is to know about Trinitarian design and to trust the process to discovery as God leads us. Later in the chapter, we include a profile strategy to help identify our Trinitarian design.

Another category of design is our redemptive gifts.

Concept 2.2
The Seven Redemptive Gifts

Our spirits are made of divine light – God's light – and this divine variegated light is capable of and actually did create a universe. You and I have within us the colors of light that hold the design and spiritual resources to create, and each of us is different, with different callings, assignments, birthrights, talents, and resources, all uniquely orchestrated by God to represent Him accurately on the earth. What brilliant and vibrant colors of God did He put in your spirit to show the world?

The seven redemptive gifts listed in Romans 12 and Table 2-1 give some clues to what God intends to release into the earth of Himself with each gift. Arthur calls these gifts our redemptive gifts because God wants to meet us in this special place of His shared essence and reveal Himself to creation through the gift, looking toward the redemption of all things.

> "The ache for belongingness is healed at the deepest level by knowing and rejoicing in shared essence."
> Arthur Burk

Table 2-1 Seven redemptive gifts

	Prophet	Servant	Teacher	Exhorter	Giver	Ruler	Mercy
Mature expression	Shines divine light into darkness	Releases God's authority to others	Releases truth for reconciliation to God	Inspires by revealing the essence of God	Provides resources to give new access to God	Builds culture and structures for freedom to follow God	Brings fulfillment and alignment for the entire ecosystem
Purpose	Faces a problem and solves it	Raises up leaders	Sees and perfects truths to establish the government of God	Expresses reality in cause and effect relationships	Births new things	Brings order and gets things done	Brings a system to rest
Struggle to maturity	Learn to forgive and have compassion for self and others	See yourself as God sees you	Have the courage to speak truth, balance rights and responsibilities	Embrace the pain and learn legitimacy in the struggle	Not be independent or selfish	Controlling, demanding, ungrateful	Stubborn, enabling, people pleaser
Wrong path	Sharp tongue and little community	Victim, shamed and belittled	Sexual perversion and religious spirit	Demand loyalty and exploit others	Rebellious predator	Militant conqueror	Exploited and abused

Our soul leads with one of these gifts, which sets the tone for our personalities, talents, dreams and passions. Once you know how to recognize the gifts, you can spot the gift in even a small child. For example, Cari is 7 years old; she is strong-willed and has a strong sense of justice and what is right and wrong. She speaks her mind fully, unedited and opinionated. She carries the Prophet gift!

As we study the gifts, it helps to compare them to some other groupings of seven in Scripture:

- Seven days of creation helps us understand the purpose of each gift as we see what God did on each day.

- Seven letters to the seven churches in Revelation where Jesus points our strengths and weakness of each gift.

- Seven words of Jesus Christ when He suffered on the cross express His passion for each gift.

- Seven pillars or principles of Wisdom (Proverbs 9) are the keys to the fulfillment of each gift.

Redemptive Gift 1. Prophet and Design

The Prophet is designed by God to receive light and release it to others. Because they are equipped to see that creation was designed to work well, they can easily spot where something is off. Out of their relationship with God, they can see the light needed to solve the problem. Arthur describes the Prophet gift as the Research and Development Department for the Body of Christ.

Revelation 1 and 2 demonstrate a fine expression of the Prophet redemptive gift when Jesus sent seven letters to the seven churches explaining in bold and vivid language what they had done well, where they were sinning and what they needed to do to move forward in their design.

The first letter is to the church in Ephesus, a Prophet church, where Jesus commended them for hating the practices of the Nicolaitans who, according to early church history, polluted and compromised worshipping God with all kinds of evil practices and idolatry. In the bold language Jesus used, He made it clear He does not hate the Nicolaitans but rather their deeds of pollution and compromise.

Purpose of the Prophet Gift

The Prophet enjoys the new and is often a bold trailblazer (see Figure 2-4) who sees far and is willing to work long and hard to cut a path for pioneers to follow. The Prophet is bold and confident to speak, sometimes impulsive in their words and their giving. They are likely to confidently believe there's a path forward when others have given up or not even tried.

The Prophet passionately needs to know how things work and make sense of things. Never say to a Prophet, "Just trust me and follow. You don't need to understand where we are going or what we are doing." Not gonna work for a Prophet!

Because the Prophet delights in fixing broken things, they like to spend time with broken people who need their solutions.

Figure 2-4 The Prophet is a bold trailblazer who sees far

 John Adams and His Personality

John Adams, the second President of the United States, appeared to carry the Prophet gift and makes for an interesting character study. Let's look at a few details of his life and personality:

- As an attorney, Adams defended the British soldiers in the Boston Massacre of 1770, because he believed every person deserved the right to counsel and a fair trial. During the trial, he said, "Facts are stubborn things... whatever our passion, they cannot alter the state of facts and evidence." He achieved acquittal for six of the soldiers.

- Having decided that independence from Britain was necessary, Adams organized a committee to draft the Declaration of Independence and persuaded the committee to choose Thomas Jefferson to write the document because "I am obnoxious, suspected, and unpopular. You are very much otherwise." Later, Adams successfully argued before the Second Continental Congress to adopt the declaration, which happened on July 4, 1776.

- During the Revolutionary War, Adams worked tirelessly in Europe raising money and other resources for the effort, and in 1789, was elected the first Vice President of the newly formed United States of America. No more than six months into the office, he wrote to his wife Abigail that the office was "not quite adapted to my character ... too inactive, and mechanical." Later, he wrote, "My country has in its wisdom contrived for me the most insignificant office that ever the invention of man contrived or his imagination conceived."

- During the 1796 presidential election, Adams was described by other political leaders as "too vain, opinionated, unpredictable and stubborn to follow directions."

- As the second President of the United States, Adams was the first to occupy the White House. He wrote, "I pray Heaven to bestow the best of Blessings on this House and all that shall hereafter inhabit it. May none but honest and wise Men ever rule under this roof."

- After having retired, he wrote, "No man who ever held the office of President would congratulate a friend on obtaining it."

02

For thought and discussion:

1. Prophets simply cannot tolerate powerlessness. They want to fix a problem and immediately move on to the next one and can go stir-crazy when asked to maintain what's already working. List the ways John Adams exhibited these characteristics of the Prophet gift.

2. Prophets are quick to take initiative and can change course quickly. Describe how the gift worked in John Adams to birth the United States.

3. Prophets gravitate to justice as a core value. How did Adams demonstrate this characteristic?

4. Prophets don't normally do community well. What is a statement Adams made that indicates he did not see himself as a people person? What is a statement others made about him?

5. Fill in the following table, listing three traits about John Adams that confirm he had the Prophet gift and three people you know personally who demonstrate one of these traits. One of these three people can be yourself.

Trait of John Adams as Prophet	A person you know with this trait

6. Do you believe one or more of the people listed in question 5 have the Prophet gift? Explain your answer.

The Immature or Wounded Prophet

The Prophet might judge others for their inconsistency, laziness and compromises. Because Prophets can shift tasks and projects quickly, they might not finish one before starting another and never look backward at the trail of unfinished projects they left behind.

A Prophet has a wide range of emotions that run deep. Because they feel deeply and work hard, they can shut down emotionally and withdraw when they feel someone they have robustly and passionately invested in have let them down.

The Prophet's Struggle to Maturity

God requires the Prophet to pay a high price in their struggle to maturity. Look at Miriam, Naomi, Ezekiel, Caleb, John the Baptist, and Peter as possible examples. Each faced multiple failures and disappointments and were equally hard on themselves until they were finally able to find reconciliation and peace with God, themselves and community. They each proved to be big people who made amazing contributions to the Kingdom.

Compassion does not come easy for the immature Prophet. In the mind of the Prophet, when you have done wrong, you need to say so and repent, loud and clear! No cheap grace! Prophets deal with sin head on! Denial can drive a Prophet to act with great boldness. And, as John the Baptist found out, cost one their head.

However, this same denial that frustrates them when another does it can keep them from forgiving themselves. A Prophet can fall into the trap of thinking they must sacrifice greatly to serve God. They can drive themselves nuts with not forgiving themselves until they can finally say to God, "God, I don't owe You anything," which is the key to ending the torment described in Matthew 18.

Redemptive Gift 2. Servant and Dominion

Although the Servant gift gets little honor in our society, it packs a mighty punch in the spirit realm. God trusts the Servant with authority generally beyond what He can trust to other gifts, primarily because the Servant doesn't usually focus on their own honor or needs but is quick to recognize and respond to the needs of others.

Purpose of the Servant Gift

The passion of the Servant gift is to get under and raise up leaders while keeping his eyes on God rather than the needs of the one he serves. In doing so, this leader has the opportunity to become an effective reflection of God they are designed to be. Some people in Scripture who most likely had the Servant gift are Barnabas, Timothy, Ananias, and Joseph, the husband of Mary. Some characteristics of the mature Servant are:

- **See the best in others.** Servants find it easy to forgive and overlook offense and give others the benefit of the doubt. Mature Servants easily give honor to others and rarely hold a grudge.

- **Obedient and alert to the needs of others.** A Servant easily sees the needs of others and finds it easy to obey God and follow their leaders. Think of Joseph who changed directions for his life based on a single dream and was able to protect Mary and the young Jesus.

- **Restoration of family.** The Servant can be the counselor and peacemaker. They are able to reach those difficult to get along with and sometimes be a bridge in building broken family relationships.

- **Love the unlovable.** They are willing and able to hug the porcupines in a community. Think of Ananias reaching out to Saul, soon to be Paul, when all others wanted nothing to do with him. And what about Barnabus embracing John Mark when others were done with him?

- **Hard-working and loyal to family.** Servants tend to be pure in motive, not working to earn favors.

- **Authority to protect boundaries.** The Servant can be adept at establishing emotional boundaries and coaching others to do the same. They are quick to see where a community is scapegoating, gaslighting or unjustly accusing someone, and are often involved in inner healing and deliverance ministries. The Servant can establish land boundaries and is often involved in cleaning projects, such as intercession to cleanse the land.

Jack Stack Gave Authority to Those He Led

Jack Stack lives out the Servant gift with authority and wisdom. In 1983, Jack had worked his way up the assembly lines and was plant manager remanufacturing engines for heavy equipment when the plant almost went bankrupt. He and several other employees purchased the plant and, over a few short years, made it a profitable company and a sought-after place to work. At the heart of their Servant-style solution to a successful business, they empowered and gave authority to everyone in the organization.

In his book, "The Great Game of Business," Jack describes what they did:

- **The fundamental problem is ignorance, and their core business is education.** Employees who don't understand how money is made and spent in the company will kill a business. They taught everyone how the business works and exactly how their particular job affected the bottom line of profitability. Jack established a corporate culture where everyone is learning and growing all the time.

- **Eliminate all the jobs and expect everyone to be owners.** Jack calls workers who think a job is just a job the "living dead" because they expect to go nowhere. Jack realized that ownership is a mindset, and he worked hard to give people hope again, to take pleasure in their work, and to make a true contribution to the company.

- **Problems are shared.** Jack operated the business with "open book management," which means the Profit and Loss statements and the Balance sheets were shared with every employee in the company. Everyone knew who made what salary, what raw materials cost, where every sales dollar was made and who made what commission, and everything else about the finances of the company. Nothing was hidden, even Jack's salary. When a problem arose, the data was available to whomever might contribute to its solution, and anyone in the company might be called on to help solve a problem. The authority to make decisions for resolution went down the authority chain to the ones nearest the problem and its solution.

- **We are all on the same team and this team wins.** Every effort was made to eliminate competition from the company culture. Employees or departments no longer competed against others for a bonus. Bonuses were readily awarded but were based on the company bottom line where everyone contributed as a team to share the win. Jack created a culture of winners winning by celebrating small wins and celebrating people. Something or someone is always being celebrated.

- **Keep the big picture out in front of everyone.** Everyone needs to see the big picture of why the company exists and where they fit in. To accomplish that, all their products were marketed to every employee, people moved around in the company so they became familiar with every area of the company, managers put people out in the field to meet their customers and hear their stories, and the company got heavily involved in the local community.

For thought and discussion:

1. Fill in the following table, listing three traits about Jack Stack that indicate he has the Servant gift and three people you know personally who demonstrate one of these traits. One of these three people can be yourself.

Trait of Jack Stack as Servant	A person you know with this trait

2. Do you believe one or more of the people listed in question 1 have the Servant gift? Explain your answer.

3. The Servant is designed by God to express God's authority on the earth. By God's design, when we have authority, we release authority to those under us. Describe three ways Jack released authority to those under his authority.

4. In Jack's company, employees were encouraged to purchase part ownership in the company. How does this bring a new level of authority to employees?

5. As Jack's company began to prosper, they offered investment opportunities to their employees to start their own companies, and his company is now known as an ongoing business incubator. How is this a win for Jack's company when some of their best employees left to start their own businesses?

6. Jack believes the primary purpose of a business is to create jobs for the community. He suggested that churches, governments, and schools have largely failed to influence or lead, and that it might be necessary for businesses to take up the slack. Describe how a business can do what we traditionally expect a church, government or school to do.

7. If you were to own your own business, what of Jack's ideas might you implement? Why?

The Immature or Wounded Servant

Because of their quiet, giving, and unselfish nature, their greatest challenge is enabling or becoming the victim to those who would exploit their gift. The Servant who is not yet mature:

- Can see themselves as insignificant, inadequate, or powerless and can be susceptible to being used by people.

- Servants easily extend honor to others but find it challenging to accept honor. Servants often cannot believe in themselves when life is not going well. They and others can take themselves for granted.

- Can enable others and make excuses for their messes so that others don't mature or clean up their messes. A Servant might be in denial about their spoiled children or unrighteous members of the family. A wise Servant will empower, not enable.

- Finds it difficult to invest in their own spiritual growth, rest, or restoration.

The Servant's Struggle to Maturity

The immense authority God designed for the Servant to walk in comes when they are doing what God called them to do rather than what people want them to do. The Servant's greatest struggle is to believe in themselves, especially when life is not going well. They can develop great authority if they can get past the lie "I'm a nobody" and be able to say no to people in need so that God is honored above all else. The struggle is to see themselves as God sees them, and to do all things for the glory of God.

When God invites us into a God-size assignment, are we willing to be a person big enough to partner with God for that assignment?

The Servant aligns with the second day of creation, the second words Jesus spoke on the cross, and the second letter to the churches in Revelation:

- **Know your essential value to community and life.** On the second day, God created the atmosphere. The air is essential to our existence, but we seldom think about it or acknowledge it. The Servant gift is essential to all the other gifts, but the Servant must see and know the vastness of that assignment at the core of their being.

- **See yourself as God sees you.** The second words Jesus spoke on the cross were, "Today you will be with me in paradise." In the middle of His deepest humiliation and destruction, Jesus still knew who He was so much that He could turn to the man on the cross beside Him and say, "Don't worry. I've got you."

- **Embrace your pure heart and your great authority.** The second letter to the churches in Revelation was the only letter that did not contain a rebuke from Jesus. Rather Jesus spoke of their authority over death and offered them a crown of great authority to establish life.

My friend Jason is a gentle Servant who loves people and serves them well, and yet struggled with his legitimacy in community. That wound was healed when Jesus told him that Jesus had made him so righteous that he could open any seal in heaven. I believe that Jesus was expressing the Servant gift when He, as the triumphant Lion of Judah and Lamb that was slain, stepped forward to accept the seal from the Father's right hand in Revelation 5.

Redemptive Gift 3. Teacher and Truth

Those with the Teacher gift are designed to have a deeply devoted and intense relationship with Jesus. They are designed by God to stand in the office of priest as a mediator or reconciler between God and man.

Some people who demonstrate the Teacher gift in Scripture are Levi, Daniel, Samuel, Isaiah, Ezra, Luke and Mary, the mother of Jesus. Read how God views the Teacher gift:

"And you will know that I have sent you this warning so that my covenant with Levi may continue," says the LORD Almighty. "My covenant was with him, a covenant of life and peace, and I gave them to him; this called for reverence, and he revered me and stood in awe of my name. True instruction was in his mouth and nothing false was found on his lips. He walked with me in peace and uprightness and turned many from sin. For the lips of a priest ought to preserve knowledge, because he is the messenger of the LORD Almighty and people seek instruction from his mouth."

Malachi 2:4-7

Although the entire nation of Israel was initially called to be His priests to the other nations, that privilege was ultimately narrowed down to the Teacher tribe of Levi because of how the Levites stood with Moses and God against the worship of idols

(Exodus 32).

Purpose of the Teacher Gift

The mature Teacher has made peace with God and passionately wants to help others reconcile with God, too. They understand the Kingdom and delight in helping others enter the Kingdom. Characteristics of the mature Teacher are:

- Passionate pursuit of **truth and life.** The Bible is viewed by the mature Teacher as a deep well of one invitation after another to experience God and know His ways and to invite others to become a friend of God.

- Passionate that **rights and responsibilities aligned** in community with people and with God.

- Because of their deep commitment to **healing and wholeness,** Teachers make wonderful listeners, statesmen, counselors, healers, and peacemakers.

- They are **careful and accurate** to represent God well. They research, validate and verify the accuracy of what they say or do. Because they are careful, they are slow to come to decisions or conclusions.

- The Teacher is an **emotionally safe person** to be around. They make great listeners and counselors and are unlikely to reject others.

- They are **slow to take risks** and can slow down the pace of impulsive leaders.

- Teachers are **loyal** to those around them, especially their leaders.

The Immature or Wounded Teacher

One way to learn about the corrupted Teacher gift, is to read about the Pharisees in the four gospels. Some characteristics of the immature Teacher are:

- Passive, tends to not take initiative where it really counts, and can be slow moving.

- Difficulty handling money.

- Poor at returning things borrowed.

- More confident in knowledge studies rather than in experiences. This can be a downfall when Teachers study the Scriptures for knowledge and insights rather than personal encounters with God.

- Religious. Jesus publicly rebuked the Pharisees many times for excluding the evidence of what God was currently doing (healing the man born blind) because He did not follow their rules (healing on the Sabbath). In doing so, they missed the heart of God for healing and freedom.

- Refusing to move forward until they have seen the big picture when God expects us to use what we have and then He gives more.

- Self-centeredness.

- Imbalance between rights and responsibilities. Jesus said the Pharisees kept the rights to themselves and put the responsibilities on the people. Matthew 23:4

- Selective responsibility. Accept responsibility in one area of their life but ignore or refuse responsibility in another area.

- Selective rights. Immature Teachers can accept the elite ruling the masses, the rights of leaders to oppress those under them, and domestic abuse.

- Emphasis on analyzing and observing, rather than engaging.

- Whereas the Prophet takes initiative and seeks to help someone in trouble, the Teacher tends to be passive and waits for a troubled person to ask for help.

Rights and Responsibilities

Allen grew up in a difficult home environment. His mom and dad were heavy drug users, and, at four years old, when his mom and dad were both in prison, he was assigned to foster care. His foster dad was a harsh angry man, and his foster mom was weak and unable to protect him from the abuse. He became extremely attached to his dog. When his dog died, life took a nasty turn and he was soon in a gang and using drugs himself.

Years later, after time in prison, he became a Christ follower and tried to put his life back together. He found a job in a hardware store where he loved to explain to customers how to use a certain tool or do a certain job. He was so good with customer service and the details of how to use tools and equipment, that he soon received raises and had gained favor in the company. After marrying a woman with a child of her own, he began to devote himself to becoming a good husband and father.

He felt justified in his angry outbursts because his stepdaughter was unruly, and he felt justified in allowing his wife to take care of the house and yard while he watched TV because he worked so hard during the day. Occasionally, he delighted his wife and daughter by offering to lead Bible devotions after the evening meal.

For thought and discussion:

1. List reasons why Allen might have the gift of Teacher. Include both positive and negative characteristics.

2. Where has Allen accepted responsibility in his life? Where is he practicing selective responsibility?

3. Where does Allen demand his rights?

4. If you were mentoring Allen and he invited you to speak clearly into his life, what three strengths might you suggest he further develop?

The Teacher's Struggle to Maturity

The single struggle toward maturity is to balance rights and responsibilities. This strategy applies to every area of the Teacher's life, including home, work, play and relationships with God and others.

The Teacher grows when they step back from religious service to God and begin to engage with God on a personal basis. The Teacher can receive revelation and truths regarding the nature and heart of God more easily than the other gifts. By these revelations and truths, they can set people free to establish Jesus as Lord and King in their lives, providing a path toward reconciliation to the Father.

> Fundamentally, the quest of the Teacher is to experience Jesus as Truth and release that truth to others so they can experience more of God and more freedom.

Consider what Daniel did in Daniel 2 when faced with the need to know truth. He asked his friends to plead with God for mercy, and then received the truth he needed in a vision during the night. Immediately, he praised God and gave glory to God for the revelation. Later, in the presence of King Nebuchadnezzar, he made it clear that it was God and not Daniel who had revealed the mystery.

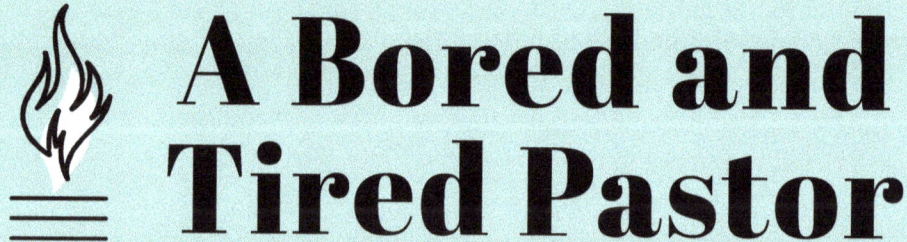

A Bored and Tired Pastor

As a boy, Dave dreamed of serving God as a professional minister and pastor. When he completed seminary and took his first position as pastor of a small congregation in his denomination, he felt like life was off to a grand start. He had prepared for this all his life. With all his seminary books and study tools in the office at his church, with great anticipation, he spent two weeks preparing his first sermon. As time went by, however, the passion and fire died down and his preparations for a sermon slowly reduced to just a few days of tedious, boring and even dreaded study.

A few of the young couples in his church who had been on fire for the ways of God began to drift off into worldly living. One husband had an affair, and the marriage was almost destroyed. A year later, the couple dropped out of church. A widow began criticizing the sermons and gossiping about the pastor to other members that maybe it was time for him to move on to a new church. Years and multiple church assignments later, Dave retired.

For thought and discussion:

1. List reasons why Dave might have the gift of Teacher. Include both positive and negative characteristics.

2. A Teacher in ministry often has a professional relationship with God, but does not engage emotionally with God, which can lead to stale thinking, also called "brain rot." How would you describe Dave's relationship with God?

3. A person with the Teacher gift sometimes struggles to confront sin. How did this struggle play out in Dave's life?

4. God does not give the Teacher the option to not confront sin. On this one issue, the Teacher will rise or fall. If you were mentoring Dave, what questions might you ask Dave to help him see the importance of putting truth ahead of relationships? What advice would you give Dave as he enters retirement?

When a painful event happens, the one we share the pain with first is the one we are most intimate with.

John Q. Adams, Passionate Opponent of Slavery

With the gift of Teacher, John Q. Adams was the sixth president of the United States and son of John Adams, the second president of the United States. He was a brilliant man who spoke seven languages. Right after his graduation from Harvard, he was appointed American minister to the Netherlands at just 26 years of age. He served in the Senate and served one term as president. Then he returned to Congress for 17 years in the House of Representatives where he was considered an independent thinker and earned the nickname "Old Man Eloquent." His 15,000-page personal diary written over 68 years is one of our best resources to learn about personal, political, legal, and public experiences in the United States up to his death in 1848.

At every opportunity, Adams passionately protested slavery. In his words, "The world, the flesh, and all the devils in hell are arrayed against any man who … dare to join the standard of Almighty God to put down" the issue of slavery. Near the end of his life, while serving in the House of Representatives, he defended before the Supreme Court of the United States 53 Africans who had revolted aboard a slave ship bound for America, killing the ship's captain and one crew member. With over four hours of arguments on each of two days, he was able to convince the Court to free the men and allow them to return to Africa.

For thought and discussion:

1. Because John Q. Adams did not win a second term as President, some deem him a failure and others say he was one of the most successful public servants. Let history be our judge. What do you say about him? Failure or success? Why?

2. Fill in the following table, listing three traits about Adams that confirm he had the Teacher gift and three people you know personally who demonstrate one of these traits. One of these three people can be yourself.

Trait of John Q. Adams as Teacher	A person you know with this trait

3. Do you believe one or more of the people listed have the Teacher gift? Explain your answer.

Redemptive Gift 4. Exhorter and Reality

Exhorters see reality in ways that seem impossible, even outrageous and scandalous, to others. Think of Moses coming to an enslaved people group and telling them to pack their bags because God is taking them out of Egypt and slavery, into the wilderness to conquer the giants in another country! Because an Exhorter is designed to introduce others to the greatness of God, they must believe in their own greatness. ==It's easy for an Exhorter to believe in their greatness, but it takes a mature Exhorter to believe in the greatness of others.== Let's see how Jesus did that.

In Revelation 14, Jesus, the Exhorter, stands on Mount Zion, the governmental mountain of God, with 144,000 of His loyal and blameless followers. The situation is dire, as the antichrist spirit had enslaved all the people of the earth. Did Jesus come as a conquering champion on His white horse when the earth was in its greatest need? No, He came as a Lamb and gave the world stage to His followers who, in *their* greatness, sang the song to the Father that Jesus had taught them.

Jesus did not confront the enemy as a great warrior or lead His followers to do so. As outrageous and preposterous as it seems, He led them to turn their full attention to the Father and sing a song of worship Him! The thought makes my heart sizzle! As they did so, Father was released to send His angels to bring even more people to Him! Glory!

Purpose of the Exhorter Gift

By design, the Exhorter introduces people to a new reality of who God is that surprises, astounds and delights. Think of Moses explaining that God wants to defeat their enemies for them, and Jesus expressing that worshipping God with a new song will invite Him to do so. Or consider the little girl in Figure 2-5 asking can her great big Daddy come play with her friends in their tiny little tent. What preposterous fun Exhorters can be! Making God's reality known is the purpose of the Exhorter gift.

Figure 2-5 "Can Daddy come in and play, too?"

Exhorters in Scripture

Three examples of Exhorters in Scripture are:

- Jesus, the Exhorter, came to earth to reconcile all things to the Father. He said, "When you have seen Me, you have seen the Father." He made it clear He did not come to do His own will, but that of the Father, to present a story of who Father is that the people had not yet seen and to make a way for His followers to approach the Father and be reconciled to Him.

- Moses was an Exhorter. He met with God and knew God better than any of the Israelites at the time. When the Israelites were afraid to come near God, Moses said, "I am trembling with fear," and yet he walked up the mountain to be with God, know Him and later, describe God to the people so they could know Him, too.

- Paul, an Exhorter, brought the scandalous and joyful message to the Gentile world that we, too, are included in the new Covenant with the Lord Jesus Christ, who has made a way for us to be reconciled to our Father.

- The antichrist spirit is an Exhorter. He is insecure, wants to be center stage and requires blind loyalty and obedience. If someone doesn't follow him, he might remove their head!

For thought and discussion:

1. Exhorters like to be with people. Compare and describe how Jesus enjoyed people, and how John the Baptist, with his Prophet gift, did not express this desire to be with people.

2. Exhorters are world changes and need followers to fulfill their birthrights. Three Exhorters, Walt Disney, Donald Trump and Vladimir Putin, all changed the world. How did each gain their followers?

3. Exhorters have big visions. Name two people you know personally who have big visions. What vision does each have?

4. Exhorters are naturally joyful and have fun with people. Name two people you enjoy being with. Perhaps they are even the life of the party.

5. Immature Exhorters demand loyalty from their followers. Name one person you know personally who expects and even demands loyalty.

6. Of the people you named, which one has at least two of the characteristics of an Exhorter? Do you think this person is an Exhorter?

02

The Immature or Wounded Exhorter

Children and adult Exhorters tend to draw people to them because they are friendly, happy people with large vision. Because Exhorters can see a different reality than most, immaturity might cause them to view the world in a reality that is biased and self-serving. Although they love having friends and followers, they might be selfish and exploit their followers.

An immature Exhorter can demand loyalty as a counterfeit legitimacy. Their immature followers, with their own counterfeit legitimacy, might crave to be in an Exhorter's inner circle. As a result, an Exhorter can be surrounded by yes-people who cannot or will not speak truth about the very exploitation and denial that prevent an Exhorter from executing their vision well. It's a legitimacy trap for all involved. (This trap baited by immature leaders and weak followers can apply to any gift, not just the Exhorter gift.)

An immature Exhorter can view life as fun and easy, largely because they are likeable and friendly and find favor in community. Embracing the productive pain to grow in character to see cause-and-effect relationships in community is non-optional for an Exhorter to come to fulfillment. Exhorters might ignore a principle, believing the means justifies the end and, therefore, live in non-reality that God cannot bless.

Raising an Exhorter Child

Janice, an 11 years-old Exhorter, loves center stage, always has something to say, loves to dance and sing, can be quite dramatic at times, and tends to be selfish and self-centered. On the way out of the school building, she asks her younger brother to carry her backpack. John, who is seven years old, says, "Sure, I'll help," and takes the backpack. His mom stops him and points out that he's carrying two backpacks way too heavy for him. She tells Janice that, yes, she does have a right to ask her little brother to carry her heavy backpack, but her brother does not have to accept that responsibility. The little brother takes the opportunity to say he no longer wants to carry the backpack and hands it back to Janice. Janice immediately has a meltdown dramatic moment in the parking lot because she has to carry her own backpack.

For thought and discussion:

1. Siblings of an immature Exhorter can get lost in the shadows, become enablers, and even take on a victim spirit. How did John act as Janice's enabler until Mom intervened?

2. Why is it important that Mom protect John from Janice using him?

3. What can Mom do to help Janice mature into accepting reality? If you were the mom's mentor, what would you do or say to help the mom parent her Exhorter child?

4. Immature Exhorters struggle with cause-and-effect relationships. They can fail to see how their negative actions and attitudes have negative effects in their lives. Do you know of someone with a big vision that is blinded to their need for character development? What might be a reason they are not growing?

5. Immature Exhorters and Prophets can make big demands of people. Do you know of someone like this? Do you think they are an immature Exhorter or Prophet? What other characteristics of these two gifts can you use to tell which gift this person has? (Hint: Look for motive. The clues to determine a gift are more rooted in why a person does what they do rather than what they do.)

The Exhorter's Struggle to Maturity

Generally, the greatest struggle for the immature Exhorter is to know that they are legitimate before God and people. They must know they don't have to prove anything to God. This vertical relationship with God is their main issue. Once that is settled, they no longer need loyal followers, attention or success. They are free to empower their followers to take the stage and unleash their gifts to express their devotion to the One True God.

Look for these qualities in a mature Exhorter:

- A mature Exhorter invites us to gaze on the beauty of God and to follow Him. Beware of any leader who expects you prove your loyalty to them.

- A mature Exhorter will invest in their followers. Blessings roll downhill. Beware of a leader who measures you by how much you invest in them, such as building their vision or serving them.

> Serving a leader is appropriate when it is done as a service to God, not to man. Jesus taught His disciples to lead by serving their followers.

02

Redemptive Gift 5. Giver and Stewardship

Each of the seven redemptive gifts become progressively more complex and multifaceted than the previous gift, a fact evident in the Giver gift. This gift is the most difficult to identify in a person because the Giver can express all the other gifts as needed for a situation. We all can do that, but the Giver is especially adept at that by God's design.

Abraham and Jacob apparently carried the Giver gift, resulting in God using this gift to establish the nation of Israel. Even today, we see the gift operating at the national level. Israel is one of the most generous nations in the world, and their giving is always strategic, designed to help the receiver lift themselves out of poverty or other crisis.

The expression of Jesus as the Giver at the Marriage Supper of the Lamb in Revelation 19 was so monumental and significant that it was the only event in Revelation that caused John to want to worship the angel who told him about it. There's much in this event we don't understand, but one thing is evident -- it involved providing **access to oneness with our King** on a level no one had ever seen or experienced before. That's the glory of the Giver gift!

We see the resulting power of this oneness in Revelation 20, when our King of Kings and Lord of Lords set out to defeat the enemy.

When I asked the Giver portion of my spirit what is the purpose of the Giver gift, I heard her say, "We birth legitimacy." Fundamentally, legitimacy is being on the inside, the inner circle, with God.

Purpose of the Giver Gift

Although the Giver is designed by God to release resources such as money, food, shelter, clothing and more, the finest resources the Giver can broker is access to God and access to community. The exquisite preparations for this access can put us in awe of God as the Giver goes all out to prepare just the right experience for someone they see who deserves the access they offer.

A Giver is a gatekeeper who has the responsibility to judge who is worthy of access to the ones they protect. Eve was most likely a Giver. In her role as Giver, she was designed to protect Adam from evil and help him have access to God. She failed miserably in both roles. However, in the redemption of all things, we hope to see the reconciliation of the genders where the wife once again is entrusted with the roles of protector for her husband from evil and helper for her husband to have access to God.

The Immature or Wounded Giver

The immature or wounded Giver does not see the privilege God has given them to manage resources and access. For this reason, a Giver can hold back for personal gain, resentment, jealousy or other unrighteous motives. An immature Giver tends to see their role as a protector of themselves and their own resources, which can lead to control and power rooted in fear of what they might lose. It can be difficult for an immature Giver to receive because they see receiving as a weakness. They might not be able to receive physical resources or wise counsel, which means they must learn from their mistakes.

Have you ever wanted to fit into a community that would not allow access? Think back through those dynamics. Perhaps a Giver was denying you access. When a Giver denies access, the shut door is heavily locked and guarded. Do you think their actions were righteous or unrighteous? Maybe God kept you out because the community was not right for you at that time, or the Giver denied access because of immaturity or control.

A Phone Call Asking for Advice

Ellie, a Giver, is from Japan and currently studying for an advanced degree in Europe. Her plan is to be a professor in a university in Asia. Although she is highly intelligent, she sometimes gets herself into difficulties in social situations because she doesn't read people well. When Ellie requested a phone call with Ken, her mentor in Japan, for his advice, Ken agreed but recognized advice was not really what she was seeking.

On the call, Ellie ranted about the problems with her housemate who owned the home, tried to put an unfair share of the work and expenses on Ellie and would not give her a fair share of the space in the house. She was so upset she was thinking about abandoning her studies and returning to Japan. Ken listened well, letting Ellie know he was fully present as she fully unloaded her struggles. Then, he gently began asking questions to help Ellie think through what abandoning her studies might mean. As Ken asked questions and Ellie thought through her answers, she devised a plan to relieve the tensions between her and her housemate.

For thought and discussion:

1. Before Ken realized Ellie is a Giver, he would often get frustrated when she would ask him for advice and then rudely reject it. What about the Giver gift makes it difficult for the Giver to receive advice?

2. Ellie's education is financed by her wealthy family. How can that arrangement put pressure on Ellie, as a Giver?

3. Housemate arrangements can be difficult for Givers. What house rules can reduce tension in these relationships?

4. Givers despise making decisions when people withhold important information. When the housemate invited Ellie to live with her, the housemate was not totally forthcoming as to what she expected from Ellie. Have you ever been in a situation where someone withheld information when asking you for help or a favor? How did that make you feel? If that was highly offensive to you, you might be a Giver!

The Giver's Struggle to Maturity

God created the Giver to be tough because they are called to do tough things. The struggle to maturity is learning to trust God with everything and everyone so they can give up the control that protects them and their resources.

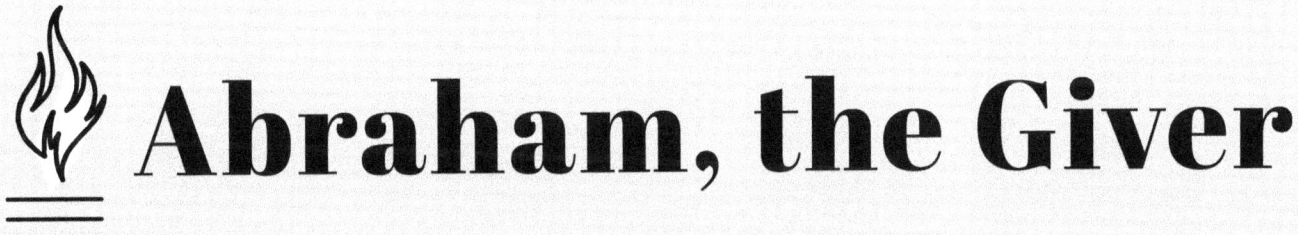

Abraham, the Giver

Abraham, a Giver, was first called by God in Genesis 12 and eventually his bloodline released life-giving generational blessings based on his covenant relationship with God. God told Abram to leave his people and go to a land that God would give him. Lot, his nephew, went with him. Because of a famine, Abram left the land God had given him and went to Egypt. He instructed his wife Sarai to say she was his sister, so the Egyptians wouldn't kill him for his beautiful wife.

Pharaoh took Sarai into his palace and, in exchange, gave Abram great wealth. God inflicted diseases on the Egyptians because of Sarai, and Pharaoh forced Abram to tell the truth that she was his wife.

Later in the story, when Sarai could not have children, she and Abram agreed for him to bear a child by her Egyptian slave Hagar. After Hagar was pregnant with Ishmael, she and Sarai could not get along and she fled from Sarai. God told Hagar that He saw her misery but, even so, to return to the family.

God established His covenant with Abraham, giving him and Sarah new names and promised Abraham his son Isaac will be born within a year. Soon after that, Abraham moved to Gerar, presented Sarah as his sister, and the king of Gerar took Sarah as his own. When God told the king that Sarah was already married, the king gave wealth to Abraham to make up for having taken Sarah.

When Sarah gave birth to Isaac, Hagar mocked her, and then Sarah and Abraham sent Hagar and Ishmael away into the desert with only the food and water that Hagar could carry on her back.

Sometime later, Abraham was instructed to sacrifice Isaac on Mt. Moriah. When Abraham obeyed, God prevented him from killing the boy.

For thought and discussion:

1. During Abraham's struggle to become a mature Giver, what are two times he used control to protect himself?

2. An immature Giver can be slow to obey God. Name two times Abram was slow to obey.

3. When and how did Abraham express his right to own the resources God entrusted to him?

4. Fill in the following table, listing three traits about Abraham that confirm he had the Giver gift and three people you know personally who demonstrate one of these traits. One of these three people can be yourself.

Trait of Abraham as Giver	A person you know with this trait

5. Do you believe one or more of the people listed have the Giver gift? Explain your answer.

Stewardship is doing someone else's job with someone else's resources. Suppose you work for an electrical service company, drive the company truck to a residence, do the work the company has ordered you to do, use the tools and materials the company provides and collect payment on behalf of the company. Your paychecks are based on your contractual agreements with the company and not based on profits you made for the company. May we all see our Kingdom assignments and service to our King in the light of this type of good stewardship!

Redemptive Gift 6. Ruler and Freedom

The Ruler is gifted with the natural ability to father and mother and passionately wants to see people free to be and do all Jesus calls them to. Rulers see structures as helpful and often essential to help people get free (see Figure 2-6) and grow to maturity.

When we are truly free, we are able to do whatever God has called us to do from a place of rest and peace.

Figure 2-6 Rulers can lead others to work together and use structures with a passion for freedom

We might see freedom as coming from outside ourselves; however, true freedom is first built on the inside. We are truly free when there are no more inside battles to fight.

Purpose of the Ruler Gift

Rulers are designed by God to build people from the inside out so that the community can build their Father's Kingdom. Mature Rulers can mother and father those they lead more naturally than others. They believe in their followers so deeply they can overlook imperfections and messy details, without judging or criticizing.

They believe in their tribe with passion. They see the best in their tribe's qualities and destinies and can draw these characteristics out with ease. They can make room for all to thrive in a culture of dignity, purpose, productivity and honor. Rulers are amazing at motivating people and teams and experience fulfillment when their tribe is synchronizing with each other and God.

Whereas the Exhorter can dream culture, the Ruler can more easily build culture.

The Immature or Wounded Ruler

Rulers who are not yet secure in their legitimacy or experienced enough of God's fathering can focus on building structures rather than building people. The immature or wounded Ruler can:

- Ignore important details
- Believe the end justifies the means and be slack with righteousness
- Easily feel betrayed and abandon a leader because of an offense
- Expect fierce loyalty from their core group of followers
- Compromise when followers are not competent (for the Ruler, relationship is more important than competence)
- Resent micromanagement from above (they generally don't need it)
- Be independent, run ahead of resources (go in debt) and not accept help when it's needed
- Avoid submitting to a committee (a Ruler does best submitting to one leader they respect)
- Be task-oriented and not good at fathering or mothering those they lead
- Stay very busy and tend to not be passionate about many things
- Drive people too hard and be heavy-handed in leadership
- Enslave people in their grand plans (Joseph enslaved an entire nation)
- Resent retirement. They need busyness.

 # Nehemiah the Ruler

In the book of Nehemiah, we read how Nehemiah asked the king permission to rebuild the city of Jerusalem, identifying it as where his fathers were buried. He explained his plan and asked for specific resources to execute the plan, which took 12 years to accomplish before he returned to the king. His first task was to build a wall around the city as a structure to protect the people. He then led them to repopulate the city by tribes and clans and to establish the protocols that empowered them to return to God and His ways.

For thought and discussion:

1. The Ruler gift is one of the easiest to identify. They always seem to have a project in mind and are always planning next steps for building it. They don't tend to judge people and are quick to recruit imperfect people into their building plans. How did Nehemiah exhibit these characteristics of the Ruler?

2. Rulers thrive under pressure and want their followers to also be under pressure. What pressure did Nehemiah apply to his followers?

3. Rulers tend to want to empower their tribe, family, or community over that of others. Give three examples of how Nehemiah did that.

4. Mature Rulers are especially good at getting projects done because they can build teams, delegate authority and empower others. How did Nehemiah, as governor, empower Ezra, the priest?

5. Nehemiah 8 and 9 describe how the people assembled as one man and a revival started. Revivalist teach that revivals start when people are hungry for God and pray, they obey Holy Spirit and their hearts are in unity. How do you think Nehemiah was able to help position the people for revival?

6. Fill in the following table, listing three traits about Nehemiah that confirm he had the Ruler gift and three people you know personally who demonstrate one of these traits. One of these three people can be yourself.

Trait of Nehemiah the Ruler	A person you know with this trait

7. Do you believe one or more of the people listed have the Ruler gift? Explain your answer.

The Ruler's Struggle to Maturity

The Ruler's struggle to maturity is to focus on building people rather than building structures and institutions. In Chapter 6, you learn about boss leaders and fathering leaders. The Ruler must become a fathering leader. In the sixth letter to the churches in Revelation, Jesus tells the Ruler church of Philadelphia to use the key of David to go through the door opened for them. The Ruler opens doors for their followers to walk in freedom to do all God has called them to do. Looking at the seven words Jesus spoke while on the cross, the sixth word is "It is finished." Rulers are charged by God to help their followers finish all the work God has assigned to them.

> In the ministry of church planting, a key to understanding the work of the Ruler is to see that we are not called to build churches by using institutional structures – we are called to build people, to mother and father people , so that Jesus can build His church.

Redemptive Gift 7. Mercy and Fulfillment

The Mercy gift is unique from the other six gifts. When you look at each of the analogies of sevens in the scriptures, the seventh item has a unique flavor all its own. Think of the seven days of creation, and the uniqueness of the seventh day when God did not create but rested and called it holy. It's truly a joy to know and learn from someone with a mature Mercy gift.

Purpose of the Mercy Gift

The Mercy gift brings a beautiful and sweet blessing simply by being present, resulting in community coming into alignment. When someone with a Mercy gift walks into a room, you can often feel the room or people coming to rest. For a Mercy person, the blessing of presence is sometimes the greatest gift he or she can give.

Worship and fellowship with God for the Mercy person are more experiences than action. The Mercy person tends to think nonlinearly with pictures that might lack continuity. They might tell a story with bits and pieces here and there and leave it to the listener to connect the dots. They often hear from God and make decisions with their feelings and intuitions.

> The Apostle John carried the Mercy gift. On the Isle of Patmos, he was all alone, and God used that time to release the most brutal, and yet most hopeful, prophecy in human history. Intimacy with God qualified him to do that. Not only was it the most brutal prophecy, it was also the most fulfilling as King Jesus was freed to set in order the alignment of all creation into fulfillment to the end of the ages.

02

The Immature or Wounded Mercy

A Mercy person can be slow to talk, process thoughts, make decisions, commit or act. They might be poor communicators and not know how to fit in community. Because they rely so much on intuition rather than logic, we can scratch our heads wondering why a Mercy does what they do.

In a group trying to make a decision, the Mercy person might know an idea being considered is wrong, but they don't know why it's wrong and, therefore, don't speak up. They are not yet confident enough to say, "This is wrong, but I cannot tell you why." Days pass and the idea obviously is not working. The Mercy gets frustrated because they knew the group embraced a bad idea. Others get frustrated when the Mercy person takes on the "I knew this was not going to work" attitude.

> King David mostly likely had the gift of Mercy, and as we read the Psalms, we can hear his loneliness and the pain of having few deep friendships with people, and yet he knew the heart of God better than most.

The Mercy's Struggle to Maturity

The Mercy generally takes longer to reach maturity and fulfillment than the other gifts, but the prize of fulfillment is greater. Fulfillment comes when they can articulate ideas. Once they are able to do that, **they can build an ecosystem in community like no other gift can.**

They are capable of reaching profound fulfillment for themselves and communities, and this process can be shorter when people in community understand how the Mercy gift functions. Mercy people are extremely sensitive spiritually and they hear from their spirits better than the other gifts. The human spirit does not communicate the same way the soul communicates. The soul mostly uses words and sometimes pictures. The spirit has a different language that uses pictures and feelings to impress ideas onto the soul. When a community knows that about the Mercy person, they can celebrate that and rejoice that God in His wisdom has given a Mercy to the group so they can better know the direction Holy Spirit is taking.

People with the Mercy gift sometimes feel lonely and misunderstood. They have unique relationships with God and tend to know God better than the other gifts.

Fulfillment comes to the Mercy when they embrace the pain of continually seeking after God. However, if the fear of pain or the fear of change blocks out everything else, including the big picture of fulfillment, they avoid pain and can miss their birthright of fulfillment.

Chris Pfohl and Fulfillment

Chris Pfohl, a veteran, retired U. S. Marshall, artist and fiction writer, runs a center for homeless veterans in my city. Chris carries the Mercy gift with Grace and Wisdom, and it's truly a gift to enjoy his friendship. As with many Mercy people, Chris has endured many rough patches in life as God has pushed and even shoved him into one difficult situation after another.

His center for vets, called "Warriors Once Again," as of the time of this writing, accommodates five vets. Chris is the sole live-in employee of this non-profit ministry and does all the work, including counseling vets, working with donors, applying for grants, managing finances, overseeing the six-bedroom building and taking the residents to doctors' appointments, job interviews and work. Recently, the center was awarded a major grant, which propelled it to a whole new level, allowing him to hire his first employee and start building out the ministry as he had dreamed it could be.

Chris recalls a few weeks after receiving the grant experiencing a moment of euphoria, "So this is what fulfillment feels like!" As we talked, I kept digging for his words to express the ultimate prize for a Mercy person – fulfillment. He described it as the essence of shalom, prosperous, nothing missing, nothing lost, all is right with the world. He knew this was what all Mercy people search for and desire, but this was the first time he felt it. We talked about all the successes and failures that led up to this current success and the hope of what the ministry would be for all the future vets that would come.

For thought and discussion:

1. Chris has been diligently seeking God and His ways for years. Why do you think he is just now experiencing fulfillment? Give five possible reasons.

2. When I first got to know Chris, he said he felt lonely and in exile even though he has many friends and associates in the city. Why do you think he felt lonely?

3. When I asked Chris would he be interested in designing the interior of this book, he said, "I see the design is essential for tying the entire message of the book together into an organic structure." What about Chris's design and his proposed book design does this statement say to you?

4. Based on his work as a U. S. Marshall, Chris wrote a page-turning fiction novel that I couldn't put down. Based on what you know about the Mercy gift, what might you guess is Chris's writing style?

5. Rulers tend to focus on the end goal and can overlook when something in community is off, but it's really hard for a Mercy to be at rest when their community is not aligned or cohesive. How does Chris's blessing of presence help him bring alignment and cohesiveness to community?

6. Fill in the following table, listing three traits about Chris that confirm he has the Mercy gift and three people you know personally who demonstrate one of these traits. One of these three people can be yourself.

Trait of Chris as Mercy	A person you know with this trait

7. Do you believe one or more of the people listed have the Mercy gift? Explain your answer.

Concept 2.3 The Seven Portions of Our Human Spirit

We are spirit, soul and body. As we learned in Chapter 1, our human spirit came from Father God into the fertilized egg in our mother's womb. Our spirits are made of the essence of God, in His image, of His divine light and with the unique design and resources from God to fulfill our destinies. Our theology about the spirit and soul is always evolving. Here are some Scriptures we are relying on to help us understand the nature and essence of our spirits:

*Watch, and pray, that ye may not enter into temptation: the **spirit** indeed is willing, but the flesh is weak.*

Matthew 26:41

*"My soul glorifies the Lord and my **spirit** rejoices in God my Savior..."*

Luke 1:47

*...and her **spirit** came back, and she arose presently, and he directed that there be given to her to eat..*

Luke 8:55

*And as they were stoning Stephen, he prayed, "Lord Jesus, receive my **spirit**."*

Acts 7:59

*The Spirit himself doth testify with our **spirit**, that we are children of God.*

Romans 8:16

*...for who of men hath known the things of the man, except the **spirit** of the man that [is] in him? so also the things of God no one hath known, except the Spirit of God.*

1 Corinthians 2:11

*For I indeed, as absent in body but present in **spirit**, have already judged (as though I were present) him who has so done this deed. In the name of our Lord Jesus Christ, when you are gathered together, along with my **spirit**, with the power of our Lord Jesus Christ,...*

1 Corinthians 5:3-4

*.. for he who is speaking in an [unknown] tongue -- to men he doth not speak, but to God, for no one doth hearken, and in **spirit** he doth speak secrets.*

1 Corinthians 14:2

*... for if I pray in an [unknown] tongue, my **spirit** doth pray, and my understanding is unfruitful.*

1 Corinthians 14:14

*The grace of our Lord Jesus Christ [is] with your **spirit**, brethren! Amen.*

Galatians 6:18

*... and the God of the peace Himself sanctify you wholly, and may your whole **spirit**, and soul, and body, be preserved unblameably in the presence of our Lord Jesus Christ;*

1 Thessalonians 5:23

*The Lord Jesus Christ [is] with thy **spirit**; the grace [is] with you! Amen.*

2 Timothy 4:22

*... for the reckoning of God is living, and working, and sharp above every two-edged sword, and piercing unto the dividing asunder both of soul and **spirit**, of joints also and marrow, and a discerner of thoughts and intents of the heart...*

Hebrews 4:12

*Then, indeed, fathers of our flesh we have had, chastising [us], and we were reverencing [them]; shall we not much rather be subject to the Father of the **spirits**, and live?*

Hebrews 12:9

*... for as the body apart from the **spirit** is dead, so also the faith apart from the works is dead.*

James 2:26

Our soul expresses one of the seven redemptive gifts, and this gift largely defines our personalities. Our spirits, on the other hand, carry all seven gifts and can flow in either gift at any time. Think of the white divine light of God that is the essence of our spirits, and that light is refracted to show the seven colors contained within the white light. See Figure 2-7.

Figure 2-7 Our spirit is divine light and can express each of the seven colors and characteristics of the seven gifts

In the spirit realm, Prophet gives off red light, Servant emits orange light, Teacher shines yellow, Exhorter is green, Giver is blue, Ruler emits an indigo color and Mercy shines brightly in violet. People who are able to see in the spirit (in Scripture, they are called "seers") might see portions of their spirits in these colors.

Learning From Our Spirit

It's possible and most helpful to get to know our spirits and be able to communicate with our spirit. Every morning, when I first wake up, I check in to see what might have happened with my spirit while I slept. Many of my breakthroughs happen when I'm asleep and my spirit is very active. I might turn to my spirit and say something like, "Exhorter, can you tell me where you are and what's happening?" At other times, I might just look into the spirit realm to find my spirit and see what is highlighted.

I often find Servant underneath things. One morning I saw a great big tree of life in the middle of my inner world. I suspected Servant was under it somewhere, and I asked him, "Servant, are you in the roots?"

I heard him say, "I *am* the roots." I had earlier seen Exhorter in the trunk and Prophet in the high top of the canopy, but until that moment it had not occurred to me that they were the tree. But then, I often think of myself as a tree, and sometimes God expresses truths to me, showing me to be a tree. Those dots were obviously not fully connected.

I began to look more closely (see Figure 2-8.) Teacher is the leaves, the life factory producing life and healing. Ruler is the branches, creating structure, and Giver is the fruit and seed. Mercy is the entire ecosystem, whom I first saw as the system that draws water and nutrients from the deepest root to the highest leaf. I had a new understanding of how spirit works to give life and godliness to me and others.

But the most amazing idea that morning was to see that I was part of that tree, too. I saw myself as the flowers on the tree, beautiful and fragrant, drawing others to cross pollinate and share life. Until that morning, I had always seen myself as a burden to community and even to my spirit.

People would just have to put up with me until they couldn't tolerate me any longer and then I would get quiet or disappear, whatever seemed necessary at the time. To see myself as beautiful and fragrant enough to actually attract others *into* community in which I was a life-giving part was a lovely new beginning. Later, I began to understand that I had always viewed my spirit as having the essence and life of God but not my soul or body. Now I understand that the spirit grows the soul and body from the essence of God, similar to how a tree grows its flowers from its own essence. We are created spirit, soul and body in His image!

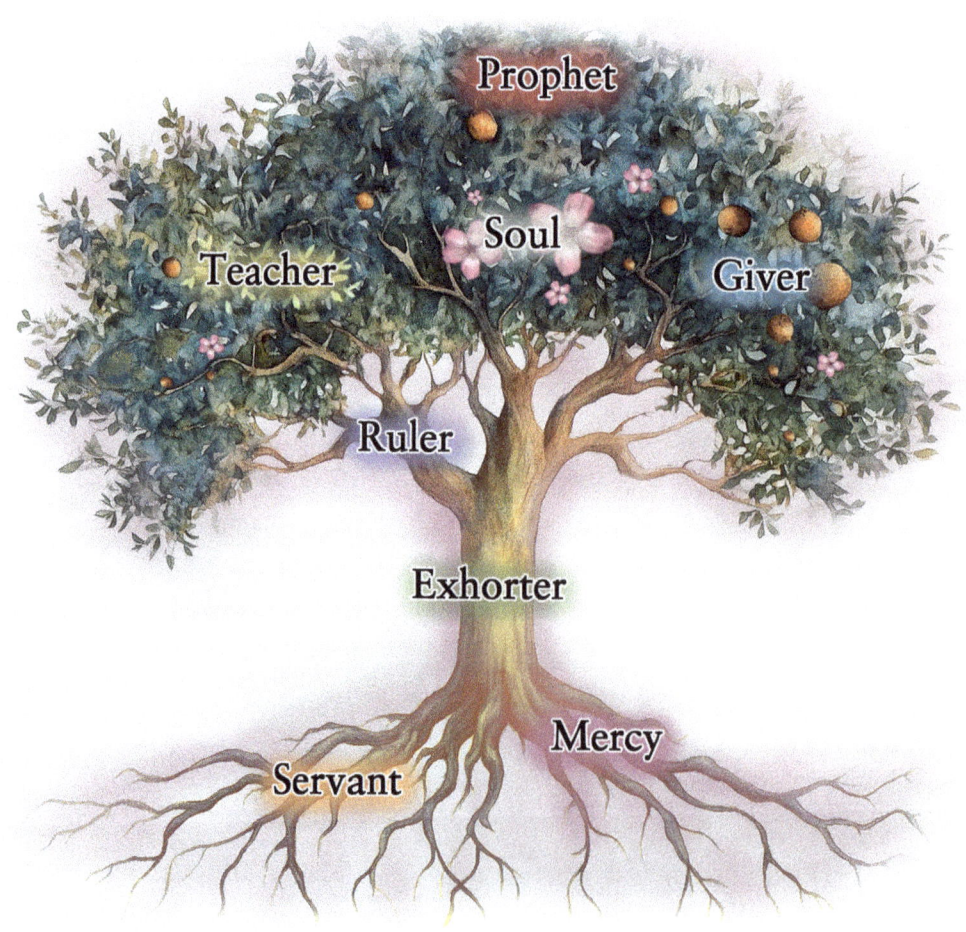

Figure 2-8 My spirit and soul as a tree

One Portion of the Spirit is the Leader

In the spirit realm, one portion of our spirit is ordained by God to lead the other six. Only God can tell us which gift is the leader. Sometimes we can see it in our passions, personalities and what the enemy has attacked in us to keep us from our destiny. The ultimate identification of our primary redemptive gift is when Jesus ordains one of the seven portions of our spirit as the leader. When that happens, there is a sense of alignment and fulfillment that only can come from God and the spirit.

Figure 2-9 The shadow of an object teaches us about the object but is not the fullness of the reality of the object.

The Spirit World

We live in a spirit world and a physical world. Each world has multiple regions, structures, atmospheres and purposes. Scripture is full of descriptions of the spirit world and our spirits who live in it, but we might have been taught to see these descriptions as simply metaphors. If, however, we are willing to accept and enter into this spirit world as a reality and not a metaphor, we can more easily meet with God there. Why? Because God is spirit, and our spirits come from Him and can more easily know Him than can our souls.

In Scripture, Father God teaches us about the spirit world by giving us shadows of realities that we can see and understand in the physical world. The shadow of a tree is not the same as a tree (see Figure 2-9). A shadow is not living, but the tree is alive. A shadow is two dimensional, but a tree has more dimensions than two.

When God instructed His people to build a physical structure, such as the tabernacle, He was inviting them to imagine what that structure might look like as a living structure and reality in the spirit world.

"Therefore do not let anyone judge you by what you eat or drink, or with regard to a religious festival, a New Moon celebration or a Sabbath day. These are a shadow of the things that were to come; the reality, however, is found in Christ."

Colossians 2:16–17

In this book, you learn much about our spirits and the spirit world, as God describes them in Scripture. God intends that our spirits nurture and lead our souls in both worlds!

"The Spirit himself doth testify with our spirit, that we are children of God."

Romans 8:16

As we study the spirit world and our spirits, keep in mind the end goal is to always know Jesus Christ more and more. We are members of His Body. That can only be understood and seen in the spirit world.

 The Current War

The movie, "The Current War," gives a glimpse into the controversy led by Thomas Edison and George Westinghouse over which type of electricity, alternating current (AC) or direct current (DC), would be used to build the infrastructure for distribution of electricity in our nation.

Edison built his case for DC on his conviction that AC was too dangerous and that it would kill people. Using fear to make his case, he demonstrated the danger of AC electricity by publicly killing animals with it. On the other hand, DC could not travel for long distances without expensive infrastructure. Ultimately, AC won out, partly because Nikola Tesla, who worked for George Westinghouse, was able to invent an AC motor that could power machines effectively. Today, we all realize that AC electricity is powerful enough to kill someone, and yet we continue to use it because it benefits us in many ways. We need to know how to respect and steward that power. For more information about the battle over current, search for "war of the currents" at *history.com*.

For thought and discussion:

1. In this book, you learn how to work with the human spirit to solve many problems in relating to God, human relationships, and building our Father's Kingdom. It's a powerful topic and can also be dangerous. How can working with the human spirit be beneficial?

2. How can working with the human spirit and in the spirit realm be dangerous or cause problems?

3. What safeguards might be put in place to make it less dangerous and more beneficial?

4. Describe how you can respect and steward the power of working with your own human spirit and that of another and in the spirit realm.

Concept 2.4 Our Authority and Power over Evil Critters and Defilements

Our weapons of warfare are all based on the victory of the Lord Jesus Christ. Jesus won!

Colossians 2 tells us He defeated death, flesh, the law, sin and ALL His enemies. In addition, He disarmed every enemy, parading them all in a public display of total defeat. His enemies remember those events and know they are a defeated, powerless army. Every encounter we have with the enemy needs to be based on this one fact -- they are already defeated.

If this truth is not deeply implanted in you, study the Word until you know it, see it and breathe it. Only then are you ready to engage the enemy to enforce the victory Jesus won.

Just as God created many physical creatures, such as bugs, spiders, cows and horses, many spiritual creatures also exist, such as demons, angels, Nephilim and Leviathans. In this book, for the most part, we call all evil creatures "critters."

Defilement of What God Has Made Holy

A holy thing is a thing dedicated to God for His purposes, and He claims it as His own. The enemy came to steal, kill, and destroy what belongs only to God, and his primary tactic is to defile what God has made holy. Here is what God made holy and belongs only to Him:

> If you think there is a battle for you to win, you are already defeated. If you know you are sent to enforce the victory Jesus attained, you have already won.

1. **Time.** God made time holy, when on the seventh day He rested from all His work and called this day holy. Specific times are set apart by and for God as holy and designated for His purposes. Genesis 2:2

2. **Land or space.** God made specific land and space holy first in Exodus 3:5, when He told Moses to take off his sandals because he was standing on holy ground.

3. **People or community.** God intended for all people in the earth to be holy and set apart for Him. However, because of sin, He set apart the nation of Israel as a "kingdom of priests and a holy nation" in Exodus 19:6.

4. **Birthright.** God further narrowed down the people set apart to the Lord in Exodus 32:29 to the tribe of Levi because the Levites stood with God and Moses against the worship to the golden calf.

5. **Office.** In Exodus 28:1, God ordained Aaron and his sons to serve Him in the office of high priest.

The enemy hates whatever belongs to God and tries to destroy what is holy. As you study this book, you will learn how to cleanse what God has called holy so that time, land, people, birthright and offices can all be restored to their original design as set apart for God for His purposes.

Am I Holy?

Do you belong to the Lord Jesus Christ? If so, you are holy. You are set apart to Him for His purposes. When you accept Him as Lord and Savior and are water baptized into His crucifixion, death, burial and resurrection, you are in Christ and Christ is in you. You are righteous and holy because He is righteous and holy.

> In Haggai 2, Haggai explained that under the old law, when a defiled thing touches a holy thing, the holy thing becomes defiled. In Matthew 8, a man with leprosy asked Jesus to make him clean. Jesus did so by touching the man and said, "Be clean." In Christ, when the holy touches the defiled, the defiled becomes holy! We will use this principle as you learn to clean up the defilement on time, land, people, birthright and offices.

Strategy to Enforce the Victory over the Enemy

To understand how to enforce the victory that belongs to Jesus Christ realize that every enemy attack is always against the nature and character of God. In the garden, the very first attack was when the enemy said to the woman, "Did God not say..." When dealing with the enemy, begin by asking is this attack against:

- The nature or character of Father God and His community
- The nature or character of Jesus Christ and His dominion
- The nature or character of Holy Spirit and His creation

Once you know which Member of the Trinity is being attacked, you can better see and address the lies. For example, suppose a friend is struggling with low self-worth. Your friend is part of God's creation, born of Holy Spirit. How dare the enemy attack the work of Holy Spirit in this way! The lie is not against your friend so much as it is against the nature and character of Holy Spirit and His creation!

SOLVING PROBLEMS

In this part of the chapter, you continue to develop your problem-solving skills. Recall that, to solve a problem, we:

1. Collect data.
2. Analyze the data looking for patterns of cause-and-effect relationships.
3. Identify the principles, which are universal, non-optional, cause and effect relationships.
4. Apply the principles in new situations.

02

The more patterns you are aware of, the more likely you will be able to identify a pattern in the data that will lead you to a principle and the problem's solution. In the last chapter, you learned to look for patterns regarding belonging, worth, competence and legitimacy. In this section, we add more patterns or filters that we can use to analyze data. The first pattern we explore is the taker-breaker-maker.

Problem 2.1 Use Story to Impart Principles and Solve Problems

People face life as a consumer (taker), predator (breaker) or builder (maker). A father or mentor knows how to grow someone from being a taker or breaker into a maker. Stories are one of the most effective tools to inspire change. As you read the following story, look for the principles involved.

Nickie has been working with Maria for a few months. Maria is a new believer and met Nickie soon after making her decision to follow Jesus. Just a few weeks after her salvation experience, her life began to fall apart. Her husband, Andy, took her to a Shaman and they both required her to take drugs to enter a psychedelic state. Soon after that, Andy moved her and the four children out of his house into a rental. And soon after that, Maria found herself escaping with the children out of the city in fear of what Andy might do next. A ten-year marriage was in deep trouble.

Settled temporarily in a new city, Maria needed legal help to protect her and the children from Andy's threats. Short on funds, Maria hired the best attorney she could afford, and a court date for full custody of the children, initiated by Andy, was looming. Maria had grown up in an affluent family where well-paid attorneys worked hard for the benefit of their clients, and Maria expected nothing less from this attorney.

She emailed, called and texted at all hours of the day and night, demanding he prepare the documents she knew would be expected in court and prep her for the witness stand. When friend Nickie tried to convince her she needed to do her own prep work, the reaction was always the same, "I've paid *the attorney* to do that. I'm *not* going to do *his* work for him." Eventually, they appeared in court, ill-prepared, and the judgement did not go well. Maria fired the attorney, pondering a lawsuit against him for failure to deliver on his agreement. By the third court date and a third attorney, Maria was at her wits end as to how to secure rightful custody of her children.

> Maria's life fell apart right after her salvation because of a curse put on her by her forefathers that anyone who became a Christ follower would bring destruction down on their lives. When this curse, called the Jewish curse, was uncovered and voided, Maria's circumstances took a sudden turn for the better. You learn more about dealing with curses in Chapter 4.

It was then that Nickie remembered a story she had heard from Arthur Burk. After a canceled flight, one woman spent all her time demanding justice from the airlines while other passengers were resourcefully finding alternate ways to reach their destination. When Nickie set the scene by describing the lady demanding the airlines fulfill their agreement, Maria gleefully broke in and told Nickie she knew *exactly* how to do that and quoted several regulations that require the airlines to fulfill their obligations. Nickie then finished the story, explaining that, while the lady was demanding justice, all the seats on flights with other airlines filled up, and the lady was left without a way to fly.

Nickie could feel the ah-ha moment settling on Maria. She got the point. Her thinking made a significant turn that day from taker to maker. As she diligently prepared for the court case with all the resources a maker can bring to bear, she reminded herself daily that she did not want to still be standing at the airline counter demanding justice from her attorney while losing a critical court case her children depended on.

Answer the following questions:

1. Nickie had observed Maria long enough (collected enough data) that she was able to see the patterns of taker, maker and breaker in Maria's life. Describe three actions by Maria that depict her as a 1) taker, 2) breaker or 3) maker.

2. Leaders who inspire their followers often do so with stories. A story that inspires does so because it teaches a principle in such a way the listener can understand the principle without feeling they are being personally criticized or attacked. What is one principle taught in Nickie's story? What is the cause-and- effect relationship of the principle?

3. In the Gospels, the stories Jesus told are called parables.

    a. Pick a parable from one of the Gospels and summarize the story.

    b. What is the principle taught?

    c. What is the cause-and-effect relationship of the principle?

    d. Who was Jesus talking with?

4. Describe a story that you have heard that inspired you and caused you to change direction in your life. What is the principle taught in the story? Have you told this story to others in hopes they, too, might benefit from the story?

5. Consider making it a habit to routinely read about the great leaders of the world and find in their lives a story that inspires. Find a story about a leader that inspires you.

6. What is one principle expressed in this story? Give at least one situation where you might use this story to teach the principle needed in the situation.

02

Problem 2.2 An Associate Often Gets Their Feelings Hurt

Kara works in a small grocery store. Jay, the manager, often gets frustrated with Kara because the least little slight by another employee or himself can set her off into a mode of withdrawing, sadness or even resentment. He never knows from one day to the next will she be easy to work with or still nursing a grudge from yesterday's offense.

Jay wants to help Kara with her lack of emotional groundedness (unstable emotions). Here is some data he's collected about Kara:

- Kara grew up without her father who left her mother when she was a baby.

- She seems to hurt the most on Mondays after she has had the weekend off.

- If Jay does not give her attention at break time, she gets hurt.

- When Jay corrects her work, she gets hurt.

- Kara can't wait to find a day off when she can hike in a nearby state park. She also loves to swim and ride her bike to work when the weather is good.

- Kara loves her mother very much and often mentions how hard her mom has worked to provide a good home for her.

A problem with relationships might have a root cause in one or more of these areas:

- **In the spirit realm.** For example, the problem might be in the generational bloodlines, such as sin, the occult and resulting covenants with evil, rebellion against God and His ways, curses or iniquities (a tendency in the generations toward evil)

- **Woundedness in the soul.** For example, rejection, abandonment, unforgiveness or fear of failure.

- **Lack of growth.** For example, a person might not have had enough mothering and fathering and not know how to stand up for what is right, get along with peers or develop his or her talents.

Answer the following questions:

1. List three types of earned authority that you believe would be the most effective in someone to best help Kara.

2. How might Kara embrace the productive pain needed to get to the root of the problem of her emotional instability?

3. If Kara asked you to mentor her, which of the three areas of root causes would you start when helping her find emotional groundedness?

GROWTH PROJECT

These projects are designed to help us grow ourselves and unpack our spirits so that we are better able to grow those we lead.

Growth Project 2.1 Learn the Basics

In the book of Numbers, God expected the Israelites to camp in certain positions among the tribes and for the men to be part of Israel's army. The camping arrangement forced some clans to live where they did not choose to live, and many of the men were not designed to be warriors. Although our goal might be to spend at least 80% of our lives living and doing what we were designed by God to do, we must all first learn the basics.

Do the following :

1. In the primary grades, we must all learn to read and write and do basic math. Later we can diversify and study subjects more fitting to our design, such as geometry or music. List five things everyone must learn when they first start a new job.

2. When we first enter a new community, list five things we must learn to fit into community.

3. When we first begin work for a new boss, list five things we must learn so that we can sync to our boss.

4. When we first are saved and begin our walk with Jesus, list five things we must learn to begin this walk with Him.

One basic skill we must learn as new Christians is to hear the voice of God and to follow Him.

"My sheep hear my voice, and I know them, and they follow me, and I give unto them eternal life; and they shall never perish, neither shall any man pluck them out of my hand."

John 10:27-28

Do the following to learn to hear His voice so that you can follow Him:

1. Have paper and pen ready. A bound journal works well for this project.

2. Invite Jesus to sit with you. Sit silently with Him without speaking. Use this time to tune yourself to His presence and get to know the feeling of Him sitting beside you.

3. Are you aware of where He is sitting? On your right, on your left or in front of you, as when you sit across the table from someone?

4. Write a few sentences in your journal about how much you love Him, and then read the statement aloud to Him.

5. Ask Him to tell you about His love for you. Jesus sometimes speaks with words, pictures, feelings, Scriptures or thoughts. Write whatever you sense, see or feel. Don't rush this step.

6. Ask Jesus to bring to your mind a story in Scripture that tells you how He sees you at this season in your life. Briefly describe the story in your journal. For example, He might remind you of the story of Saul being chosen as king of Israel or the story of Zacchaeus climbing a tree to get a better view of Jesus.

7. Ask Jesus what lesson He wants you to see from this story. For example, He might show you that Saul didn't think he was ready to be king, yet God had chosen him anyway, and it was up to Saul to agree to the assignment.

8. Ask Jesus to show you what is the most important thing He wants you to see now. Write down the first things that come to mind. Do you have any questions for Him about what He just told you?

9. Practice this type of hearing from God each day for seven days. After seven days, if this method of hearing from God is not working for you, ask others how they hear from God and try a different method. Jesus knows you well, and He will help you find the best ways to hear His voice based on your design.

Growth Project 2.2 Discover Your Trinitarian Design

We are each designed to have a personal relationship with each Member of the Trinity and to thrive in community, dominion and creation. At different seasons in our lives, we might grow our relationships in one area or the other. Ultimately, however, our greatest fulfillment will come when we partner with the Member of the Trinity in our area of design who can best release us into our birthrights.

Do the following:

1. It's difficult for us to see our own design because it comes so naturally we might miss it. For that reason, work with a partner as they ask you these questions:

   a. What were your childhood pleasures that brought you the greatest joy?

   b. Where were you attacked in early childhood? (The enemy knows your design and will do his best to destroy you in that area before you destroy him.)

   c. What do you spend much energy on that you don't have to do but you love doing it? It might not even be productive.

   d. What assignments has God given you?

   e. What assignments have people talked you into or were a misfit?

   f. Ask your friends to identify your dominant characteristics.

   g. What do you do for downtime?

   h. What do you do for fun social times?

   i. Where did you thrive in school?

   j. What was your greatest difficulty in school?

   k. Where do you thrive at work?

   l. Describe what it is like for you to be at a family reunion.

2. Working with your partner, draw some conclusions and give a percentage spread of your Trinitarian design, such as:

   o Community and Father God: 50%

   o Dominion and Jesus Christ: 20%

   o Creation and Holy Spirit: 30%

3. We're all on a journey. Which Member of the Trinity are you currently focused on building a relationship? How can you use community, dominion or creation to build that relationship?

Growth Project 2.3 Identify Your Redemptive Gift

It can take years to identify your redemptive gift, so don't be concerned if this project keeps on going for some time.

Do the following :

1. Interview someone who knows their redemptive gift. How did they decide? What tools did they use? Did someone tip them off? Did they try on for size another gift first? If so, what did they learn about themselves or how did they grow as they practiced this gift? What about this gift did not fit them?

2. Find some redemptive gift assessment tools online. Based on these tools, what redemptive gift do you have?

3. Try the gift on "for size" for a few weeks. Discuss your findings with your discussion group or partner. Do you think you have identified your gift?

4. Help a family member, spouse, child, sibling or a close friend identify their redemptive gift. Describe how the process went. How confident are you that you have identified their gift?

SPIRIT PROJECT

The Spirit Projects are designed to help you develop and enlarge your spirit, get to know your spirit world and better sync with God.

Spirit Project 2.1 Cleanse the Generational Bloodlines

Our lives can be greatly influenced by junk we inherit from our family lines. The two tools most effective to cleanse the generational bloodlines of an individual or family are the Blood Covenant we have with the Lord Jesus Christ and water baptism into His crucifixion, death, burial and resurrection.

Although you can pray these prayers alone, it helps to work with a partner who is a seer. While you speak, your partner can report what they see so that you can respond to what is happening in the heavens as you pray.

If the person you are praying for is present and engaged, ask the person to confess the sins of their forefathers and their own sins, according to James 5:16. The more detailed and specific, the better. As you pray, encourage the person to interject and help in any way they are led. These prayers are most effective when the person is emotionally engaged with deep repentance toward God and truly wants to change. Here are the general guidelines for prayer.

To learn more about water baptism as a deliverance tool, listen to the video "Water Baptism" at *FromHisTable.com*.

Use your own words as you follow the guidelines:

1. With purpose and intention, enter the courtroom of heaven and ask Father God to take His seat in judgement of the accusers of this person and their family as the Righteous Judge of the Universe, Creator of Heaven and Earth.

2. Ask Jesus to be our Power of Attorney to say/do/correct anything we mess up or leave out in these prayers.

3. Ask Father God to require all the accusers against this person to come into the courtroom in the area designated for the accusers of the brethren that Father God has chosen to be present for this particular legal action.

4. Ask Father God to bring forth into the courtroom the books for this person and all the books that have influence in these proceedings including the books of all forefathers, both by blood line, marriage, adoption or any other relationships. Ask Him to open the books.

5. Acknowledge to Father God that He was justified to allow whatever bad has happened because somebody did something somewhere in sin, iniquity or rebellion to God, which gave the enemy access to us.

6. Then clearly state the biggest BUT in the universe! BUT this person has a Blood Covenant with the Lord Jesus Christ. Based on this Blood Covenant, all sins, iniquities, and rebellion have been forgiven. Ask Father to apply the Blood, to go through every page of every book present, searching for any sin, iniquity or rebellion against God and blot it out, applying the Precious Living Blood of the Lord Jesus Christ. Wait until you sense this work has been done. It can take a while. A sense of Awe often settles over the proceedings. Worship and gratitude are most appropriate at this point!

7. Acknowledge that this person has been water baptized into the crucifixion, death, burial and resurrection of the Lord Jesus Christ. Romans 6. Acknowledge the old man or woman is dead, crucified with Christ.

8. Ask Father God, because of this death and according to Romans 7 and Isaiah 28:14-22, to annul and make void any covenants, contracts, and subordinate covenants and contracts and agreements appropriate for these proceedings. Acknowledge the person that was once included in these covenants and contracts is now dead, and the person is now a new creation, made holy unto God. Acknowledge this person's Blood Covenant with God is superior to all other covenants.

9. Ask Father God to declare a verdict on behalf of this person and include their seed, both physical and spiritual seed up to 1,000 generations. Ask Father God to execute this verdict against all accusers present and including any accusers not present in the court as Father God views appropriate at this time.

10. Declare Isaiah 28:14-22. It is sometimes appropriate to read these Scriptures as part of the verdict. Wait until you sense the courtroom is cleared of all accusers. This might take some time. If a seer is present, ask the seer to make sure all accusers have left the courtroom. Sometimes one might stay to make its argument of ownership, which you can often clear up quickly by reminding the accuser that the one they once owned is now dead.

11. Ask Father God to install the plumbline of Righteousness (Amos 7:7) in the person from the top of their head down through their bodies to their tailbone, and to install the measuring line of Justice horizontally through the head and hips and wherever else Father God sees as appropriate. Ask Him that Justice and Righteousness be established in the person's life as He sees fit. See Isaiah 28:17.

12. Ask Father God to cleanse the time, land, communities, birthrights and offices assigned to this person of all critters and all defilement, reestablishing these as holy and set apart for God. (More about this in later chapters.)

13. Ask Father God to establish the cross and the Finished Work of the Cross in the timeline of this person to segment time before and after the position of the cross. From this position of the cross, the time going forward is holy unto God and all the bad and evil before the cross cannot leak into the future timeline past the position of the cross.

14. Ask Father God or Jesus to pronounce a blessing over the person and their family. This part of the proceedings can be especially emotional and tender as the person gets a sense of the inheritance finally released to them.

Cleansing the bloodlines is not a one-and-done event, but a process. As the person walks in righteousness with God, more need for repentance will emerge. Encourage the person to be alert to times when God might want the person to go back before Him to ask for more deliverance, cleansing and release.

Spirit Project 2.2 Explore the Seven Portions of Your Spirit

In Chapter 1, you learned to bless your spirit and the spirit of another. In this project, you learn to dialog with your spirit and the spirit of another.

It's an easy and natural conversation, such as when a grandmother asked her 8-year-old granddaughter, "Liz, may I speak to your spirit?"

"Sure."

"Spirit, would you like to talk with me?"

"Sure."

Grandmother asks, "Liz tells me she has bad dreams at night. Do you know why?"

"Yep, it's a demon. It stands at the window."

"Could you ask Jesus to drive it away?"

"Yes. I just did that and it's gone."

The bad dreams stopped that day. I know that sounds way too simple and powerful at the same time. And, yes, it really is! Try it with someone!

Do the following:

1. Working with a partner who has given you permission to speak to their spirit, ask, "Spirit, would you like to talk with me?" Pause and wait for a response.

2. If the spirit is able and willing to talk, start with simple binary questions (those with only two choices), such as, "Do you feel safe?" or "Are you surrounded by darkness or light?"

3. Try to connect with each portion of the spirit. It goes something like this:

   a. Spirit, may I list the seven portions of the spirit and you tell me which one you identify with?

   b. Is it okay with you if I speak with Teacher?

   c. Teacher, may I speak with you?

4. After a few questions and answers, trade roles and give your partner permission to speak with your spirit.

When you ask to speak with someone's spirit and no one answers either by feeling, sensing, hearing or seeing, some clean-up might be necessary to release the spirit from oppression or bondage. Begin by cleansing the generational bloodlines using Spirit Project 2.1 as your guide. Then bless the spirit as you learned to do in Chapter 1. You will learn other tools for setting the spirit free in later chapters of this book.

Spirit Project 2.3 Build Friendships by the Spirit and Design

When you first invite a new person into your community, you can use this strategy to create a clear path to build relationships based on the principles of design and holiness.

Do the following:

1. Use Spirit Project 2.1 to cleanse the generational bloodlines of the person before or soon after you begin the relationship. For example, a teacher might do this for each child in their classroom before the first day of school.

2. Bless the spirit of the person as you learned to do in Chapter 1 and then ask the person's spirit would he or she like to speak with you, as you learned to do in Spirit Project 2.2. The person doesn't have to be present when you do this. Use good social manners and don't push or intrude. Invite the spirit to have a relationship with you. When talking with a human spirit, never try to manipulate, invade or control.

3. When you first meet this person, try to notice what they are emotionally invested in and ask honoring questions about their interests. For example, a teen is wearing a T-shirt sporting their favorite band. You can ask, "What is it about this band you like? Is it the music or the musicians?" Be sure to not judge their tastes. The idea is to discover their design.

When talking with the spirit of a child, know that a child's spirit is more adult like than the soul of a child. You can have an adult-like conversation with the spirit of a child, even one still in the womb.

For more discussions of how our spirits and souls relate, see the blog Spirit Talk at *FromHisTable.com.*

"I am in awe of the God who cherishes walking with me"

"He walked with Me in peace and equity, and turned many away from iniquity." Malachi 2:6

CHAPTER 03 GROWING IN RESPONSIBILITY

"Because we are like our Father God, we think and act like God in all we do."

03

PRINCIPLE

The principle of truth empowers us to develop a healthy reconciliation model that allows us to walk in unconditional love with God and people, even when we are wrong. When we raise our children with this principle, they grow into people who delight in following God and His ways.

The Principle of Truth

The **principle of truth** brings life and sets us free. When lies permeate our thinking, death and bondage result. Truth comes with both rights and responsibilities, and God expects us to level up both in our lives so that we are neither powerless nor entitled. See Figure 3-1.

Rights

Responsibilities

Figure 3-1 God expects us to bring equity to rights and responsibilities in all we do.

An older brother asks his little sister to carry his backpack. She agrees and struggles to get both backpacks to the car on the way to school. Does the brother have a right to ask his sister to carry his load, and, thereby, relieve himself of his responsibility to get his backpack to the car? Yes. Does the sister have a right to say yes or no? Yes. However, if the sister feels she must accept an unfair and unjust responsibility because her brother can and does overpower and bully, does she really have a right to say no?

This situation leads us to consider righteousness and justice. See Figure 3-2.

Righteousness
(Hebrew "Sedaqa")

Justice
(Hebrew "Mispat")

Figure 3-2 Righteousness and justice are the foundation of the government of God

*Righteousness and justice are the foundation of your
throne; love and faithfulness go before you*
Psalm 89:14

The throne of God is the seat of the government of God, and this verse shows us that the government of God is seated or established on righteousness and justice. For rights and responsibilities to be in proper alignment, we need both righteousness and justice. Let's define both:

- **Righteousness** comes from the root word meaning "to be straight." It refers to an ethical or moral standard and describes the character or nature of God. A great picture of righteousness is the plumb line described in Amos 7:7.

  This is what he showed me: The Lord was standing by a wall that had been built true to plumb, with a plumb line in his hand.

- **Justice,** sometimes translated **judgement,** means "to decide a case and execute that decision." When God judges, He always judges for righteousness because that is His character. The government of God is built on righteousness and the execution of righteousness.

Can you see how this happens in Amos 7:7? When the Lord Jesus stands on a wall and holds the plumb line of righteousness in His hand, what happens? The execution of righteousness happens, and the wall conforms to plumb. Jesus was explaining to Amos that if the people would allow Him into their affairs, He would synchronize them to Himself through His plumb line of righteousness.

The heart of the third principle of truth and the third gift, the Teacher gift, is to enthrone Jesus, who is Truth, in our hearts and in our land. In Chapter 6, you learn more about what it means to literally enthrone Jesus in our hearts.

Sons of God love to sync to Him and their leaders, but slaves don't see value in syncing to others.

> *However, some of them paid no attention to Moses; they kept part of it until morning,*
> *but it was full of maggots and began to smell. So Moses was angry with them.*
> Exodus 16:20

This chapter is about syncing or reconciling with God and His righteousness through principles and values, also called moral standards. When we do so, we enthrone Jesus on the inside and on the outside.

HERE WE GROW

During the third stage of growth, we learn how to move from wrongness to rightness with dignity and unconditional love and without shame.

Growth Stage 3.
As I Learn Right from Wrong, I Can Give Life to Others

Ever wonder why some people live their lives out of strong convictions of what is right and wrong, and it seems like other people just go through life doing whatever they like with little regard for moral standards? People who lack moral standards, a sense of right and wrong, missed part or all of this third stage of growth, which is designed by God to happen in our primary grades.

A child isn't born with a moral compass or moral standards; left to themselves, a child often chooses what is wrong. Parents, grandparents and other leaders in a child's life must show the child the principles of God (see Figure 3-3) in such a way the child consistently wants and chooses what is right when parents and other leaders are not overseeing.

God desires that we choose life so that He can bless us and our descendants:

> *This day I call the heavens and the earth*
> *as witnesses against you that I have set*
> *before you life and death, blessings and*
> *curses. Now choose life, so that you and*
> *your children may live.*
> Deuteronomy 30:19

Figure 3-3 A moral compass based on the Word of God leads to fulfillment with Jesus as our life-giving King

When we choose life, we choose Him and His ways because He is the way, the truth and the life:

> *Jesus answered, "I am the way and the truth and the life.*
> *No one comes to the Father except through me."*
> John 14:6

When a seed has soil, water, air, and light, it can grow into a plant and produce new life. The very first leaf that appears has this capacity to create new life. In this third stage of growth, we invite a child to be a leaf – to be a factory that produces new life.

At this early age, a child generally decides how they will relate to other people and the physical and spiritual worlds around them for the rest of their lives. Parents and teachers have the great responsibility and privilege to show a child how he or she is a life giver to others and this life they give comes from God.

When we relate to God, people and creation in righteousness, we can:

- Live at peace with ourselves, our community and God. We can live in harmony with those who are not like us. We can even live with something that is painful.

- Be a life giver to ourselves and others, even when we or the other person have not fully arrived. The more we draw near God, the more light is in us and the more life we give to others.

- Be a blessing because we have been blessed.

Learning to walk in righteousness as a life giver is a process and we will most certainly make many mistakes along the way. The process or pathway from wrong to right is called **reconciliation**.

God's Examples of Reconciliation

Scripture, from Genesis to Revelation, is a story of reconciliation. Under the old Law, God provided for the ministry of reconciliation through the Levites, who were priests. For example, leprosy was unclean, and God required someone with leprosy to live outside the camp. The entire community knew to stay away from this person. If they were healed, the priest coached the person through an elaborate process of reconciliation to community. The priest's glorious words, **"You are clean!"** meant the person could reenter community, and the process was finished.

In covenant with the Lord Jesus Christ, Jesus, as our High Priest, has reconciled us to the Father, to ourselves and with each other.

> *For God was pleased to have all his fullness dwell in him, and through him to reconcile to himself all*
> *things, whether things on earth or things in heaven, by making peace through his blood, shed on the cross.*
> Colossians 1:19-20

When a child makes a mistake, he or she might feel they are separated from community because of their wrongness (see Figure 3-4). It's vital a parent help a child move from wrongness to rightness in community without bullying, despising or rejecting so that the child feels loved and honored through the *entire* process. With a loving reconciliation model, a child grows up delighted to live a righteous life and knows how to do that.

Figure 3-4 A loving path to reconciliation teaches a child that God always receives them, even when they are wrong.

Father God's Discipline Feels So Good

My church leaders had so offended me that I had refused to go with them on a missions trip to a foreign nation even when God told me to go. I knew I had disobeyed God but I was so angry at the leaders I was neither repentant nor remorseful even when their trip went badly and my presence on the trip would have prevented the debacle. I was wrong – very wrong.

Early one morning, an angel woke me up with a big beautiful smile and said, "Get dressed quickly. Exciting things are happening." When I got to my prayer room, the presence of God was powerful, loving and welcoming. He gently explained to me that because I had disobeyed Him and had such a bad attitude about it, He was stopping all ministry travel for one year. I had multiple trips on the calendar, all of which, for one reason or another, got canceled that year. At the end of the year, the invitations started again.

That's what happened, but more importantly, I want you to know how I felt because of what God did. I felt honored. I felt cared for. I felt enveloped in love. I felt immense awe for my good Father who loved me so much He disciplined me in this way. I was so proud of my Daddy! I felt proud to be His daughter. I felt secure in our relationship more that year than ever before. I learned I could trust Him to discipline me with unconditional love and acceptance when I needed it. I was so grateful. It's hard for me to find the words to express how loved I felt through that discipline. It proved I was His daughter. It changed me from the inside out.

For thought and discussion:

1. Read Hebrews 12:1-11. List all the benefits of God's discipline in these Scriptures.

2. When you discipline someone, how do you want them to feel in the process?

3. How does this Scripture and my story change the way you might discipline others?

If our family systems didn't provide a loving reconciliation model built on strong moral standards, we must learn these skills as adults. In this chapter, we learn about many principles of righteousness, and we explore how to implement a healthy reconciliation model.

CONCEPTS

Values are principles that motivate; they explain why we do what we do.

Similar to the ingredients in a cake, values come together and are baked in to make the culture in which we live. See Figure 3-5.

Figure 3-5 Our core values are baked into our culture like the baked-in ingredients of a cake

When first building a community, select only a few values to get started and add others later. For example, for a new school we are building, we decided to start with four values: continually moving toward God, design, trust and reconciliation. After we feel confident these values are baked into our culture, we will add other values.

03

We all have baked-in values whether we realize it or not. In learning to become a son who can build, we must reassess our values and choose those that Father God values the most. We must also discard the ones that oppose God and His ways. In this part of the book, we examine several values that we believe are valuable to God for growth and transformation in a community of sons who know how to build. You'll learn more about these values later in the book.

Value 1. We Value Continually Moving Toward God

Often, we don't understand God or what He has done or might do. We might not trust God. Even so, will we move toward God or away from Him? Moses said, when he was walking up the mountain toward God, "I am terrified and trembling." (Hebrews 12:21) But still he kept walking toward God. The Israelites made a different choice.

> *When the people heard the thunder and the loud blast of the ram's horn, and when they saw the flashes of lightning and the smoke billowing from the mountain, they stood at a distance, trembling with fear.*
>
> *And they said to Moses, "You speak to us, and we will listen. But don't let God speak directly to us, or we will die!"*
>
> *"Don't be afraid," Moses answered them, "for God has come in this way to test you, and so that your fear of him will keep you from sinning!" As the people stood in the distance, Moses approached the dark cloud where God was.*
> Exodus 20:18-21

The better we know God, the more in awe of God we become and the more we celebrate Him and worship Him out of profound and deep gratitude to Him.

Daily, many times a day, we all make this same choice. Even when we don't know God, trust Him or like what He's doing, we choose to risk on God. We are committed to continually discover God and know Him better and better. We refuse to step back from God even when we perceive He has let us down. We recognize in these situations, our perceptions must be wrong because God is always giving us His best

"When people say they are content with their walk with God, most of the time they are lazy."

Credited to John Dawson

(Psalm 84). When we step back from God, our relationship with Him is dulled and it becomes more difficult to hear His voice.

We move toward God to better know His nature, character, ways, commands, protocols, systems, judgements and righteousness. We want to know what God wants -- what pleases Him. All the days of our lives, may we never settle for our current relationship with God. Every day, may we discover more of Him.

The Gates of Nehemiah

In the book of Nehemiah, we learn about the ten gates to the city of Jerusalem. These gates represent the authority we gain by getting to know our God. For the purpose of our study, we look at two gates – the sheep gate and the fish gate. The sheep gate is in place in our lives when our hearts are to follow Him. We are surrendered to God and His ways.

However, when we first give our lives to Him, addictions, bad habits, curses, lack of knowledge of Him and all sorts of hindrances can prevent us from *actually* following Him.

The water gate is in place when we accept that, in order to *follow* Jesus, we must *know* Jesus. Think of a fish. When God first created fish, He spoke to the water, "Let the water teem with living creatures." Fish cannot live without water. If a fish attempted to live on dry land, it would flop about for a while and then it would die. A fish, by God's original design, requires water to live.

When God first created man, He spoke to Himself, "Let us make mankind in our image, in our likeness." Just as a fish came from water and requires a relationship with water to stay alive, we came from God and we must have a relationship with God to stay alive. When we are immersed in God as a fish is in water, the authority of the water gate is functioning in our lives. When we don't stay immersed in God, we will flop about for a while in dry places and then we die.

To know God better by discovering more of His character and His nature, read through the Principle sections at the beginning of each chapter in this book.

03

Keep Discovering God

In Exodus 8, we read where Pharaoh asked Moses to pray to his God to remove the plagues from the land. God answered every prayer Moses prayed. Pretty impressive stuff. But the time came in Exodus 32-33 when the Israelites sinned, Moses prayed and God refused to answer his prayer. He sent a plague anyway.

What was Moses's response? Did he get angry with God, step away from Him or blame himself for not praying hard enough? He did none of that.

Moses recognized that he needed to know God better and so he went *toward* God. He built a tent of meeting and started to hang out there. He said, "If you are pleased with me, teach me your ways so I may know you and continue to find favor with you. Remember that this nation is your people."

For thought and discussion:

1. Describe a situation in your own life when God did not answer your prayers as you expected.

2. Describe your response. In the situation, did you step away from God? Did you point blame at God, at yourself or at others? Or did you step toward God and purpose to know God better?

3. What is one thing you can change in your daily lifestyle to get to know God better?

Our Perspective and God's Perspective

I had a dream to build schools and thought it was from God. But one day God told me that I would not succeed at building schools and led me to the story of David and his desire to build the temple.

I spent several days in disappointment, blaming and accusing myself of not being worthy of building and wondering who was the spiritual son that might be chosen to build. Then my mentor challenged me to sit with God and **ask God for His perspective on the situation**. When I did that, God showed me that David got very excited about God's offer for his son to build the temple and yet I was disappointed. Somehow, I had totally missed the blessing God was offering me.

As I read the Scriptures to see exactly what it was that God offered David, I realized it was the opportunity **to father the builder**. I saw it. God was saying to invest my time and effort in fathering people who would build schools. I was reminded of when some pastors stay so busy pastoring their church, they don't have time to pastor their people. It brought such joy and hope that day to see God wanted me to father sons who would build schools.

For thought and discussion:

1. My perspective was one of disappointment when I thought God was denying me something I felt He had called me to do. Have you ever felt the same way? How did you handle the situation?

2. Think of a disappointment in your life. Spend time with God in your own "tent of meeting" and ask God to show you His perspective of the situation.

Value 2. We Value Love

God is love. "For God so loved that He gave." Love is how we behave towards others, and love is a feeling. In a healthy community, we act with love toward one another in these ways:

- **Patience.** We exercise self-control toward others.

- **Kindness.** We are kind and we lead with kindness. When we are kind, we give attention, appreciation and encouragement to others. We are active listeners. Most people think of listening as passive (be silent when another is speaking), but it's actually a difficult skill to learn to give a speaker our full attention, to be fully present for the speaker.

- **Humility.** We are authentic, real people willing to be seen for who we really are and purposing to know ourselves as God sees us.

- **Respect.** Simply put, we treat others as we want to be treated. We are honest and trustworthy

people. Trust is built over time by honesty and respect.

- **Selflessness.** We listen to others and meet the legitimate needs of others.

- **Forgiveness.** We give others who have wronged us the gift of freedom from what they have done. No more resentment or reminding them of past mistakes.

- **Commitment.** We stick to our choices.

- **Honesty.** Complete honesty with empathy is love in action and necessary if problems are to be faced and solved.

- **No condemnation.** We can correct and lead without a condemning tone or put down that can make the other feel less than.

03

Love is behavior and feelings. We cannot always control our feelings, but we can commit to always being present for the other person. In this way, we can love people, even when we don't particularly like them.

When we all love well, the atmosphere of our community becomes a culture where people can grow. Think of a garden with good soil, water and sunshine. When these elements are present, a plant can grow. We can't make a plant grow, but we can provide the culture or atmosphere where growth can happen naturally.

Handling a  Commotion

For about 15 years, I traveled extensively with a mandate from God to "Take My love to the nations." One trip took me to another continent where the pastor of the church had heard that I followed Holy Spirit and experienced revivals. He told me before the service that he wanted to see what a service looked like led by Holy Spirit and for me to take charge of the service.

During the worship, a woman on the front row began to make loud, strange noises. So loud they were beginning to disrupt the worship team and then the entire room. When the noises turned into loud wailing, I knew something had to be done. I turned to Holy Spirit, "What do you want me to do?" I waited but heard nothing. So I did nothing, but I was uncomfortable as I didn't want the noise to distract others from the powerful worship happening.

Then my friend Judy, who had accompanied me on this trip, went to the lady, stood in front of her and wrapped her arms around her, drawing the woman to herself. The woman melted into Judy's arms, and they both ended up on the floor in tears of love and ultimately peace. The lady stood up with a smile on her face, and Judy slipped back to her seat as the worship ended. I was greatly relieved that, even though Holy Spirit didn't want me to handle the situation, He did lead Judy to do so. Praise God!

Later, I asked Judy what Holy Spirit told her in that moment. She said she prayed but heard nothing. Then she remembered that a pastor had told her that when there's not enough love in a situation, inject *your* love. So, she acted on that principle and decided the right thing to do was to love this lady who obviously did not have enough love!

For thought and discussion:

1. Judy was willing to act on principle when she didn't hear from Holy Spirit. Why was this effective?

2. Recently, I read a news story about an Olympian swimmer who sank to the bottom of the pool during practice. Her coach jumped in and brought her to the surface, saving her life. The coach later explained, "She was under the water far too long." The commentator said, "A friend is someone who doesn't allow us to stay under the water too long." How can you be a friend like that to someone you know?

Value 3. We Value the Dance

The Word of God teaches us about the dance between receiving and giving, as expressed in Scripture as the roles of the Bride of Christ and the Sons of God. All followers of the Lord Jesus Christ are part of the Church that Christ is building, and we are also growing into the sons of God, who are building our Father's Kingdom in every area of life. See Table 3-1.

Table 3-1. The dance between receiving from God and building His Kingdom

Bride mode	Son mode
Female	Male
Bride of Christ	Sons of God
Church	Kingdom
Intimacy	Dominion
Receive	Give, make or build
Mothering (teaching a child to receive)	Fathering (teaching a child to give and build)

Each of us, regardless of our gender, have both male and female tendencies and needs. The Bride of Christ receives from God, and a Son of God gives out of what God has given him. Each of us is part of the Bride of Christ and also a Son of God. We all must learn the dance of moving between receiving and giving.

- If we don't spend time in the female mode of receiving, we stop growing and burn out.

- If we don't spend time in the male mode of giving, we fail to reach our potential in Christ.

I am in awe of the God who wants to marry us.

The Fractals of Two in Our Design

Jesus perfectly reflected this pattern of receiving and giving (which can be an example of a fractal of two). He spent much of His time giving to people in male mode, and yet also spent time alone with His Father in the female mode of receiving.

In this passage, Jesus expressed His female role of receiving:

> *As they were walking along the road, a man said to him, "I will follow you wherever you go." Jesus replied, "Foxes have dens and birds have nests, but the Son of Man has no place to lay his head."*
>
> Luke 9:57-58

When someone lays their head on another's chest, they can feel the rest, protection and nurture of the other. Perhaps this is what the Shulammite woman meant when she said, "I belong to my beloved, and his desire is for me." Song of Songs 7:10.

Is Jesus acknowledging here that His followers could not provide the support and intimacy that only His Father could give? If this is so, surely we can accept we need the same. By design, we might lean more toward the receiving mode or giving mode in our lives. We see this design in children as the "up and over" child who climbs and builds and the "down and under" child who likes to hide in cozy places and draw their stuffed animals to them. Although God designed us in specific ways, we all need to learn the dance as Jesus did to receive and give in our seasons.

Solution using Bride Mode

I invited a few people to a three-day retreat at a short-term rental house to learn more about Bride mode of receiving from God. Father planned a quite impressive imagery of Bride mode the first night at the retreat. The basement reeked of the smell of mold; nonetheless, two ladies agreed to sleep in the two basement bedrooms. The next morning, they both announced, "There's no way we will sleep there tonight. We were tormented all night with ghosts and demons in the basement." We made some changes, and I agreed to sleep in the basement.

Because of weak lungs, I cannot tolerate breathing in mold. I silently asked Father to deal with the mold on my behalf. When I went downstairs to bed that night, to my delight, the space smelled free of mold, and I slept well all night.

The next morning, I invited everyone downstairs. The air was clear, there was no oppression and someone noticed even the stack of towels in the bathroom smelled as if they had just come from the laundry. The topic was discussed at the first teaching session, as everyone wanted to know what had happened. I explained that I did not speak to mold, ghosts or demons. When I laid my head on the pillow, I laid it on my Father's chest and simply went to sleep.

Sometimes we are called to deal with a problem in Bride mode and sometimes in Son mode.

For thought and discussion:

1. Which mode is David speaking of when he said in Psalm 23:5, "You prepare a table before me in the presence of my enemies?" How can you demonstrate a similar mode when solving a problem in your life?

2. Which mode is David speaking of when he said in Psalm 18:37, "I pursued my enemies and overtook them; I did not turn back till they were destroyed?" How can you demonstrate a similar mode when solving a problem in your life?

3. List two more Scriptures where David received in Bride mode and gave in Son mode.

4. Give an example in your own life where you have received from God in Bride mode. Given to people in Son mode.

5. Which mode is more prominent in your life? What changes can you make to bring more equity between Bride mode and Son mode?

How High Can We Build?

Two pillars are needed to possess our birthrights. The tree and left pillar in Figure 3-6 represent our inside character built through our intimacy with God. The castle and right pillar in the figure represent the ideas, strategies and systems we use for building His Kingdom in our communities. We need the dance between intimacy and dominion to build both pillars.

Building inside character
through intimacy with God

Birthright

Ideas, strategies
and systems to
build the Kingdom
on the outside

Figure 3-6 How high can we build?

Bride Mode and
Son Mode Solutions

A ministry is building a food pantry service for the community with the goal of evangelizing the people when they come to receive free food. Suppose you are the leader of this ministry and are trying to learn to lead by asking strategic questions.

For thought and discussion:

1. In measuring their success over the past six months, the ministry tracked that it gave away 120,000 pounds of food. It also saw two people surrender their lives to Jesus Christ as their Lord and Savior. The staff is discussing what can be done to increase the number of decisions for Christ. Looking at the structure of Figure 3-6, what questions would you ask the staff members to determine whether the problem stems from a need to work on Bride mode or Son mode?

2. Suppose everyone decided the problem was not enough attention given to Son mode. What questions might you ask to get to the root of a problem with Son mode?

3. Suppose everyone decided the problem was not enough attention given to Bride mode and all admitted they needed to spend more time in prayer. What questions might you ask to get to the heart of the issue of not receiving from God?

Value 4. We Value Mothering and Fathering

We are all born into this world as takers, fully dependent and demanding of others to meet our every need. Eventually, and not too long after birth, we are expected to start the long, hard journey to take less and less, and learn how to give and build. We need both mothers and fathers to help us with this. We've crafted new, active definitions for these familiar terms:

- A **mother** can be a male or female leader who teaches people *how to receive* in an ever-changing environment. We will be receiving from God and man all the days of our lives, and it's vital to recognize when and how we might need mothering.

To learn more about mothering and fathering and which to use and when, see the album "Colors of Love" by Arthur at **theSLG.com**.

- A **father** is a male or female leader who looks for the treasures in people and teaches them how to give and build out of these treasures. A son will always be giving his entire life, serving God and man, building the Kingdom of God.

It's important we have the right balance of mothering and fathering in our lives (see Figure 3-7). Any leader needs to know how to mother or father those they lead and when it is appropriate to do one or the other. This skill is especially important as parents raising our children.

We are all leaders. We lead when we help a co-worker learn a new job or give directions to a stranger at a street corner. In both these situations, think of yourself as mothering. When that same co-worker continues

Mothering

Fathering

Birthright

Figure 3-7. We need a healthy balance of mothering and fathering to grow to maturity

to come to us for help when they really should be figuring it out for themselves, it might be time to do some fathering to help empower them to take initiative.

In principle, we all need more mothering when we are just getting started learning something new and more fathering when we are learning to master that same skill. Later in the book, you learn more about the wisdom of knowing when to mother and when to father those you lead.

Synchronizing to the Leader

Leaders who know how to mother and father those they lead help their followers synchronize to them. A person with the heart of a son syncs to the leader and expects those who follow them to sync to them. The key to synchronizing with our leaders is to share their same values, and a leader is responsible for communicating their values to their followers.

A servant might find it difficult to sync to a leader because a servant does not always share the same values with their leader. A leader can grow a servant to a son by imparting their values and teaching a servant to sync to them.

One way to discover whether a leader is also a father is to ask the followers to list the top five values of their leader. They can then rate themselves as to how aligned their values are to the values of the leader. For this to be successful, the leader must:

- State their values often and explain their values so all the group can know why the group does what it does. Masters and servants focus on rules – what to do. Fathers and sons focus on values – what to do as well as why we do it.

- When our values align with the values of our leader, relationships can blossom. The authority the leader has is then seen as a blessing and not a hindrance because the leader is taking us where we truly want to go. When a leader senses a follower is syncing to them, they are more likely to delegate authority to this follower.

- Sometimes a leader will sync to their followers, such as when an employee is in a personal crisis and everyone on the team supports the person in crisis.

You learn more about synchronizing in Chapter 4.

In a community, taking initiative is not usually welcome until a person has first learned to sync with the community. Another way of saying that is people don't want to hear what we know about their weaknesses until they first know that we care about them and are willing to sync with them.

First Weeks on a New Job

Sammie had just started a new job as an events planner at a mid-size manufacturing company. She was excited that John, who hired her, would also train her. On Monday morning, John explains that she will first learn to do some basics that everyone in his department knows how to do. She will then be evaluated on how she manages her time and how well she organizes her work.

It was a total letdown when he explained her first assignment is to inventory three containers of furniture and supplies – and there is no air conditioning in those containers! John hands her a laptop, gives her the keys to the containers and tells her to check back in with him before she leaves for the day. Oh, and he mentions that Excel is installed on the laptop.

Two hours later, John sticks his head in the door to find Sammie sitting on the floor with her eyes closed. Sammie jumps up and John asks how far she has gotten. Sammie sheepishly reports she has started a spreadsheet and made a few entries. Truthfully, Sammie is bored stiff and has already lost interest in this "exciting new job." John suggests she not sit down until half the container is inventoried.

Just before noon, John appears again. This time, Sammie reports she has worked her way to near the back of the first container. John smiles and asks her to meet him in the cafeteria in 20 minutes. 'Darn,' thought Sammie. She had planned to meet her girlfriend for lunch.

At lunch, John explains that meeting occasionally for lunch is a good way to build relationships and suggests they have lunch together on Thursday. He also looks at her inventory spreadsheet and suggests a couple of changes.

At the end of the day, Sammie finds John. He checks her spreadsheet and asks how far she got through the containers, and how much time did she expect to take to finish the assignment.

Fast forward two weeks. Sammie is in the swing of things and has gotten to know several of the workers. But big event planning? Not happening. John checks on her at least once during the day and she is still required to report to him before she leaves for the day. Other workers tell her they only report to John at the end of each week, and some days they never see him. They hint to her that John is the type of guy who likes to share why he does things, appreciates those who take initiative and doesn't like to just dole out orders.

Finally at a staff meeting weeks later, John tells Sammie he's ready to assign her first job for an event, putting together the guest list, invitations and seating. He hands her names and phone numbers of every salesperson who will invite customers to the event, and asks for her plan by noon tomorrow. Well, it's a small start for event planning, but at least it's a start.

For thought and discussion:

1. A father gives less flexibility to servants and more flexibility to sons. What can Sammie do differently to gain John's trust so that she would be observed and evaluated less often?

2. Why do you think John checks on and evaluates Sammie more often than other workers?

3. What are some goals that Sammie could set to grow her value in the company?

4. What questions could Sammie ask John to better sync with him as the leader?

5. In your opinion, is Sammie a servant or a son? Explain your reasons for your opinion.

Tough Love

A leader with an official position as leader is responsible for the culture or atmosphere in their area of influence, organization, studio group or team. Sometimes tough love is required. James Hunter, the author of "The Servant," calls tough love *legislating behavior*. When someone refuses to follow the leader, it's up to the leader to decide whether the appropriate response to the resistance is kind love or tough love.

Kind love intends to reduce the pain the person is feeling. Tough love allows the pain to increase in hopes that the person might be motivated to change their attitude.

The Ritz Carlton, Lou Holtz and Jesus Christ Legislating Behavior

A not-so-wealthy man tells the story of taking his wife to a Ritz Carlton hotel so they can experience the delightful atmosphere. When he asked a bartender about the extraordinary respect the employees show the guests, the bartender stated the hotel motto: "We are ladies and gentlemen serving ladies and gentlemen." When the man prodded for more, the employee explained: "If we don't behave this way, we don't get to work here. Is there anything about that you don't understand?"

Another story about legislating behavior comes from Lou Holtz, a former Notre Dame football coach. When asked how he was able to get his team and staff to always be so enthusiastic, he replied, "It's really quite simple. I eliminate the ones who aren't."

In John 2, we read a story where Jesus legislated behavior:

When it was almost time for the Jewish Passover, Jesus went up to Jerusalem. In the temple courts he found people selling cattle, sheep and doves, and others sitting at tables exchanging money. So he made a whip out of cords, and drove all from the temple courts, both sheep and cattle; he scattered the coins of the money changers and overturned their tables. To those who sold doves he said, "Get these out of here! Stop turning my Father's house into a market!" His disciples remembered that it is written: "Zeal for your house will consume me."

As leaders, one of our finest motivators is zeal for our Father's house. This is especially true of parents struggling to find the courage to require our children to obey. Jesus was not motivated to drive out the cattle and sheep and upset the selling and exchange of money from a selfish position. His motivation was zeal for His Father's house.

For thought and discussion:

1. You're building your own company and are writing the policy manual. Decide what your first core value will be and now you will legislate it.

2. Legislated behavior is not nearly as effective as imparted or baked-in values. Remember that behavior is what you do; a value is why you do it. List five tasks or activities everyone in the company might routinely do to bake your value into the culture.

3. In the list you created, which items express tough love and which express kind love?

Value 5. We Value Design

Our design comes from Father God and perfectly matches our assignments, our other resources and our birthrights. As discussed in Chapter 2, it can take years to discover and unpack our design, discover our assignments and step into those assignments.

Most of us find it difficult to see our own design because design is such a natural part of us and so obvious to us that we can miss it. It takes mothers and fathers (and others) who know us well enough to point out what we do naturally. To discover your design, look for what you do easily and naturally that no one trained you to do. Two other points about design:

- The enemy knows our design and may clobber us before we find it. Sometimes we can see our design by looking for where we have most been attacked or wounded.

- Woundedness can cover or mask our design. Healing might need to happen first before our design emerges.

In an organization, our managers should do their best to see that our assignments match up with our design because:

- We can do more with less when we operate out of our design. The company benefits, and we are happier and more fulfilled.

- Creativity emerges out of our design.

Value 6. We Value Always Growing

When a plant or animal stops growing, it begins to die. When we as humans with spirit, soul and body, stop growing, we, too, begin the dying process. We cannot settle where we are. Just as when someone swims upstream against the current and stops, they will drift downstream.

For many of us, however, our growth stagnated at some point in the seven stages. We find ourselves in adult bodies without the spiritual, social and emotional skills we need to live a prosperous and fulfilled life. In this situation, Father God is perfectly capable and desires to father us. He may even send a spiritual father to come alongside us. It's a good idea to keep our eyes open for those people willing to help us grow. This book is all about growing.

> "I'm about to turn 76 years old. I'm healthy and active. I feel young and I have many things I plan to do with my life. The key to my good health is exercise, keeping a good diet, and continually seeking God." Dennis Cudd

Value 7. We Value Transformation

Each of us still has some junk in our trunk. No matter how hard we try to deal with character flaws, wounds in our spirits and souls or critters that vex us, no one has totally arrived. The only one who was able to walk out life fully whole and free is Jesus Christ. In fact, if someone insists on having arrived with all the solutions and answers to life, it's highly unlikely they will be authentic, trustworthy or a team player.

Let's look at some guidelines that will help us toward personal transformation.

Become More Authentic

If you're new to a journey of transformation, one good way to start is to learn to become more authentic. Authenticity is being real with people. We are real people with real problems, challenges, successes and failures. To be authentic:

- **Trust or risk.** We must trust a person to allow them to see who we really are, as real people with real problems. If someone has not yet earned our trust, we can, at the least, decide to take a risk on them to allow them to see us as we truly are, toe fungus and all.

- **Confidentiality.** As a community, we cannot afford to be authentic unless confidentiality is protected. When we tell someone something bad, we must be assured they will protect our place in community.

In an authentic community, we can say when we're having a bad day. When our lives at work or at home are in chaos, we ask for appropriate help, and we learn to deal with our junk without hiding it.

> We all know it's not wise to grant tons of trust to a stranger. A person must prove themselves trustworthy gradually over time with a thousand little decisions and actions. Before we trust someone, we can decide to risk on this person, hoping they prove themselves trustworthy. Even so, we use wisdom in deciding how much risk to take.

Look for Cause and Effect

To deal with our junk, we need to apply the principle of cause and effect. Every event has a cause. If we cannot save money or even meet our monthly budget, there's a reason. If we cannot get through a family meal without an argument, there's also a reason. As people willing to deal with our junk, we accept responsibility and search for the cause of these problems. It could be "somebody did something somewhere" that is affecting us. Life has its ups and downs, and we cannot expect pure bliss, but we do need to identify destructive patterns, explore root issues and implement solutions.

Embrace Productive Pain

See a problem as an opportunity to grow and be transformed. God carefully crafts certain problems and puts them in our lives so that we can grow and become all that He designed us to be. When you are looking for why you are here at this time and in this place, look at the greatest problems you have had to consistently face in your life. These problems are most likely the most significant clues as to your assignment from God. ==Our birthrights stem from the greatest problems we are called to solve and will require all of our resources and experiences with God to solve them.== See Figure 3-8.

When the Israelites first came out of Egypt, with few exceptions, they were all slaves in their hearts. A slave will not trust himself or God enough to tackle a problem they can avoid. God gave them a God-size problem – kill the giants in the land so they could possess their land birthright. They were not willing to embrace that problem and lost their birthrights for an entire generation. Not embracing the problem that God wanted to help them solve cost them dearly.

> When we gossip about someone, we are using their story as currency to gain connection with the person we gossip to. Gossiping to a righteous person does just the opposite... they discover we are not trustworthy. Rather than gain connection, we lose trust.

> When we value transformation, we dedicate time and energy to solving our problems at their root.

Our Birthright
Our Life Messages That Others Need
Our Experiences With God
Our Greatest Problems

Figure 3-8. Our birthrights bring solutions to our greatest problems

Job and Skyscrapers

To replace a three-bedroom house with a skyscraper, you first must destroy the current house and dig down deep into the ground to pour a deeper and stronger foundation that can support the skyscraper.

God found Job, the most righteous man among the people of his day, worthy of such an upgrade. His friends, however, saw it differently and tried to convince Job that his destruction was because of his sin (Job 5:17). But when Job asked his friends what was that big sin they were sure he had committed, they could not answer him. Job asked God the same questions:

"Will you never look away from me, or let me alone even for an instant? If I have sinned, what have I done to you, O watcher of men? Why have you made me your target? Have I become a burden to you? Why do you not pardon my offenses and forgive my sins?" Job 7:19-21

Basically, Job said, "God, stop testing me!" It gets worse. Later, Job accuses God of being in the wrong: *"Though I cry, 'I've been wronged!' I get no response; though I call for help, there is no justice."* Job 19:7

Finally, God had heard enough of Job's friends falsely accusing Job and Job falsely accusing Him. God said to Job, *"Will the one who contends with the Almighty correct him? Let him who accuses God answer him!"*

By the end of this discourse from God, Job responds, *"Surely I spoke of things I did not understand, things too wonderful for me to know."* Job 42:3

Everything in our lives is Father-filtered. In the trials of life, a key to trusting God is to know that, even though He might not like what is happening, He allows it, knowing that He can use the problem to give us His upgrade.

For no other foundation can anyone lay than that which is laid, which is Jesus Christ. Now if anyone builds on this foundation with gold, silver, precious stones, wood, hay, straw, each one's work will become clear; for the Day will declare it, because it will be revealed by fire; and the fire will test each one's work, of what sort it is. I Corinthians 3:11-14

Long ago I decided I didn't want structures of wood, hay and straw in my life, but I knew I had built plenty of that. So I prayed a very dangerous prayer, "God, judge me now. If what I have built can burn, let it burn sooner than later!"

03

For thought and discussion:

1. Name two upgrades that God was able to give Job at the end of his time of testing.

2. Are you currently facing a significant problem in your life? Ask God who put this problem in your life. Did the problem come from:

   - The enemy trying to distract you?

   - People trying to use you?

   - God trying to grow you up?

3. How does knowing the source of a problem change the way you face the problem?

Trust often revolves around the issues of protection and provision. The Israelite former slaves could not trust God for either. We tend to trust God in one area more than another. David was able to trust God for provision but found it more difficult to trust Him for protection.

Jesus tried to explain to Peter more than once that He would die, but if Peter would trust God for protection, he would pass the test to stand with Jesus. When we're about to face a big problem, God in His goodness often prepares us for the test if we will let Him.

Value 8. We Value Trust

Trust is an emotion, a feeling that we can safely rely on a person, group or thing. We can't legislate an emotion. The emotion of trust must be built over time by a thousand little actions that allow our feelings to trust.

Why do we need to develop trust with God and within our team or organization?

- **Transformation.** I must trust someone before I can be completely honest about my deepest concerns, fears and wounds, which is necessary for transformation. I must trust the other person that I will not be judged or condemned, and they will help me with empathy and love.

- **Teamwork.** To work together as a team, we all must be willing to say what we need to say for the common good without fear the other will be offended, withdraw, attack, quit the team or question our good intentions. Where there is trust, we can be completely honest with empathy and without fear.

Lack of trust especially can be a problem in a Christian organization where we work hard to be nice and not offend others.

When cultivating trust in another, these questions can help:

- **Will you hurt me?** I know an employer who decided not to hire someone based solely on the fact he did not wash his hands after using the restroom. His reasoning was, "If I can't trust him to protect me from germs in the restroom, how can I trust him with more important matters of my business?"

- **Will you hurt my place in community?** A friend once said about her family, "If you're not **at** the table, you're **on** the table." Will you criticize or belittle me when I am not present to defend myself?

  Can I say unpleasant things or be misunderstood and still know that you will not reject me or put me down?

  Will you speak up to defend me or my group when we are being disparaged behind our backs?

- **Will I be safe in community if I tell something bad to you?** Pastor Jim asked another pastor to walk with him as he struggled to get free from a pornography addiction. At the next pastor's association meeting, almost every pastor present offered to pray for him. Pastor Jim was so hurt by the betrayal of trust, that he vowed to never ask another pastor for help the rest of his life!

To stand up for what is right requires a level of maturity many don't have. To learn more, listen to the audio album "MRI of Fathering" by Arthur at **theSLG.com.**

- **Will you hear me?** Joseph, the Director of Operations of a small company, wants to tell Sally that her program's resources are being wasted with some glaring inefficiencies. However, when he had pointed out a problem in the past, she would accuse him of being critical of her. Joseph is putting off the dreaded conversation with Sally, afraid she will see it as an attack and slander him to his boss. In the meantime, the problem goes unaddressed.

- **Will you hurt my future?** Susie heard that Jane was applying for a promotion within the company, a promotion Susie herself wants. At lunch one day, she casually dropped some negative thoughts about Jane in the presence of those on the selection committee. A friend of Jane's was also present and told Jane what happened.

- **Will you see my value?** Thomas works every Saturday as a volunteer at a local non-profit thrift store. Steve, the store manager, doesn't like Thomas, especially the way he doesn't follow all the rules posted in the breakroom for volunteers and employees. One Saturday, Steve speaks harshly to Thomas about his actions, and Thomas leaves the store offended, feeling unappreciated and unwanted.

- **Can you see what I have already unpacked?** We might be a mess in one area of our lives and exceptional in another. We can help a person grow through their mess at the same time they help us with a problem we have. Doing so is life giving and brings dignity to each of us.

- **Will you see what I can become in my future?** When you first start to mentor or lead someone, look through the eyes of Jesus to discover the unpacked gifts and treasures in this person put in their original design, as God created them. You can believe in this person more fully when you see them as God sees them. Lead with the goal of searching out and unpacking design and treasures within.

- **Will you risk on me?** You might not yet trust a person, but you can take a risk on them, one small risk at a time, until they prove themselves trustworthy.

  Betsy offered to show Anne, a new employee, how to use the lunchroom equipment and occasionally has lunch with Anne. Then one day Betsy overhears Anne criticizing her to other employees. Betsy decides that Anne is not the potential friend to invest more time in.

- **When I lead, will you sync with me?** When followers don't sync to a leader, the leader is seriously limited as to what can be accomplished on the team.

  Lydia is learning a new shipping job in the organization she has worked at for ten years. Jack, her co-worker, works beside her and does not always follow procedures. Lydia is now uncertain as to how she should do her new job.

- **Can you hear my priorities are different than what you are used to?** When we first start a new job, most of us come to work with our old boss still in our heads. Ask yourself, "Am I doing things this way because it was required in the old job, or am I purposely studying my new boss for her priorities and values?" No boss wants the old boss in the mix.

- **Can I fail without harm?** Many of us unconsciously expect our leaders to be perfect and resent them when they are not. Every leader or follower will fail. A healthy model of reconciliation makes it possible to deal with failure, learn from it and move on. In doing so, trust is built. Perfection is not the goal; knowing how to fail forward is a worthy goal.

- **Will you accept the new me?** When I deal with my mess and it's now in the past, will you accept the new me? Or will you refuse to see whom I have become or even resent that I have changed?

Comfort when Life is Tough

When we risk on others and they fail us, or when life is tough in other ways, where can we turn for comfort? It might be comforting to talk about our pain, especially with someone who has experienced similar pain. Veterans, physicians, police officers and teachers often gather in their own groups to talk about difficult and painful situations they have endured in their profession.

Jesus is our comforter. We can search the Gospels for where Jesus suffered pain similar to ours. Here are a few examples:

- At the Last Supper, Jesus listened as His disciples clashed over who was the greatest. It's painful when we invest much in people and they still don't "get it" or mature.

- In the Garden of Gethsemane, His disciples fell asleep at the moment Jesus needed them the most. Have you ever thought someone would walk with you but found out they could not or would not?

- Jesus, with fury, cursed the Pharisees when they put unnecessarily heavy burdens on the people but they themselves were not willing to lift a finger to help. Have you ever been furious at the way people are oppressed by their leaders who save the best for themselves?

- When John the Baptist was executed, everyone was traumatized. Jesus was faced with wanting to help the crowds and also help His apostles who wanted to leave the crowds and go away to rest. Scripture says His "intestines were tied in knots" over the stress of the situation. Have you ever been in a difficult position where people you love are pulling you in one direction and others you deeply care for are pulling you in a different direction?

This last situation brings me to tears when I think about the time I moved away from family to live in another state where I had few friends or connections because I knew God was leading me there. My little granddaughter called me one day, crying over how much she missed me. I cried, too, and then she felt badly about that and later called to apologize that she had made me so sad. Jesus experienced all this pain and more; sharing the pain with Him helped so much.

For thought and discussion:

1. Think of a difficult time in your life when you were in pain. Search the Gospels for when Jesus endured similar pain. Then pause and connect with Him over that shared pain.

2. Ask a friend or family member to describe a painful situation. Find the situation in the Gospels where Jesus experienced similar pain and share the story with your friend or family member.

Value 9. We Value Good Communication

Ever try to fit into a group when the group refuses to accept you and no one is willing to tell you why? It's been said that people cannot change until they (1) Have enough love they can change, (2) know how to change and (3) want to change.

When building a culture and community for growth and transformation, we must all be willing to communicate. This helps people who don't fit in or are new to the group have every opportunity to understand the culture and expectations. Someone can also love us enough to explain to us where we are missing the mark and to offer a path to change. Then we have a choice with feet on it. If we choose to change, there's a way to do so. If we decide we don't want to change, then we might not belong to this group and need to move on. Clearly to have that choice is based on good communication.

The right to help someone change is earned by:

- **Friendship.** We must be a friend when this person needs a friend. We must build some sort of relationship first before we have earned the right to explain to someone their problem fitting into the group.

- **Authority over the problem.** Have you earned authority to help a person through change? For example, if you overcame rejection earlier in life and see a person reacting to the slightest rejection by others in the group, your earned authority gives you the right to help this person also overcome rejection.

- **Communication.** We must be an active listener, be able to put words to the pain someone is feeling and talk about solutions.

- **Walk beside.** Walk with the person as they go through what can be a painful process to change.

Value 10. We Value Reconciliation

We all fail in relationships, and it's vital we know how to repair a damaged one. Regardless of who is at fault, everyone is responsible to try to reconcile:

- If I owe a debt to my brother, I go to my brother. Matthew 5:23
- If my brother owes me a debt, I go to my brother. Matthew 18:15-20

Poor Reconciliation Models

We all have some type of reconciliation model. A poor reconciliation model (see Figure 3-9) does not take us through to complete reconciliation and we settle for less than a fully restored relationship.

Wrongness

Rightness in Community

Figure 3-9 A poor or missing reconciliation model can destroy community.

Did you grow up with any of these reconciliation models?

- **Rage-aholic home.** Jan grew up with a father who expressed excessive anger. In their rage-aholic home, the number one rule was, "Thou shalt not make dad mad."

  If dad did get mad, to "reconcile," Jan would get out of the way as quickly as possible (if possible, run!) and hide. She would stay out of harm's way for a while and then carefully peek into the room where dad was. If dad was watching TV, she knew it was safe to return to community. No real reconciliation happened. She never knew where she stood with dad and often didn't know what she did wrong or right. She had little opportunity to learn the moral standards that allow us to receive God's blessings and thrive in community. Even as an adult, this is still a mystery to her.

- **Outcast with no safe return.** When David disturbed the family peace, going to his room was the usual punishment. His mom might say, "Go to your room and don't *dare* come out!"

  Waking up in the morning, he wondered, 'Is mom still angry? What to do? Is it safe to get my breakfast? Will I be shamed if I ask? Do I go on to school without breakfast? When I get home, will mom still be mad?'

  When an event is forgotten over time, some might get over it, but others don't. The mindset might be, "I'm over it and you should be, too." The issue has been swept under the rug. But wait. Do we just pretend nothing happened? And the next time I make mom mad, will she bring up this old issue? Or is it really behind me?

- **Someone is scapegoated.** In a healthy community, each person has an appropriate balance between rights and responsibilities. When there's a problem, it's recognized that each person in the group plays a part in the function or dysfunction of the group.

03

When rights and responsibilities are not appropriately shared, the group tends to finger point, blame and scapegoat. Scapegoating fogs up the real issue because people conclude, "This issue is the only issue," and others in the group who are not the chosen scapegoat don't have to face their junk.

Lucio grew up in a family where he usually ended up getting blamed for whatever problem the family was enduring. Mom had no workable system to keep the kitchen clean and yelled at Lucio for leaving his plate on the table. When they were late for school, Lucio frequently heard, "Next time, don't make us all late!" When he was sent to his room for punishment, he often spent time wondering what he did wrong.

As an adult, Lucio cannot afford to be wrong because the expectation is being wrong will get you blamed, scapegoated and outcast. Because Lucio cannot be wrong, he usually resorts to fighting, fleeing or stonewalling.

- **Wear the shame hat.** The guilty party must be shamed for a time. Mary confessed she messed up, but still everyone rejected her until they were over being mad. "I must wait until they allow me back in the group. There is no reconciliation, just waiting. I'm in the doghouse for now."

"Please forgive me." "No, I've not been mad at you long enough!"

In a toxic home, it might not be safe to be wrong or to speak up when we have been wronged. When we cannot own our junk or address a wrong, we might have an emotional meltdown, hide, shut down, point fingers at others or run away.

Indications We Don't Have a Healthy Reconciliation Model

Thoughts and feelings that indicate we need to develop a better reconciliation model:

- Mistakes, conflicts and confrontations leave an uneasy feeling in the group. We would love for the air to be cleared, but don't know how to do that. The process feels too painful.

- We might feel resentful, accused or guilty. Can I work with this person? Do I still belong? Are they glad to see me? Am I welcome? What must I do that I don't know how to do to set things right? Do I try to engage or draw back? Is it safe to open my heart again?

- What is the right thing to do here? What is everyone expecting of me? How will I know?

- Without opportunity to talk things through to reconciliation, each person tends to settle into their own version of what is right or wrong (moral standards) without applying them to a plumbline of righteousness. "Every man for himself."

Giving a Sincere Apology

We all need to know how to give a sincere apology, which can help all parties process their emotions and repair a relationship. Learn to include these five parts in an apology:

1. What happened with complete honesty

2. Why our actions were harmful

3. How the other person might have felt

> Sometimes the offense is so insignificant that we can brush it aside and it does not cause tension in the relationship. A sincere apology or a process of reconciliation is needed, however, when the event brings tension or distance to the relationship.

4. What we could have done differently

5. Our plan to make things better

For example, "I apologize for correcting you in front of the others. I realize that damaged your relationship with them, and I suspect it embarrassed you. I should have talked with you in private. From now on, I intend to always correct in private."

Simple and Loving Reconciliation Model

When the damaged relationship cannot be repaired with a sincere apology, everyone affected needs a sit-down conversation. Let's examine a simple three-step reconciliation model, shown in Figure 3-10. Sometimes a parent or leader needs to walk the person through the three steps without anger or shaming. ==Not even a hint of rejection or abandonment!==

Figure 3-10 A simple three-step reconciliation model

Here are the three steps:

1. **Own your junk.** Be specific and completely honest about what you did. Don't hold back. No fair saying something like, "If I have hurt you, please forgive me." If you think you hurt someone, say what you did, how that was harmful, and acknowledge the pain you caused others. If you don't think you hurt someone, you can ask, "Have I hurt you?"

2. **Clean up the mess.** Parents, the boss or whomever is in charge accepts responsibility for cleaning up the mess, and everyone involved is expected to help. How are **WE** going to fix this problem together?

3. **Make changes.** What could we all have done differently? What can we ALL do to prevent this from happening again?

> "A teacher is responsible for the errors of his pupil." -Gandhi
>
> We messed up the human race, and Jesus accepted responsibility to clean up our mess by laying down His life for us. This was planned before the first one of us messed up. He became the path to reconciliation with our Father.

> In a family, when a child does wrong, and parents approach the child with love and kindness, ready to walk with them to return to rightness in community, the child learns to know the heart of God who is not angry nor rejects when we do wrong. The loving kindness of God leads us to repentance.

Moving Past Reconciliation

After the reconciliation has happened, we all agree that this issue is settled and will not come up again as ammunition in a later conflict.

Sometimes a problem is one-and-done. We made the mistake, and we know it will never happen again.

Sometimes a problem is reoccurring because of some deep root like a soul wound, spirit wound, generational curse, generational sin or covenant with evil in the family line. By design, our lives work. If something is not working, we need to find the root cause and fix it. Inner healing and deliverance might be needed.

> Sometimes people cannot or refuse to reconcile. In these situations, we can follow Matthew 18:17 to treat them as a "sinner or tax collector." In other words, treat them as Jesus does to fully forgive and love unconditionally!

Developing Intimacy Over Time

As trust is built and transformation happens, intimacy grows over time. We can purposefully grow intimacy by being aware of and practicing the seven stages or levels of intimacy listed in Table 3-2. Determine which level you are at with an associate and notch up the intimacy level one step at a time. Take it slowly, and don't try to develop too intimate a relationship that is not appropriate for the circumstances.

Suppose a husband comes home late to dinner, already on the table. The wife asks, "How was your day?" Table 3-2 describes each level of intimacy the husband might choose.

Table 3-2 Seven levels of intimacy

Level of intimacy	Husband's response
1. Cliches	"It was okay." "It was fine." "I'm fine."
2. Facts	"I had to work late."
3. Opinions	"I had to work late, but it was not my fault."
4. Feelings	"I had to work late, and I'm really angry about that. I feel badly I'm late to dinner."
5. Affirmation and condemnation	"I had to work late. The boss didn't manage our time well today, and he's the reason I'm late. But your dinner looks amazing!"
6. Confession and forgiveness	"I had to work late. The boss didn't manage our time well today, and I got more and more frustrated. By the end of the day, I had forgiven him and brushed it off. But I'm really sorry I'm late."
7. Dreams and disillusionments	"I had to work late. The boss didn't manage our time well today. I forgave him for that. But it still hurts my heart that I didn't make it home at the time we agreed to. I'm sorry I'm late"

No More Finger Pointing

The day I wrote this section about finger pointing, I received a past-due invoice by email. The invoices had been mailed to the wrong physical address for five months. Later that day, Matthew, the person who had been receiving the invoices, texted me to apologize for holding on to them for so long. I accepted his apology.

Because the payment was so long past due, I called the company to pay the bill over the phone. After giving the bookkeeper my correct mailing address, I explained to her that Matthew was the one who had held up the invoices, which is why I was late paying. Ugh! Jean! Practice what you preach!

For thought and discussion:

1. What could I have said to the bookkeeper about the situation and still protect Matthew's place in community?

2. Is there a situation in your life where you felt embarrassed because someone of importance caught your mistake and to cover up, you blamed another? Explain how you could have handled that situation, while being trustworthy to the one you had blamed.

3. Write the seven stages of intimacy on an index card. Post the card at your workstation or wherever you find yourself talking with other people.

4. Select someone with whom you would like to build intimacy. What level of intimacy do you practice now? Work your way up the intimacy levels slowly over the next few weeks. Listen for the response from your friend. Are both of you developing intimacy or does your friend resist your efforts?

Value 11. We Value Failures and Problems to Help Us Grow

Failures, problems, mistakes and mess-ups contain hidden opportunities, which can serve us well to help us grow and be transformed. An organization fundamentally faces its problems in one of these ways:

- **We settle with our problems.** The Post Office, some governmental agencies, public education, professors in universities, pastors in some Christian denominations and many organizations with a built-in tenure system often create an atmosphere of settling into less than what is possible. Contentment is often laziness to not change. Where tenure is engrained, the mindset is, "*We will be here until retirement, even if we don't grow. I'm counting the years to retirement!*"

- **We eliminate our problems.** Examples of eliminating problems are major league sports, authors working with high-profile publishers and news anchors. My friend was a television news anchor in Los Angeles. When he gained 25+ pounds, he was fired and replaced by a more fit anchor.

- **We beat our problems into submission.** Examples of this include Amazon, the U.S. Army and other branches of the military. If you can't measure up, you get pushed and forced and commanded until you are compelled to perform.

- **We solve our problems at the root.** Examples of solving root problems are a hospital ER and Navy Seals. When a patient dies in the ER, staff meet later to debrief. Everyone arrives at the meeting having studied all the data and parts they were involved in. The team discusses what happened, what could have been done differently and how to keep it from happening again. Root causes of the problem are identified and addressed appropriately. In the ER culture, each team member expects this scrutiny as part of their job.

<mark>In our organization, we value solving our problems at the root.</mark>

To solve problems at the root, most often we need help. We need to sit, talk and process what happened in a healthy way, and we all need to be truth tellers, totally honest with each other about our behaviors, attitudes or values. <mark>Truth telling about negative behaviors and attitudes without a kind, gentle, and loving tone is painful and cruel.</mark>

> "A person able to build community is one who can identify a problem, see its root cause, and provide a solution so that an asset who is not fully contributing to the common good, can do so."
>
> Arthur Burk

Solving a Problem Might Require Risk

Paige has worked three years for a research company. All employees are expected to work on a variety of tasks, nimbly change direction at any time, be cross trained in every task, and function well in teams. It's a fast-paced, demanding job with expectations that everyone is growing and learning as they work. A new employee, Diana, who is still on probation, is struggling to learn her job in this wild and weird new culture. Paige, her co-worker, is aware of her slowness to adapt and says to her, "I don't want to tell you what to do, but I can assure you that if you would allow my help, I could coach you what to do."

Diana responds, "No, thank you. I'm sure I can figure it out on my own."

Later, as Diana doesn't progress, Paige asks her, "Why are you here? Are you here for yourself, your paycheck or the Kingdom? Being here for the Kingdom changes your perspective about everything."

For thought and discussion:

1. Diana didn't report to Paige in an official way. Why do you think Paige offered to mentor Diana?

2. In a culture committed to growth, it must be safe to take a risk on someone. What risk was Paige willing to take to help Diana?

3. List three values in the company culture that would motivate Paige to volunteer investing her time to help a new co-worker succeed. For each value, describe two ways the value could be baked into the company culture.

4. Discuss with others how you might answer Paige's question about why you are in your current organization. What does it mean to you personally to be here because of the Kingdom of God?

"If we're growing, we're always going to be out of our comfort zone." John C. Maxwell

Value 12. We Value Teamwork and Synergy

Most people these days want to work independently and be given clear goals to accomplish and objectives for evaluation. Father God, however, is focused more on family and teams. In John 17, Jesus prayed that His disciples would be one as He and the Father are one. Here are some advantages of working in teams:

- **We are better together.** One can chase a thousand, and two can put ten thousand to flight. The synergy of working in teams makes us more productive than each of us working alone.

- **We better express the nature and character of Father God.** Father is all about oneness and teams. "Let us make man in our image, after our likeness." We were designed by God to be like Him – to work in teams.

- **We are more creative in teams.** Each of us have a unique design, gifts and talents given by God. When we synchronize with God around these strengths, we are better able to align with others also synchronizing with God. As we flow organically in teams synchronizing with God, we see how our strengths enrich the strengths of others. In this organic atmosphere of alignment, God is able to draw out the best in us and we can flow in creativity. Working in synergy in this way is exhilarating and fun. See Figure 3-11.

Figure 3-11. A team that can sync with each other is fulfilling and fun

Syncing at Lunch Time

Julia, the senior partner in a dental practice, closes the dental office from 11:30AM to 12:30PM each day. Everyone brings their own lunch, and at 11:30, all go to the kitchen to prepare so that all are seated at the table promptly at 11:40. The kitchen is small, and it takes some synchronization to pull it all together. Someone standing in front of the microwave must step to the side so another can open the fridge door. Only two can work at the stove at one time. Everyone has their assigned prep spot at a counter and their assigned spot around the lunch table.

Julia requires that everything in the office, from dental instruments to the utensils in the kitchen, have their place and be put back in their place when someone finishes with it. Kitchen cleanup is done by rotation, and everything is put back exactly where it belongs.

When Jeffrey Stone started work as the new staff dentist, he was shocked at how everyone in the kitchen was quick to correct him, "Dr. Stone, you dry your hands with this towel, not that one."

"Dr. Stone, put the knife in *this* drawer and turn it *this* direction." By the end of the first lunch, Jeffrey was wondering what kind of strange dental practice Julia had!

At lunch that day, Julia discussed with the staff why she refused to do pro bono dental work for one patient but offered it to another. She invited discussions and questions, especially the "why" questions, about her pro bono work. And then she invited questions and discussion about why she requires the staff to pick up the trash in the parking lot as they enter and leave the building.

For thought and discussion:

1. Julia sees lunch time as the time to build her core values into her partners and staff. List as many lunch activities as you can that exhibit the core values of a builder.

2. Identify three core values that Julia wants for her dental practice.

3. Julia has decided that one goal for next year is that each staff member, including herself, grow in team leadership skills. What is one activity she can add to the lunch routine that might help grow the staff in this area?

4. Charlie, a dental hygienist, begins leaving the office at 11:00 and returning at 12:30 each day. Julia asks Pam, the office manager, to discuss the company policy with Charlie about all staff being present at lunchtime. If you were Pam, what are the points you would make to Charlie? What questions might you ask?

Ernest Shackleton and His Men

"MEN WANTED: FOR HAZARDOUS JOURNEY. SMALL WAGES, BITTER COLD, LONG MONTHS OF COMPLETE DARKNESS, CONSTANT DANGER, SAFE RETURN DOUBTFUL. HONOUR AND RECOGNITION IN CASE OF SUCCESS. SIR ERNEST SHACKLETON"

This ad was placed in a London newspaper in 1914, and 28 men responded, including a physicist, meteorologist, photographer, surgeon, cook, artist and one stowaway.

Shackelton was attempting to cross the Antarctic for the first time and carefully selected his team. On January 19, 1915, the *Endurance*, froze fast in ice, and Shackleton ordered the crew to abandon ship just before it began to tear apart. After almost two months camping on ice, the party finally made it to Elephant Island, over 300 miles from where the *Endurance* sank. During that time, Shackleton suffered frostbitten fingers because he had given his mittens to a crewman who had lost his.

After setting up camp on the island, Shackleton decided to risk taking a lifeboat, along with five crew members, over 700 miles to a whaling station on South Georgia Island. It would take them over four months to make the round-trip carrying provisions in a tugboat back to the crew isolated on Elephant Island. On August 30, 1916, the men spotted Shackleton's boat in the distance. As the boat was drawing near, all 22 men intentionally positioned themselves spread out across the horizon.

For thought and discussion:

1. Why do you think the 22 men stood on the horizon spread out the way they did?

2. What does this tell you about their feelings for Shackleton?

3. What qualities do you look for in a leader that make it easy to sync with him or her?

4. Think of a leader you have had in the past that you admire. What qualities do you admire most in them?

5. List three qualities that you purpose to grow into to become a leader who inspires.

Value 13. We Value Verifiable, Measurable and Sustained Change

Every organization needs goals by which it measures success. Many businesses measure success by the bottom line of money, which can be measured as profit earned over time or the profit margin.

In general, success can be measured as short-term or long-term change. For example, a church might measure success as the average number of people who attend each church meeting for the first time (short-term success). Or they might count the families who moved from poverty to a sustainable income (long-term success).

Long-term success is best measured using three types of metrics:

- Verifiable – change can be confirmed yes or no - change happened
- Measurable – the degree of change from not much to a lot

- Sustainable – the change is permanent and not temporary

Listed below are some successes that are verifiable, measurable and sustainable that an organization might use to track its success.

- Net profit earned or profit margin
- Money donations or grants
- Number of full-time employees
- Decisions for Christ
- Pounds or tons of food given away
- Degrees or certifications awarded
- Classes completed
- Businesses started
- Homeless people in long-term housing with a sustainable source of rent
- Unemployed people who find jobs
- Average number of people who attend meetings per year
- Out-patients treated per year
- Number of couples who had decided to divorce but stayed together and are living in peace

> Profit margin is the amount an organization saves each month, expressed as a percentage of income. For example, if a company brings in $10,000 in sales, and spends $8,000, its profit is $2,000 and its profit margin is 20%. The company is able to save 20% of every dollar it earns.
>
> A family can also measure profit margin. Suppose a family income is $3,000 each month and it spends $2,900. Its profit is $100, and its profit margin is about 3%.

Some organizations, especially non-profit ministries or churches, may have operated many years without considering what they see as successful or how they want to measure success. Even for-profit businesses can simply measure success as "we are still in business after all these years."

It can be transformative for an organization who has not measured its success to go through a process of evaluating success:

1. What do we consider to be success? (for example, a church decides success is decisions for Christ)

2. How will we verify our success? (written testimonies of decisions for Christ)

3. How will we measure success? (number of testimonies compared to number on staff)

4. How will we measure sustainability? (number of new believers who are still attending our church after three years)

By evaluating success this way, or in similar ways, problems become evident so that solutions can emerge, improvements are made and people in the organization grow and are transformed. When we don't measure success, we can drift backwards or not grow without realizing it. When we measure success, we tend to get better and better.

> What is monitored and measured improves.

Value 14. We Value Independent, Life-long Learning

The day we stop learning is the day we stop growing. The day we stop growing is the day we begin to die. According to Daniel Pink in his book "Drive," we are all driven by one or more of four motivators:

- **Extrinsic reward.** In traditional education, rewards are grades and credentials. In commerce and business, typically, the reward is money.

- **Autonomy.** Some are motivated by the right to work independently at their own pace and in their own way. Autonomy is one major reason a person is an entrepreneur who builds their own business.

- **Mastery.** Some people are so committed to excellence, their primary motive is to complete a task well. For these people, to be pulled from a learning experience before the task is mastered can demoralize.

- **Contribution.** This motive is considered the highest motivator and can even drive a person to lay down his life for another. Many people reach a maturity in life where it becomes terribly important to make a difference and leave a legacy for the next generation.

Can you think of other motivators than these four?

The Garbage Disposal and Raising Rabbits

Alan rushed off to work one morning and accidentally left the kitchen water running and the garbage disposal turned on. When he returned a few hours later, the garbage disposal was not working, and water was all over the kitchen floor. Call a plumber or search YouTube? Wanting to learn how to do his own house repairs and also save money, Alan searched YouTube.

A group of teenagers in Myanmar (Burma) live together in a home that is supported by donations from overseas. Money is tight for groceries, so they decide to grow their own food, starting with a garden and rabbits. For a few months, they watch YouTube videos on raising rabbits, try a few rabbit breeds, and learn that some cages don't keep rabbits in or dogs out. They also learn how to kill and clean the rabbits and cook the meat. After about a year of experimenting with rabbits, they conclude rabbit meat is not the best source of protein and move on to chickens.

For thought and discussion:

1. What do you think was the primary motivation for the teenagers in Myanmar to learn how to raise rabbits? Was it extrinsic reward, autonomy, mastery or contribution?

2. Our primary motivator changes from time to time and in different situations. What is your primary motivation for learning from this textbook?

3. Think of three things you've learned in the last year. Why did you learn each and how did you learn it? Is this skill you learned still of value to you?

Value 15. We Value Excellence and Order

Excellence is taking the time and making the extra effort to do things well. Excellence is a way of life and applies to everything we do, from making our beds in the morning to how we perform on the job. Excellence does not require perfection.

Most of us were not born with a commitment to excellence, and we acquired it from a parent, teacher or boss who valued excellence. Or perhaps we learned excellence through life experiences that shaped us.

"Two Logs Crossing" by Walter D. Edmonds

The book "Two Logs Crossing" touched me deeply as a youth and is one reason I chose excellence as a personal core value. The story is of John Haskell when his father died in the 1800's and left 16-year-old John to care for his mom, five younger siblings and one more on the way. Because of his father's bad reputation, John could not get full-time work. By working odd jobs and growing a garden, by the end of the summer, he had saved up enough food, firewood and coins to get them through the winter.

When he met Seth, an Indian trapper, the local judge took a risk on John and loaned him $75 to go with Seth that winter to learn the art of trapping in the woods. John worked harder than he had ever worked in his life, and by early spring, Seth estimated John had enough furs to pay his debt to the judge with enough money left to finance debt-free next winter's trapping.

Seth begged John to stay with him until the snow melted, but John got anxious to get home. He was homesick and ready to stand before the judge and his mom in victory with a backpack of pelts. Seth's last words were, "Now listen to Seth. If creeks open, you cut two logs crossing. You mind Seth. You cut two logs. One log roll. Two logs safe crossing water."

"Yes, sure," agreed John, as he hurried on his way. On the long walk home, for several days, John faithfully cut two logs each time he crossed a stream.

When he reached the last stream, fast running with melted snow, so close to home, he found a single hemlock tall enough to reach across. With no other tree nearby, John reasoned he had safely crossed all the other streams on only one log. Surely this time was no different and he started across. The log shifted, John survived the tumble, but lost everything.

Still wet, he walked into the judge's office and told the whole story, even about Seth's warning "two logs crossing." He was surprised when the judge didn't get angry, only sent him home to meet his new baby sister.

That summer was hard, but they made it through. In the fall, he found a job at the local tannery for winter work. Then the judge invited him to his office and made an offer to finance him to trap for the winter. John could barely say yes, as he came closer to crying than when he lost his pack in the stream.

Coming out of the woods the following spring, loaded with furs, always crossing the streams with two logs, he took an extra three days and came home with his furs.

For thought and discussion:

1. How did the first winter trapping affect John for the rest of his life? What role did the judge play in his life to encourage excellence?

2. On a scale of one to ten, how committed are you to excellence? How committed do you want to be? What changes might you make if you decide to raise your level of excellence?

3. List three things (for example, brushing your teeth, cooking a meal, or working on your job) that you can focus on doing with more excellence. Make this commitment with your discussion partner and report back in one week how or if excellence improved.

Value 16. We Value Dignity and Respect

Without dignity and respect, we feel like second-class citizens before God and in community. In Mark 5, Jesus delivered and healed the Gadarene demoniac. When the healed man asked to follow Jesus, Jesus said no and sent him back to his community. Although having been delivered and healed by Jesus gave the man great dignity, he also needed his dignity and respect in community restored.

Many of us have been alienated from God and community because of shame. Shame makes us feel less than and keeps us from approaching God to receive the intimacy, healing, respect and dignity we need.

> Dignity originates from having a place of intimacy with God and is completed when we function as a life-giving part of community.

The Mom's Story in "Two Logs Crossing" by Walter D. Edmonds

In the book, "Two Logs Crossing," discussed earlier, John Haskell's mom had her own part of the story. Right after John's father had died, the judge had told John that his father owed him $40. At the end of that first summer, John saved enough to pay the judge $5 of that debt.

When he told his mom, John thought she would be glad to know he had paid part of the debt, but instead she cried bitterly. Because John had done so well that summer, mom had gotten her hopes up there would be enough money for the seventh baby to be born with the dignity of their paying the cost of the doctor and nurse rather than "on the town." Her bitter tears flowed from the fact that the $5 John had used to pay against the debt was the exact amount the doctor and nurse would cost.

John didn't quite understand his mother, but he did realize he had somehow taken from her something deeply precious. Later, he explained to the judge that he needed the $5 back to make his mom "feel respectable." The judge seemed to understand and gave him back the $5.

For thought and discussion:

1. In the mom's story, what was the dignity she needed to feel respectable in community?

2. Is the mom a taker, breaker or maker? Explain your answer.

3. Do you know someone in your life who lacks dignity? Without revealing their name or identity, tell their story to your discussion partner or group. What must happen for this person to have dignity?

Value 17. We Value Gratitude and Celebration

God loves celebration! In Chapter 1, you learned about the value of gratitude and celebration toward God that is necessary to grow our minds and to see and accept the perfect will of God.

Here are some reasons to celebrate and honor people:

- **Every small or large effort.** An affirming kind word or pat on the back for showing up and trying something new can keep us going and motivate us to embrace productive pain. We celebrate persevering.

- **Birthdays.** We celebrate you. We are glad you were born and we are glad you are with us.

- **Achievements earned by hard work and focus.** When someone has worked hard to do a difficult thing and finally achieved it, we celebrate!

- **Group achievements.** A team celebrates goals attained. One wonderful goal worth celebrating is when each member of the team has made a solid contribution to the team goal.

- **Overcoming a weakness.** A boy in our classroom is selfish and doesn't help others. The day he helped a younger student accomplish a difficult assignment was truly worth celebrating!

One metric to measure the success of an organization is the number of times you celebrate in a given week. If celebration is not part of your culture, keep a chart. When you have increased your celebrations by 50% in a single week for three weeks running, celebrate your learning to celebrate!

> What we celebrate we get more of. It is imprinted in our culture and our brains and will live on as our legacy for future generations.

03

SOLVING PROBLEMS

Recall that we solve problems in four steps: (1) Collect data, (2) look for patterns, (3) identify principles, and (4) apply these principles to new situations.

When looking for patterns, it helps to have grids of previous patterns to apply to the data. The more pattern grids we have, the better our chances of identifying patterns and underlying principles. Some grids discussed in earlier chapters include:

- True legitimacy built on the love of God through belongingness, worth and competence
- Legitimacy lies and counterfeit legitimacy that can misguide us
- Pain management (avoid pain or embrace productive pain)
- Identity built as a servant of God or son of God
- Resources seen or not seen (servants often don't see resources God has provided)
- Taker, maker or breaker
- Problems in the spirit realm, such as generational covenants, sins, rebellion and iniquities
- Soul wounds
- Our design, including our Trinitarian design and redemptive gifts

Throughout the book, we add more grids to use as filters to identify patterns. In this chapter, we build some grids based on our core values.

Problem 3.1 How We Face a Problem

In this exercise, you learn more about looking for patterns in the data collected. Here are five stories to consider:

1. Peter bullies others on the playground, telling them what to do and how to do it. When his teacher tries to explain to him that he needs to learn how to get along better with other children, he says, "They always pick on me and I have to stand up for myself."

2. Jessica is always slow getting her work done and is falling behind with her self-paced curriculum. Her teacher has tried using a stopwatch and check sheets to mark tasks completed. Nothing works.

3. Jerry manages a restaurant and can't keep workers. They work for a few days and quit. In just the past month, Jerry has lost seven workers and lack of staffing is affecting the restaurant income.

4. Jan manages an office team. Lucy is causing trouble on the team and is challenging Jan's right to direct the team, claiming she could do better.

5. Stan drives a delivery truck for a major corporation. His manager has asked him to falsify his time sheet so that the manager can meet the time-billed quota demanded by her boss.

Do the following:

1. List as many grids or filters that might be used to identify the principle involved for:

   a. The teacher helping Peter

   b. The teacher helping Jessica

   c. Jerry solving his staffing problem

   d. Jan protecting her team

   e. Stan responding to his manager

2. For each story, select the most likely principle being violated or otherwise in play.

3. For each story, what is one question you can ask the person to discover whether your guess is right?

To help you get started, here are possible solutions for the first story, but you might find more:

Possible grids:

- Peter is a taker or breaker, rather than a maker.

- Peter has soul wounds.

- Problems in the spirit realm are affecting Peter.

- Peter is not embracing the values of love, teamwork and/or good communication.

Most likely principle in play: Peter does not embrace the value of love and does not treat others as he wants to be treated.

Questions the teacher can ask Peter: "Peter, which child would you most like to play with? How do you think he felt when this happened? What could you do or say so he would want to play with you?"

Problem 3.2 Build Trust and Other Resources

Every time we risk and it's safe, our trust grows. For some important relationships, we want to build real trust and not just risk.

Do the following:

1. Trust often involves trusting for protection or trusting for provision. To discover where you personally have the greater trust, answer the following questions:

   a. When you were a child, which was more consistent and abundant, provision or protection?

   b. As an adult, which is easier for you to trust God for, provision or protection?

   c. Can you think of a situation where it was difficult to be at peace and trust God? What were you needing to trust God to do for you?

2. Priya grew up in extreme poverty and is now married to Marcus who grew up in wealth. She gets nervous and irritated whenever Marcus charges an unnecessary item to their credit card even though the card is paid off at the end of each month. Which of the following next steps would help this couple resolve their conflict? Select as many as you like. For each next step, identify the principle or core value involved.

   a. Priya is designed by God to steward money and needs to better understand her design.

   b. Priya needs to learn to trust God for provision.

   c. Marcus needs to help his wife by paying cash for unnecessary items.

   d. They need to stop using credit cards for purchases.

   e. Priya and Marcus need to better understand the emotional needs of the other.

3. Issac is new at school and finds it difficult to fit in. He has already been in a couple of altercations with schoolmates and has begun to withdraw from class discussions. He recently told his mom that the other kids don't like him. The mom has asked to talk with the teacher about the problem, and the teacher realizes she doesn't know enough about Issac and his family. She wants to collect more data. For each of the next steps the teacher

might pursue to resolve the problem, create two or three questions she can ask the mom or others to decide the best course of action.

a. Inclusion and love: Encourage other students to make it clear to Issac that they enjoy him and want to hear what he has to say in discussions.

b. Rejection: Help Issac to learn to hear God's voice and to ask what does God enjoy about him.

c. Essence: Assign to Issac curriculum on our essence as sons of God, and help Issac ask God questions about his essence.

d. Belongingness: Be keen on making sure all Isaac's needs are consistently met.

e. Growth: Coach Issac on how to get along with peers.

f. Spirit realm: Address generational iniquities of rejection.

Problem 3.3 The Challenge of Finishing Well

Read the story of Jehoshaphat, a king of Judah, in 1 Kings 22, 2 Kings 3, and 2 Chronicles 17-20. Jehoshaphat began (2 Chronicles 17:3-6) well but did not finish well. Name one principle that Jehoshaphat applied that caused him to prosper. Name another principle that Jehoshaphat violated that caused him to not prosper.

Problem 3.4 Building a Healthy Reconciliation Model

We all need to know and practice a healthy reconciliation model in every relationship at home, work, at church and in the larger community.

Answer these questions:

1. Describe the reconciliation model in your family when you were a child.

2. Describe your current reconciliation model. How does it differ from the one you practiced as a child?

3. Analyze your reconciliation model with the three-step model suggested in the chapter:

a. When you are reconciling with someone, is there good communication? Are you able to "own your junk?"

b. Give an example of how you or another were alienated in community. What did you do to attempt to reconcile the situation? Did your reconciliation work?

c. What did you do to keep the problem from reoccurring?

4. If you don't have good examples of your reconciling with another, is there someone you need to reconcile with now? Try the model with that person.

5. For reconciliation to work, there must be a commitment to good communication. What are three things you can do to improve how you communicate when there is a need to reconcile.

Problem 3.5 Brave Truth Telling with Empathy

In Christian organizations, we want to be nice and not offend, which can keep us from saying difficult or uncomfortable things. But to solve a problem, we must talk about it. When a problem in community arises, have you ever not said something because:

- The other person might get angry
- Feelings might get hurt
- You don't know how to say it
- They might not know you mean them well
- They might not understand your approach to the topic

With your discussion partner or group, discuss how good communication can happen so that relational problems can be resolved in community. You can start the discussion with a question, such as, "Have you ever not said what you need to say because you think the other person might get angry?"

Problem 3.6 Identify Mothering and Fathering Needed at Each Stage of Growth

As we mature through the seven stages of growth, we need mothering and fathering to help us through to adulthood. In the following table, the stage and a situation at that stage are listed. Identify which is needed to mature a child, mothering or fathering. Then describe how an adult might meet that need. Try to remember the good parenting you received as a child or wished you had received. If you need help understanding each stage of growth, see the sections *Here We Grow* near the beginning of each of the seven chapters. Also remember that either parent (male or female) can express mothering and fathering.

Stage	Situation	Mothering or fathering	Description
S1. Belongingness	At 8 months, I cannot go to sleep.	Mothering	My dad gently rocked me to sleep.
S2. Know myself	At 3 years old, I want to play in the water.	Mothering	My mom enjoyed watching me play in a creek near my home.
S2. Know myself	At 3 years old, I can't stand loud and sudden noises.		
S3. Moral standards	At 7 years old, I talk back to my dad.		
S4. Peer relationships	At 11 years old, I went to the school dance, but no one asked me to dance.		
S5. Develop myself	I love piano but I don't have the self-discipline to practice.		
S6. Stand and build	I want to not eat sweets, but my friends just invited me for ice cream.		
S7. Become my own person	I find myself getting angry and shouting at my children, just like my father did to me.		

GROWTH PROJECT

These growth projects are designed to help us grow and to learn how to help those we lead to grow.

Growth Project 3.1: Identify Your Individual and Family Core Values

Remember that a core value is what motivates us and is a principle or truth with a cause-and-effect relationship. Sometimes a core value is called an anchor truth. Recognize that core values can change from one season of our lives to another.

Do the following:

To identify your personal core values, ask yourself how does a value motivate you. Suppose you chose valuing failures and problems as one of your core values:

1. List three of your greatest successes and three of your greatest failures. How do you define success? How do you define failure?

2. How do you see these failures or problems as beneficial to you?

3. Do failures discourage you? If so, explain the discouragement.

4. Does the fear of failure prevent you from trying something new?

5. When one of your followers fails, how do you handle it?

6. How do failures motivate you?

Identify your personal core values:

7. Make a list of 5 to 7 core values that you think are yours or that you would like to embrace. You can pick some core values from those

discussed in the chapter and/or other core values not in the chapter.

8. For each core value, write questions to ask yourself or others to help discover if this value truly motivates you.

9. Finalize your list of core values as best you can. Order the values from most to least important in this season of your life.

10. Ask someone who knows you well to list 5 to 7 core values they believe you have. How closely does your list and their list compare?

11. Does their list change your list of core values?

Now that you have your personal core values identified, identify the core values in your family:

12. Ask each family member to go through the steps above to identify their personal core values.

13. In a family discussion, look for values everyone embraces.

14. In the discussion, did some core values come up that the family would like to embrace together?

15. Write the list on paper that is visible at family meals. An occasional discussion as to how the family is doing embracing new core values can be life-giving to all involved.

Let's go deeper into core values. Identify an **anchor truth** in your life from Scripture:

16. In your list of personal core values, what is the primary core value for this season of your life? This is the one you put at the top of your list.

17. Find scripture that expresses this core value. For example, if your primary core value is gratitude and celebration, an anchor truth might be in these Scriptures:

O give thanks unto the LORD; for he is good; for his mercy endureth for ever.
1 Chronicles 16:34

In everything give thanks: for this is the will of God in Christ Jesus concerning you.
1 Thessalonians 5:18

For the LORD God is a sun and shield: the LORD will give grace and glory: no good thing will he withhold from them that walk uprightly.
Psalm 84:11

18. Restate the core value and Scriptures as your personal statement of an anchor truth, such as, "I thank God for all things because He is always giving me His best."

Growth Project 3.2
Become a Life Giver

Every adult and child has the opportunity to be a life giver in community. The fundamental principle is described in Deuteronomy 28 when God said:

And it shall come to pass, if thou shalt hearken diligently unto the voice of the LORD thy God, to observe and to do all his commandments which I command thee this day, that the LORD thy God will set thee on high above all nations of the earth: And all these blessings shall come on thee, and overtake thee, if thou shalt hearken unto the voice of the LORD thy God.
Deuteronomy 28:1-2

God goes on to describe in detail the many blessings He wants to release to His people who follow His ways, including life, provision for ourselves and others, protection, reputation and agreeable weather. With these blessings functioning in our lives, we are most certainly a life giver for others. Practically, how do we walk this out?

Do the following to make a plan:

1. What is your most important primary core value that you identified in Growth Project 3.1? This is the value that you restated as an anchor truth.

2. Identify where at home, school or work this core value could make the most difference in community. Be as specific as you can.

3. Sit with Jesus and journal the details of how Jesus wants to guide and help you bake in this value.

4. Over the next few weeks, record in your journal how this character improvement project is going and the results in community as you become more of a life giver.

Growth Project 3.3
Communicating Values

In the book of Numbers, we can read many instances of how God taught the Israelites His values as He grew slaves to sons. Masters and slaves generally focus only on obedience, but Fathers want their sons to know their hearts and encourage them to ask the why questions.

In the busyness of running a family or other organization, leaders can easily get caught up telling others what to do without explaining why. However, it's the responsibility of a leader to communicate their values to their followers.

If you lead a group, do the following:

1. Ask the group to list your core values. It might surprise you that they might not have a clue what's really important to you and why.

In some cultures, it's considered rude for a follower to ask why something is done a certain way. In the Kingdom culture of growth and transformation, sons are encouraged to ask the why questions. We must all learn to simply obey our leaders at times and know when it is appropriate to ask the why questions.

2. Make a plan to be intentional to explain why you do what you do. For example, you can require your team to have lunch together and use this time to discuss the why questions. Families can use evenings or dinner time to do that.

3. When you bring a new person into your organization, make a plan to spend whatever time is needed to help the newcomer know and understand your values. For example, one manager required a new team member to ask a why question at lunch each day for the first few weeks on the job.

Do the following if you report to a manager or other leader:

1. Write the list of core values you believe your leader embraces. Ask your leader how close you are to his or her correct list.

2. Find an appropriate and honoring way to ask the why questions. For example, you can say to your leader, "To help me grow, I really want to understand what you're thinking and why you do things the way you do. Can you explain to me why you decided on this course of action?" Most leaders very much appreciate a follower wanting to understand their motives.

Growth Project 3.4
Learn to Celebrate

When we celebrate an event or what someone has done, we imprint that in the community and will get more of it. Think of starting a campfire. Blowing on the first little flicker causes the flame to surge. That's what celebration does!

When a father celebrates a child, that celebration is imprinted on the office of fathering. The child will grow up to celebrate his own children in this way when he steps into the office of father.

Do the following to learn to celebrate:

1. List who, what, when and how your family or other group celebrates.

2. Discuss with your group your list and make changes as needed to accurately evaluate your current culture of celebration.

3. How do you and the group want to improve celebration in community?

4. Make an intentional effort to change the ways you celebrate where you see a need to change. Track your effectiveness by observing if what you celebrate grows in community.

SPIRIT PROJECT

These spirit projects will help unpack and enlarge your spirit and help you know God better. Some of the projects in this chapter show you what is possible. It is our hope you will use them as the need arises.

Spirit Project 3.1 Cleansing Time

In the spirit realm, we each have a river that flows through our spirit world. Jesus mentioned this river of life and John described it as the life of the Spirit flowing through us.

On the last and greatest day of the festival, Jesus stood and said in a loud voice, "Let anyone who is thirsty come to me and drink. Whoever believes in me, as Scripture has said, rivers of living water will flow from within them." By this he meant the Spirit, whom those who believed in him were later to receive. Up to that time the Spirit had not been given, since Jesus had not yet been glorified.

John 7:37-39

Some can see the river in their spirit world. In the spirit, it represents our timeline here in time and space. The river begins at the Spring of Conception when we were sent by Father God into time and space and ends when we return to eternity. Normally, the river flows from east to west.

Trauma Bonds to Time and Negative Emotions

In the spirit realm, you might be able to see areas in the river where trauma happened. With the help of Holy Spirit, these areas can be healed and set free from past wounds. Some areas in our timeline can be so wounded and traumatized, they still affect us today.

Even if you cannot see your spirit world or communicate with your spirit, you can still cleanse and heal trauma bonds to time.

Do the following:

1. Look for situations where old negative emotions keep arising even though logically, these emotions should have healed long ago. For example, whenever you take a test, an old fear of failure and shame resurfaces. You might have identified a trauma bond to time.

2. Ask Holy Spirit to show you where the original wound or trauma is. For example, a teacher in the early grades greatly humiliated you when you did not do well.

03

3. Look for judgements you made, especially one against God. For example, you might have judged that "no matter how hard I try, God will not protect me and I will be humiliated."

4. Repent to God for making this judgement about yourself, others and Him. Ask Him to remove the effect of this judgement. Ask Him to heal and cleanse your timeline. If you are a seer, you might see the river made right. For example, a gorge or rocky structure in the river might disappear.

5. Ask God to bless what was defiled by the enemy. For example, when you take a test, the old fear is gone, and you are able to pass with confidence.

To learn more about cleansing time, listen to the audio album "Trauma Bonds to Time" by Arthur at **theslg.com.**

When I ask Father God to remove a curse, I see Father taking the curse off of me and placing the curse on Jesus as He hangs on the cross. "Christ has redeemed us from the curse of the law, being made a curse for us: for it is written, Cursed is every one that hangs on a tree." Galatians 3:13

It's a terribly painful event as I recognize yet one more time how Jesus suffered to set me free from all I did that violated His commands.

Curses on Time and Devouring

When a curse is active in our lives, the enemy can devour and destroy. A curse on time can happen when we believe lies or otherwise sin against God, ourselves or others.

Do the following to remove a curse on time:

1. Look for devouring that happens in a time cycle. For example, every June, your finances take a big hit. Curses on time can happen the same time each year or can happen in cycles of multiple years, months or days.

2. Ask Holy Spirit to show you the original situation that allowed the curse, such as in June, 20 years ago, your business failed.

3. Ask Holy Spirit to show you what lie or sin allowed the curse. For example, when your business failed, you accepted the lie, "It is God's will that I be poor and always in need." Sometimes we are under a curse because of the sins of our forefathers. In these situations, be sure to cleanse the generational sins as you learned to do in Chapter 2.

4. Repent of the lie or sin and ask God to set you free from the curse.

5. Ask God to bless the time that the enemy had previously cursed. Know that the enemy wants to curse whatever it is that God wants to bless. For example, it's highly likely that God intends that June be your most prosperous month of the year.

To learn more about breaking off curses, listen to the free audio album "Spiritual Warfare" by Arthur at **theSLG.com.**

Spirit Project 3.2
Your Spirit and the Trinity

We are designed by God to have a unique relationship with each Member of the Trinity. Recall that our spirits often present as seven portions: Prophet, Servant, Teacher, Exhorter, Giver, Ruler, and Mercy. Each portion of our spirit needs to meet each Member of the Trinity, and each portion will know which Member of the Trinity they relate to best.

When working in the spirit realm, purpose to connect to each portion of your spirit and for each portion to connect to each Member of the Trinity. This can take weeks, months or even years to accomplish. This journey grows you immensely. Expect you and your spirit to grow with each encounter with God!

In Chapter 2, you learned to connect with your spirit. The next step is to ask each portion of your spirit about their relationship with the Trinity. The conversation can go something like this:

1. **Me:** Giver, may I speak with you?

2. **Giver:** Yes, I'm here.

3. **Me:** Can you tell me about your relationship with Jesus?

4. **Giver:** Oh, yes! Jesus and I meet in the wide-open space in the North. We dance together there. It's our favorite way to celebrate!

5. **Me:** Oh, I love that! Can you tell me where you meet with Father?

6. **Giver:** Sure. I have a cave in the North. It's my hiding place and I go there to meet Him. Sometimes, when He hugs me, a new gemstone appears on the walls of the cave. The gemstones remind me of all I have received from Him. They are my most precious possessions.

7. **Me:** So wonderful! Thank you for allowing me to see your cave.

8. **Giver:** When you need a hug from Father, I will take you there.

9. **Me:** Then I think your cave is your most precious possession! Thank you! Can you tell me about your relationship with Holy Spirit?

10. **Giver:** I meet with Holy Spirit in the wind. When the West wind begins to blow, I quickly go there. I LOVE to flow with Holy Spirit and Wisdom.

Sometimes you might need a friend to help you connect with your spirit and the Trinity. The conversation might go like this:

1. **Friend:** Larry, would it be okay with you if I talk with Teacher?

2. **Larry:** Yes

3. **Friend:** Teacher, can you talk with me?

4. **Teacher:** Yes, I can.

5. **Friend:** Teacher, would you like to meet with Jesus?

6. **Teacher:** Yes, I would love that.

7. **Friend:** Could you ask Jesus to come to you?

8. **Teacher:** Jesus, will you please come to me? ... I see Him standing at a door to a classroom. He's inviting me in. ... We're in the classroom and He is at the whiteboard. He's motioning to me to take the front seat. His class is about to begin!

9. **Friend:** I see you're connected to Jesus now. I will leave so you can focus on Him.

Do the following:

1. Try connecting to your spirit as you learned in Chapter 2. If you are unable to do so, ask a friend to help.

2. Connect to each portion of your spirit and explore how each portion of the spirit connects to each Member of the Trinity.

3. When you are ready, ask one portion of the spirit to include you in connecting with God. Would you like to receive a hug from Father God? Which portion of the spirit would love to help you with that?

Spirit Project 3.3
Peter Needs More Love

Earlier in the chapter, in Problem 3.1, you read about Peter who became a bully because he felt others were picking on him. One way to address this problem is to work with his spirit. The principle is you can't give what you have not received. Peter can receive love in the spirit realm more easily than he can in the physical because God is love and our human spirits are made of God's love. Our spirits can receive love from God

easier than can our souls and then our spirits can love the soul as God designed us to do.

The process would go something like this:

1. Connect with Peter's spirit with or without Peter's cognitive involvement.

2. Ask Peter's spirit would he like to meet a Member of the Trinity and receive a hug from him. Work with Peter's spirit until you sense his spirit is comfortable with and has received enough love from God to be secure in that love. This can take some time.

3. Talk with his spirit about his connection to Peter's soul. Are they connected? Sometimes the spirit is so apalled by the soul's behavior, the spirit withdraws from the soul and can even build a wall between spirit and soul. Explain to the spirit how God designed him to lead the soul and love the soul to life. Also explain that Jesus will help the spirit love the soul to life.

4. Work with the spirit to minister to the soul. A daily walk with the spirit purposefully loving on the soul can change a life. However, don't push the spirit to interact with the soul before the spirit is ready to do so.

5. If you are able to connect to each of the seven portions of the spirit, know that each portion will have different ideas and methods to help the soul. Here are some examples:

   a. Prophet releases light and the Prophet portion of the spirit might want to shine light on and through the soul. This is especially beneficial if the spirit doesn't feel comfortable getting near the soul.

   b. Servant enjoys executing authority over evil. Servant might want to send an East wind to drive demons away from soul.

   c. Exhorter is often a hugger. One big hug from the spirit can make overnight changes in the behavior of a soul!

6. When Peter is ready for the conversation, ask Peter if he can feel his spirit helping him. Can he feel God loving him? Invite him to receive a hug from God.

Spirit Project 3.4 Heal the Brain

The spirit is designed by God to heal the body. In this Spirit Project, we use the power of testimony to show you what's possible.

Lizzie had a stoke while in the womb, and when born at 26 weeks, she was diagnosed with CP and opioids in her body. At 8 years old, she was able to read but was not able to do arithmetic. A friend asked to speak with her spirit. After a time or two talking with her spirit and gaining some trust, she asked Lizzie's spirit would she look at the brain for anything that just didn't look right. She said there was a messy area where the wires were all tangled up. She had described the exact location where the MRI had shown the stroke.

Spirit invited Jesus to come sit with her and heal the area. She watched as Jesus meticulously rewired most of the area, sprinkled gold in the area and left. The friend asked spirit could she create a detour around that area until it was completely healed. Spirit said yes and agreed to help Lizzie when she was doing math.

Figure 3-12 shows two screenshots of her math the day before prayer and the day after prayer. Her mom gave her no new instructions. This was in March, and Lizzie was in the middle of second grade work. By June, she had finished second grade and all of third grade, passing the state standard exams for third grade, 80th percentile in math. The following year she worked through fourth grade along with her peers.

Figure 3-12. Lizzie's math the day before and the day after prayer

Lizzie did not have fine motor skills. When her friend was ready to address that, she asked her spirit to look at the pons. She described it as a half sphere with the top half missing, and Lizzie asked Jesus to heal the pons. For four days, spirit watched the pons grow. On the fifth day, she drew the picture in Figure 3-13 and said the pons was completely healed and was now a full sphere. She also said God was there.

With her friend's help, the spirit asked Jesus to activate the pons and do its job of helping the two lobes of the cerebellum communicate. Figure 3-14 shows a photo of Lizzie a few days later, clipping her own nails with her right hand. Before this time, she could hardly hold clippers in her right hand. Within a few weeks she learned how to swim and dive and walk a balance beam.

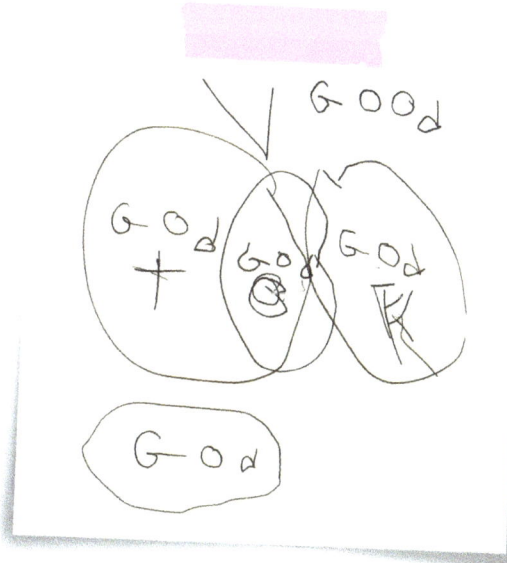

Figure 3-13. The pons is healed and God is there

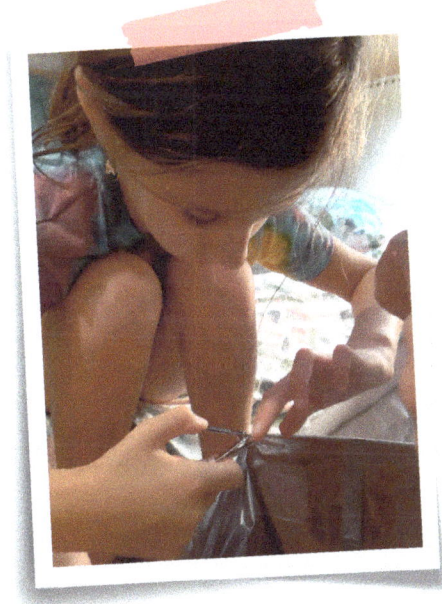

Figure 3-14 Lizzie was able to clip her own nails a few days after the pons was healed and activated

Fine motor skills and balance are controlled by the left and right cerebellum, which communicate with each other through the pons positioned between them. The pons relays this information to other areas of the brain.

For more information about the spirit healing the mind and brain, listen to Arthur's series of albums, "Blessing Your Brain," at **theSLG.com.**

CHAPTER 04 GROWING IN RELATIONSHIPS

"We love each other, and our love and joy shape and align our world."

The Principle of Reality

Reality is sometimes painful. As I was making breakfast, I noticed small droppings in my kitchen cabinet and suspected there might be a mouse. No way! I hate that thought so I ignore it. Two days later I noticed the droppings again. Maybe I should set a trap. I hate that thought so I ignore it, too.

PRINCIPLE

God designed the Exhorter to release to people a new reality of God. No wonder facing reality is sometimes difficult for the Exhorter. The enemy often attacks our greatest asset.

While I choose to stay in denial about mice in the kitchen, the problem doesn't go away. In fact, it might get worse. If months pass and I continue in denial, I might have a full-blown mouse colony in my house. At that time, will I be able to face reality and admit that I'm the cause of my house being overrun by mice because I didn't deal with the problem when it was small?

Every event has a cause. There's a reason a house is overrun with mice. Somebody did or did not do something somewhere. In chapter 1, we learn that life by design works, because God designed all of His creation to work and work well. When life does or does not work, there's a cause.

God wants to bless us. He told Abraham in Genesis 12 that He would bless Abraham and, because he was blessed, Abraham would bless others. Later, in Deuteronomy 28, he told Abraham's descendants that many blessings would come to them if they would obey Him, and warned them of all the curses that would come on them if they did not obey. Father God was explaining to the Israelites the **principle of reality**: Reality is acknowledging that what is happening, either good or bad, has a root cause. The reality of cause and effect. What a joyful and blessed life we can have when we learn to live life God's way!

Five Areas of Holiness

Recall from Chapter 2 that Father God made holy time, land, community, birthright and offices. What He identifies as holy is what He wants to bless. In this book, we focus primarily on community. In community, sons love to synchronize to their fathers, but slaves find little value in synchronizing to those they view as masters. Slaves might even see disobedience as a means to an end, as did the slaves recently released from Egypt.

Nevertheless, some of the people went out on the seventh day to gather it [manna], but they found none.
Exodus 16:27

In this chapter, we look at how to synchronize with God and His ways in community. Among the seven "I will's" of God in Exodus 6, the fourth "I will" is "I will take you as my own people." We identify our core strengths or treasures in our current circumstances of life, and we look at ways we can passionately enjoy God and community. When these relationships don't work, we learn to face reality and cause and effect. Just like a mouse in the kitchen, we might not see the mouse, but reality says it's there and we must deal with it!

HERE WE GROW

In the fourth stage of growth, we learn to thieve in peer relationships.

Growth Stage 4
I Can Thrive in Peer Relationships

Do you love being with people? Some of us crave our privacy and some prefer peopling all day and through the night. During the primary grades and through middle school is the time when children learn to be life giving and comfortable in peer relationships. Smaller children need adults or other leaders to supervise our relationships, manage our resources and resolve conflicts. As we mature, we learn how to do this for ourselves (see Figure 4-1).

Figure 4-1. As we grow and mature, we learn to navigate peer relationships.

04

When this stage of growth is complete, we can work or play peacefully with peers, and we find a way to fit into community:

- **I can fit in.** When I sit down at a table with four people playing cards, I can watch and enjoy the game, offer to keep score or go get drinks. I can comfortably find my place in this community.

- **I can honor privacy.** I walk into a coffee shop and see two of my closest friends talking privately. We acknowledge and greet each other, and then I sit down in a different part of the shop. I can still be an honored part of their community without invading their private time together.

- **I can get along.** When I first join a team at work, I can find a way to fit in and get along. I don't have to turn to the team leader to require I be accepted or to settle a dispute.

- **I don't need to manage or lead.** When I'm sitting at dinner with friends, I can be comfortable not leading the conversation. I can watch a friend be silent and the host not try to engage her and be comfortable with that. I don't have to manage or lead.

- **I can find dignity.** Our boss assigns a team to plan a company event. When the team meets, I discover the leader has already assigned responsibilities. Someone is finding a venue, another has activities covered and another is planning the food. I realize I was excluded from the assignments. I consider my options, decide not to have my feelings hurt and offer to handle communications regarding the event. In doing so, I move from a place of exclusion to an honorable position (I find a way to fit in).

When we are at peace with peer relationships, we can form social contracts for our community as needed:

- **Social contracts with peers.** The boss assigns a team project and does not assign a team leader. Our team sits down together. We make some rules, allocate responsibilities and resources, and decide when to meet. We also decide how to monitor team progress and how we will ask for accountability as needed.

- **Manage a conflict.** I work for a non-profit with a staff of five. I know what to do if there is a breach of ethics, such as a client was not served well, or gossip is happening in the breakroom. I handle the situation and don't run from it. We work it out with good emotional boundaries and a minimum of negative emotions.

When We Missed This Stage of Growth

When we have not fully grown in this stage of maturity, our relationships will look much different:

- **Reluctant.** I watch four people playing cards and wish I could join them. I sit alone at a different table waiting for an invitation. I will not initiate.

- **Passive.** I come to a team meeting and realize I did not receive an assignment as did the others. I sit silently wondering why I was left out. Was I not good enough? Was the team angry at me? I might get angry or sad.

- **Compliant.** In a group, I agree with the strongest person or loudest voice. I will not risk or take a stand for what is right. Or if I do speak up and receive opposition, I quickly cave and blame myself for the conflict. When making decisions, I often decide based on what another wants or asks without considering my needs.

- **Wavering.** As a leader, my team gets frustrated with my slowness to make decisions or changing my mind too often. Sometimes the team doesn't know what to do because I don't make my wishes clear or refuse to confront followers who are stronger than me.

- **Afraid to hold people accountable.** A carpenter does some repairs on my house. I don't check his work but "trust" he has done all that I asked. After I pay him, I notice some of the work was not done well. I'm embarrassed to call him back, so I pay another carpenter to finish the job.

> During the fifth stage of growth, we learn to stand up for what is right, which comes from a different motive than standing up for our rights.

- **Controlling.** I'm not aware of your needs and simply barrel through to get the job done. I control everything because I'm concerned you might hurt me or hurt others. I cannot give up control even when I see it is hurting you.

Did you identify with any of these dysfunctions in peer relationships? I know I did. As adults, to grow into this stage, we can:

- Recognize this problem must be solved. We cannot thrive in community or possess our birthrights without healthy peer relationships. Simply recognizing the problem and our responsibility to find a solution can take us far.

- Ask God to teach us how to thrive in peer relationships and then watch carefully what He does. Does He put us on a team or in a group where we immediately have challenges? Rather than look for a way out or fight for our rights, which psychologists call flight or fight, we can look for ways to fit in and embrace the productive pain of growing in relationships.

- For each relationship, try to see God's purpose for the relationship. What does He want us to learn? Press into the uncomfortable situation to find that purpose.

> When we don't trust another person, we can still take a risk to build a relationship. For more about that, see the section in Chapter 3 on "We Value Trust."

- Start with temporary relationships and build on that. For example, you can look for opportunities while waiting in line at a grocery store or waiting for your car to be serviced where you can engage with a person also waiting. Try to find common ground or acknowledge what you admire about someone. A comment about the T-shirt with a brand you like or message you appreciate can start a friendly conversation. In the moment, sync to their needs and their likes.

- Ask a mentor to help you understand how to get along in relationships rather than running from them or demanding things go our way.

- As we talk with people, pay attention to the tone of our voice. Change our tone as needed to be more appropriate for the conversation, such as more friendly, gentle, bold, or kind.

- Our spirits can help us build healthy relationships. Invite your spirit to connect with the spirit of another person and then catch the sound of your spirit. Is your spirit confident, kind, affirming or intimate?

- Pick our battles. As you're learning to build peer relationships, don't start with difficult people. Pick people you like or have something in common. As your people skills grow, you can grow out your sphere of friends to include some difficult ones.

CONCEPTS

When we are learning to sync with another emotionally, we begin with joy.

Concept 4.1 Learning to Sync with Others

People get along in community because they synchronize emotionally with each other. To learn to sync, we must first learn to connect emotionally with others, and that requires trust. We first learn to sync with God and others by emotionally syncing with our parents and leaders. When children don't sync with their parents, it can look like this:

- Constant bickering or conflicts
- Chaos and generally a lack of flow
- Low family productivity and creativity
- Newcomers to the family find difficulty fitting in

We learn to sync as early as the womb. Studies have shown that the heartbeat of a baby in the womb syncs with that of the mom when two things are true: (1) the mom breathes rhythmically and (2) the baby is healthy. Throughout childhood we continue to have opportunities to sync with parents, siblings, teachers and friends. If these opportunities were not positive, we may need healing. Early childhood trauma or lack of instruction can prevent us from learning to empathize and sync with others.

Enjoying the Joy of Another

When we are learning to sync with another emotionally, we begin with joy. Can a child or adult watch another child or adult have fun and recognize the joy in the other person and enjoy their joy?

To help someone learn to sync, watch their reactions as another person is joyful, laughing or otherwise having fun. Can your friend enjoy their joy? For example, Americans typically enjoy the joy of others through watching sports. Can your friend watch a game and recognize when the players are enjoying themselves – celebrated a touchdown – can they celebrate the team's touchdown with joy?

> I once asked a child's spirit does she sync with her mom. Her spirit said, "No, mom syncs with me." I knew that was true as her mom tended to be controlled by her daughter's bad behavior. I also asked does she sync with her father. Her spirit said, "No, we cannot sync with dad. He makes too many bad decisions." We will not sync with those we don't trust. When we don't trust or sync with our parents, we won't learn to empathize with others.

Do they like a particular player on the team? Can they watch that player and tell when the player is happy with what is happening? Can they enjoy their joy?

If we cannot do that, we cannot expect peace and harmony in relationships. As Arthur would say, "The hardware is not there to install the software on."

Building Internal Structures to Process Emotions

We develop the hardware to process emotions when our parents use all kinds of cute and delightful activities to make us smile when they smile, laugh when they laugh and enjoy life when they enjoy life. If that stage is missed, we can still build these internal structures to process emotions. Start like this:

1. **Can the person language various emotions?** Print out an emotions wheel that lists 10 to 20 emotions. Put the sign in places where conversation happens, such as the family dinner table. Can the person language the emotions of others around the table?

Sit with the person in a public place, such as in a car in the parking lot of a grocery store. Observe a mom and child going into the store. Is the child frustrated, happy or angry? Is the mom angry? Watch body language and identify emotions.

1. **Can the person language two emotions?** If 10 to 20 emotions are too difficult to work with, reduce the list to two. Work with "happy" and "sad" until the person can identify each in other people.

2. **Can the person observe details in others?** If the person cannot language emotions, try working with non-verbal activities. Start with observing bodies. Go for a walk with the person. "Today we are going to look at feet. Every person you see, look at their feet. Tell me about feet." See Figure 4-2. The idea is to teach the person to be aware of and observe details in others.

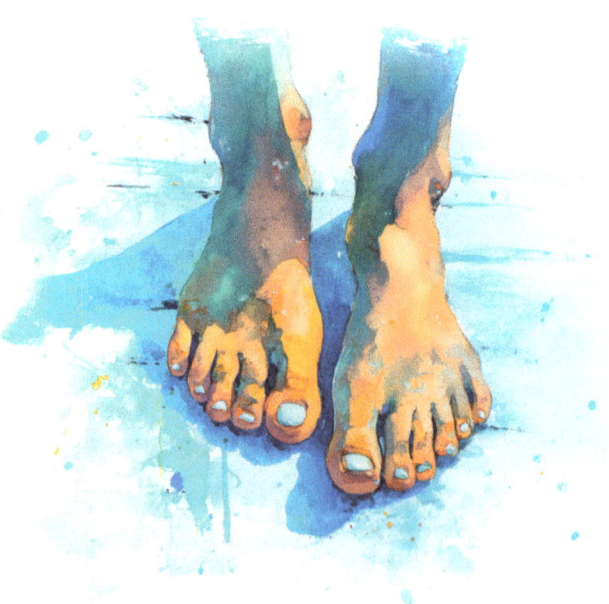

Figure 4-2 Today we watch feet!

04

After the person can observe details, work your way up to emotions. Can the person enjoy the joy of another?

Followers should not sync with leaders who make bad decisions and are not synchronizing with God. As leaders, the better we sync with God, the better our followers can sync with us.

Let's turn our attention to identifying our core abilities and core passions.

Concept 4.2
Identifying Our Core Passion or Core Strength

We know that Father God built into our design a core passion or core strength that perfectly matches up with what is needed for us to possess our birthrights. When this passion is awakened, our hearts burn:

> *And they said one to another, Did not our heart burn within us, while he talked with us by the way, and while he opened to us the scriptures?*
> Luke 24:32

Where does our heart burn within us? Discussions and prayer can help find that passion, and having a few grids to explore can also help:

- **Our Trinitarian design.** Our relationships with each Member of the Trinity can help us see the playing fields (community, dominion and creation) we were designed to thrive in. Look for what excites you the most.

- **Our redemptive gift.** Recall from Chapter 2 that our redemptive gift helps us see how our personalities align with our core passions. The corresponding principle of Wisdom can help identify our core strengths.

- **The redemptive gifts of land.** God put in land gifts for us to draw from and enjoy. If you know the redemptive gift of the land on which you most thrive, the clue can tell you something about your core passions and strengths. I built a thriving business on Prophet land and then moved to Servant land where the business shrank. Prophet land releases high visibility and Servant land releases low visibility.

Early trauma can prevent a child from learning to empathize and sync with parents. Trauma happens when a child is hurt so badly they cannot connect to people, God or themselves. One powerful way to heal trauma is to work with the human spirit. Ask the spirit to give the trauma to Jesus. Jesus is the only one who can and wants to take our pain.

- By observing the difference, I was able to see I thrive when I'm highly visible, which is essential to my passion to change nations in a big way. When I moved back to Prophet land, visibility returned.

- **Intimacy or dominion.** We each walk in a degree of intimacy with God and dominion to build His Kingdom. Try to identify which of the two is your core strength or core passion.

- **Process or product.** I find more satisfaction and passion in the process to develop a product rather than the finished product. Which are you more passionate about? Can you identify why the process or product stirs up more passion?

- **Woundedness.** When children are attacked by the enemy, especially when they're very young, consider it a left-handed compliment from the devil. What does the devil know that God has put in this child to make the devil work so hard to push the child down? Look for significant wounding in the first six years of life. How does this woundedness point to a core passion or core strength?

- **Legitimacy.** Which legitimacy lies tempt you the most? Where are you solidly grounded in true legitimacy? Both can help you identify a core passion or core strength.

- **Current emotions.** What strong emotions surface often? Learn to pay attention to these. Emotions that you thought were negative might actually be coming from your design and core passions.

- **What makes you angry?** Anger is often an indicator of your core passion. For me, it makes me angry when I see people despised and judged, especially when the despisement is about the group of people they are identified with. I want to shout, "But God made *these* people, too!"

- **What draws you.** What discussions, topics, careers, vacation spots, movies, music, sports, books, or hobbies draw your attention?

- **The wild, weird and wacky.** In your life, what doesn't fit? What sticks out as unusual? This is often a big clue to your core passion.

- **Resources.** What's in your hands? A friend, almost by accident, met a man who owned a valuable three-story building. In a quick and casual conversation, he asked her would she have a purpose for the building because he was thinking of giving it to her at a deeply discounted price. Her life-long dream to build a dance school suddenly exploded to the surface in a single God-ordained connection!

- **Your favorite Bible story when you were 5 to 8 years old.** Once you've identified the story, ask yourself what about the story stirs up your passion. For me, it was the story of David and Goliath. My passion about the story is *David defended God's honor.* Even as I write this, I can feel the fire of that passion rise up. Your chosen story and its passion in you likely comes from the core of your spirit.

- **Our greatest obstacles to overcome.** Recall that our birthrights are the greatest problems we have in life that God has called us to overcome using His strategies and His resources. Look for an obstacle, such as poverty, bad health or toxic relationships, that might lead you to clues about your core passions or strengths.

Beware of negative passions birthed out of woundedness that are defensive in nature and there to protect us from more pain:

- Fear

- Desire to please

- Desire to achieve

- Desire to mother someone, to enable them

We might need to work our way through these negative passions before we can see the core passions God has put there.

The goal is to do what you truly, really want to do and that can be the most difficult thing.

The Dream is Not in the Coat

About 30 years ago, I received a short prophetic word, "The dream is not in the coat." I understood the word was about Joseph and his coat of many colors given to him by his father. I also understood it had to do with the dream Joseph had had about ruling over his family. I had no idea what the word was saying in principle or how it applied to me.

Just a couple of years ago, I finally understood while listening to Arthur's audio album "Birthright." He made the comment that we are partly able to possess our birthrights because of what we gain from our journey, including the anointing, favor, maturity, wisdom and earned authority.

When he said that, I suddenly remembered that short little prophetic word from decades earlier that had always been a mystery. I get it now! I have been working all this time to overcome the hardships of my journey without realizing all that work was preparing me to fulfill the dream I carried. I was mistakenly expecting that one day all my useless hard labor would end when God would miraculously launch me into the dream of my life.

For thought and discussion:

1. Read the story of Joseph in Genesis 37-41 up until the point in his story when he was suddenly promoted to the office of prime minister of Egypt. Before this promotion, Joseph grew in maturity, wisdom and earned authority. What do you think Joseph gained in either of these three areas during his time in Potiphar's prison?

2. A friend spent years with a disease as she pleaded with God to heal her. One day, God said, "If I healed you now, you would not know Me." What do you think He meant by that? If you were my friend, what would you say to God in response to Him?

3. Do you know someone who has an obstacle in their life that they have endured for some time? How can you use the story of Joseph to encourage this person?

4. Has God ever put you in an unjust, unfair or unreasonable situation? Does He have you there now? How can these obstacles in your journey grow you? How can they help you identify and develop your core passions and strengths?

04

Job's Testing

How we view the book of Job can enlighten how we currently see God and help us discover our core passion. A young man described the story of Job as God and the devil got in an argument one day, and poor Job was caught in the middle as the bet made by God. In the process, Job got tired of being the bet and yelled to God, "Stop testing me!" God backed off and gave Job everything he had lost in the God-and-devil match up plus some extra to make up for how God had used him.

For thought and discussion:

1. Do you agree or disagree with the young man's interpretation of the book of Job? Explain your answer.

2. What about the interpretation, if anything, makes you upset or angry?

3. In one short paragraph, how would you describe the story of Job?

4. How does your version of the story help you identify your core passion?

Concept 4.3 Resources to Help Me

Once we have identified our core passions, we can begin to form a vision of where we are going and look for resources to help us. The following questions can help.

We need the right people in our lives to build our birthright:

- Who in my life is trying to hold on to the version of me I was in the past?

- Who is encouraging me to become all I can be?

- Do I need to let go of some friendships and purposefully build other friendships with people who share my current core values and passions?

> One owner of a company routinely asks each employee what percentage of their time they spend in their core strengths.
> He expects, for their first year with the company, an employee does what they have to do, but by the third year, they should be working 50% or better in their core strengths.

God is helping me:

- How is God strengthening me in my strengths and core passions?

- Where or what is the trail of Grace today?

- What is He breathing on and blessing?

- Is it possible for me to put more of my focus there?

- Can I language my resources? We can have a room full of resources but no language for them. For example, if we have earned authority and can't language it, we can't use it. Learn to language the resources you have. Learn to language the resources for another. In doing so, God can draw out of us the resources we need for the journey in this current season.

- Do I need to develop my core strengths? Developing ourselves is the topic of the next chapter.

Among the resources we all need are the blessings of God on our lives and communities. To release these blessings that God wants to give, we might need to address curses operating in our lives.

Concept 4.4
Curses and Blessings on Birthright and Community

For us to possess our birthrights, we need God's blessings. He blesses us progressively and sequentially as we mature. Little by little, we are able to steward more and more of His resources. We need community to possess our birthrights, and many of God's blessings involve community.

The book of Judges describes seven lies about our legitimacy that tempt us to sin, which can open doors to the seven curses. A curse stops us from building or destroys what we try to build. In the spirit realm, I see an incoming curse like a black bomb. If allowed to land, it can do great damage to what we are trying to build. See Figure 4-3. When a curse is at work, we can feel demoralized, frustrated or exhausted.

When we believe a lie, we can take a wrong turn that brings down on us a curse. The sins that come when we believe the lie and bring on the curse are always the result of a slight

> To prevent us from living in healthy communities, the enemy tempts us to sin so that curses come on us, thus preventing blessings from flowing in community relationships.

diversion from our original design. For this reason, as you read about the curses in this chapter, you might stumble on a clue to your design and your core passion.

In addition, the blessings and curses described here all apply to community and can influence our peer relationships.

The seven lies and curses align with the seven redemptive gifts. However, each of us can have any or all of these curses at work in our lives. See Table 4-1.

Figure 4-3 A curse prevents or destroys what we try to build.

Table 4-1 Redemptive gifts, curses and blessings on birthrights

Redemptive gift	Curse on birthright and community	Blessings needed for effectiveness	Legitimacy lie "I am legitimate when.."
Prophet	**Aramean curse** Can't get justice	Blessing of Hosea Favor from God and man	I fix your problem
Servant	**Moabite curse** No help getting started Boundaries not secure	Blessing of Esther Secure borders	I use my authority to benefit you
Teacher	**Philistine curse** Lack key resources	Blessing of Daniel Supernatural truths and strategies	I have truth you don't have
Exhorter	**Canaanite curse** Oppressive workload	Blessing of Moses Time to develop finest abilities	I have a following

Redemptive gift	Curse on birthright and community	Blessings needed for effectiveness	Legitimacy lie "I am legitimate when…"
Giver	**Midianite curse** Devouring of money or family relationships May be seasonal devouring	Blessing of Job Accruing capital	I can resource you
Ruler	**Jotham curse** Betrayal from within	Blessing of Nehemiah Synergistically life-giving social structures	I have an institution
Mercy	**Ammonite curse** Barrenness	Blessing of John Possessing our birthrights	I have earned God's favor

How to Identify and Break a Curse

Curses always involve devouring or destruction, and can be put on us by ourselves, other people or God. According to Deuteronomy 28, when we obey God, He blesses us, but when we are disobedient, He allows curses to come. God sent Jesus, His beloved Son, to remove these curses from us.

Repentance, renunciations and a change of lifestyle will lift off a curse. Here are the basic steps to remove a curse and receive the blessings that God intended us to have:

1. Identify the curse. Most often, we do this by identifying repeated patterns of destruction in our lives.

2. Root out, confess and repent of the sins that allowed the curse. (An undeserved curse finds no place to land. Proverbs 26:2) This step can take some time but is essential to getting free. The sin that brought on the curse might have been done by our forefathers, but it's important to keep looking until we find where we ourselves have agreed with or participated in the sin.

3. As much as possible, be reconciled with all involved.

4. Acknowledge to God that He was justified in allowing the curse because of His righteous ways and our sinful actions.

5. Ask God to forgive us and our people for our actions, applying the Blood of Jesus all the way back as far as the generations involved.

6. Break the curse or ask someone with more authority over the curse to break it off us. Ask Father God to take the curse off us and our people and put it on Jesus in His position on

In Chapter 3, you learned about trauma bonds to time or land. The difference between a trauma bond and a curse is a trauma bond presents as negative emotions that don't fit the current situation, and a curse presents as devouring and destruction.

the cross. Galatians 3:13 A curse must yield to the finished work of the cross.

7. Ask God to remove any effects of the curse, including evicting critters, cleansing defilements, and removing spiritual structures and devices.

8. Ask God to release the blessing that He originally intended to give us as we walk in the oppositive spirit of the sins that brought on the curse. Galatians 3:14

9. Make specific lifestyle changes designed to earn authority over the curse and to be life-giving to others in such a way that God can release the blessings.

> A slave cannot set a slave free. Those who have the most authority over a curse are the ones who have consistently walked in the opposite spirit of the curse.

How to Receive the Seven Blessings

God expects all of us to pursue our birthrights so that we can effectively build our Father's Kingdom. To possess our birthrights, we need all seven of the blessings operating. As we consistently live a righteous lifestyle, over time God is able to release one blessing after another until all seven blessings are functioning in our lives.

For more information on identifying and breaking curses and releasing the blessings, see the audio album "The Seven Curses and Blessings" and the video album "Seven Curses" by Arthur Burk at **theSLG.com**.

God will help you in the process! Watch for setups by God designed to give you opportunity to make right choices so that He can more quickly release a blessing. Enjoy the journey!

Curse 1.
Aramean Curse and Blessings of God's Favor

God wants to bless us with His justice and favor in all we do. He's free to do that when we are passionately committed to complete the assignments He has given us, with His supernatural help and favor.

Indication of the Curse

I have to be careful; when I see someone in need or hurting, my first reaction is to jump in and help. And at other times, people ask for my help and I say no because the problem seems too big and overwhelming. I invite the Aramean curse when I accept a problem that God did not assign me or refuse a problem He did assign. I can also invite the curse when I try to solve problems in my own strength without His supernatural resources. It's sobering to think how many of us might be under this curse!

When the Aramean curse is at work in our lives, we cannot get justice. For example, court systems, business dealings, zoning boards, promotions at work, insurance claims and other financial transactions work against us and not for us.

Legitimacy Lie

The Prophet gift is specially designed by God to fix problems. The legitimacy lie is "I am legitimate when I fix your problem." Jesus was designed to fix problems, but He refused to perform miracles when it was framed as a challenge to prove His legitimacy. "*If* you are the Son of God…" questioned His legitimacy. To have authority over this curse, we fix only the problems that God has assigned us relying on the resources He gives us with a heart that we will not receive one ounce of legitimacy for having done so.

> When our legitimate calling from God gives us legitimacy, it defiles us. We must receive all our legitimacy based solely on God's love for us.

Sins That Bring on the Curse

Ways we may activate this curse:

- We decide to live with or ignore a problem God has assigned us to fix.
- We fix a problem the wrong way, without God's help or even compromising God's ways. We can think the end justifies the means.
- We try to solve a problem God did not assign us.
- We build our legitimacy in community by fixing problems.
- We whittle down a God-size problem into a me-size problem. Then we can fix it without relying on God.

Blessings and Earned Authority

The blessing that comes when the curse is broken is justice and favor. We have God's favor and the favor of man to accomplish more with less. We experience God's supernatural help, and wonderful people offer to help us.

We gain earned authority over this curse when we risk on God. We take on God-size problems and realize that, if He does not help us, we will fail miserably.

Othniel Defeats the Arameans

God assigned to the Israelites a God-size problem of driving out the enemies from their land birthrights and promised that He would back their efforts and destroy their enemies before them. In Judges 1, however, we read the people allowed some of their enemies to live in the land. They decided to settle for less and to turn these enemies into slaves who would serve them. As they did so, they began to compromise with their enemies and ultimately worshipped their gods.

In Judges 3, God finally had had enough, and He sold them to the king of Aram (allowing the Aramean curse to fall). After eight years, the Israelites cried out to God and He raised up a deliverer, Othniel. When the Spirit of the Lord came on Othniel, he went to war and overpowered the king of Aram, setting the Israelites free. The land then had peace for 40 years while Othniel was Israel's judge.

For thought and discussion:

1. Read Judges 3:1-11. Was it Othniel's idea to fix the problem of enslaved Israel, or was the problem assigned to him by God? Did Othniel have supernatural help from God to fix the problem?

2. In the events listed below, identify the actions that might invite the Aramean curse. Describe what must happen in each situation to walk in the opposite spirit so that the curse can be broken.

- A pastor moves money from the building fund to the general fund to cover a shortfall from Sunday's offering. At the end of the week, he shifts the money back to the building fund.

In the months that follow, the church cannot get approval from the city zoning board to allow their new construction project.

- A minister gets legitimacy from her ministry of praying for people and seeing them healed. Many people routinely come to her for prayer, and God answers her prayers. On one occasion, she prays for the daughter of a prominent Christian leader and the daughter does not get healed. She explains that God is not ready to heal this week and suggests the daughter return next week for more prayer.

- A businessman is negotiating a large deal with the local government. Several government officials belong to a social club that is known to be involved in the occult. They invite the businessman to a dinner to recruit people into the social club. He attends the dinner but denies the invitation to join the club.

3. To avoid the Aramean curse, be careful not to judge your worth by your success. Explain how someone might bring on the Aramean curse by doing so. Give two or three examples.

4. Can you think of a problem that you fixed or tried to fix that, in hindsight, you realize God did not assign you? In fixing the problem, did God back you with supernatural power or did you work on the problem using only human resources? How do you think these actions might have contributed to the lack of justice in your life?

5. When God calls on us to fix a problem beyond our skill set, what does He expect of us?

6. Describe a problem in your life that you know God wants you to fix but you don't know how to fix it. Have you decided to just live with the problem or are you actively seeking a solution? How might you be tempted to fix the problem without relying on God and His ways?

7. Can you see the effects of injustice in your life? What can you do to change the situation?

8. Describe clearly what sin leads to the Aramean curse and what repentance is needed to break the curse.

9. What change can you make in your life to intentionally earn authority over the Aramean curse and to allow God to release the blessing of more favor into your life?

Curse 2.
Moabite Curse and Blessings of Secure Boundaries

Great leaders build people. They create platforms and processes to help their followers to magnificently reflect God and possess their birthrights. They help us secure our boundaries so that we are free to grow and build.

Indication of the Curse

Ever felt like the one you had hoped would build you up is the very one holding you down? Do you work hard for your leaders but they seem to be more focused on their own visions and needs while neglecting yours? The Moabite curse might be keeping you in this languishing place. Parents, grandparents, husbands, bosses and pastors might always be expecting more. Promises of being released, supported or promoted are made but not kept. The rules of the game seem to change to suit other people. We tend to see ourselves as victims, find it hard to say no and wait, hoping someone will set us free.

Legitimacy Lie

The Servant gift has much authority and God intends for that authority to be used to support and raise up others. The legitimacy lie is "I am legitimate when I build a platform under others so they can succeed." Believing this lie can give us a savior mentality and prevent us from withdrawing our support when it's enabling others in their dysfunction. When others fail, the person can feel responsible or feel like a failure.

Sins That Bring on the Curse

To bring on the Moabite curse, two players are involved: A leader who is not life-giving and a follower who responds incorrectly in one of two ways:

- Passively accepts the pain. We feel used but won't confront the leader.
- Breaks free in the wrong way or at the wrong time.

The curse doesn't come through the leader but the follower. Some examples:

- A daughter works in the family business for low pay, long hours and few rewards. She loves her parents and refuses to change jobs, even though she recognizes the job is preventing her from getting the training and experiences she needs to fulfill the call of God on her life.
- A pastor uses his church members for his own vision and purpose and does not build up the members. Even so, God makes it clear to a young couple to stay in this church for a season while they mature under the intense challenges. The couple get dissatisfied and leave the church prematurely against God's guidance.

God intends for leaders to help us secure our boundaries. But the curse can happen when leaders violate our boundaries, and we allow the violation. Boundary violations can happen in these areas:

- **Spirit realm.** For example, we try to manipulate the human spirit of another person to do what we think is best.
- **Relationships with people.** For example, we allow a bad business deal because the other business person bulldozes through the deal.
- **Physical realm.** For example, we try to control a hurricane that God never intended for us to control.

Blessing and Earned Authority

The blessings that come when the curse is broken are secure boundaries and the freedom to move about as God directs to possess our birthright. To earn authority over this curse, we learn to use God's authority to build up and help others as God leads us without building our identity on our work. We also are free to walk away from the work when God says we're done.

Our authority over the curse comes when we are (1) submitted to God's timing and (2) willing to risk everything (even being murdered) to do the right thing and possess our birthright.

Ehud Goes on a Suicide Mission

When Israel sinned, God gave them over to Eglon, king of Moab, and he took possession of Jericho at the border between Israel and Moab. Eighteen years later, God raised up Ehud, a left-handed man and a Benjamite. He was selected by Israel to lead a group of men to go pay tribute (a tax) to King Eglon. After the tribute was paid, he sent away all his men and then returned to King Eglon, asking for a moment to speak with the king in private. In that moment, he killed the king with the sword he had concealed under his clothes. He was then able to lead Israel to defeat the Moabites, and the land had peace for 80 years.

For thought and discussion:

1. Read Judges 3:12-30. Ehud made sure his men were not put in harm's way when he attacked King Eglon. The process to break free from oppressive leaders must be done in the right timing and the right way. How can someone leave a family, job or church and not do harm to others? Give two or three examples.

2. Moab was the grandson of Lot and the son of Lot's older daughter. In Genesis 19, you can read that Lot was hiding in a cave and not doing his job as a father by finding husbands for his two daughters. The older daughter took matters into her own hands and lay with her father. By doing so, describe how she brought a curse on herself and her descendants.

3. Ruth was a Moabitess. In the book of Ruth, Naomi took Ruth under her care as her mother-in-law, supported her and raised her up to ultimately become an ancestor in the linage of Jesus. Describe how Naomi played a fathering role in Ruth's life to support her and build a platform for success under her.

4. In your own words, describe how David disobeyed his leader, King Saul, and yet still stayed within God's law and favor. Can you describe a situation in your own life or someone you know personally who had to disobey their leaders to follow the direction of God in their lives?

5. Do you feel that your leaders, currently or in the past, have supported you and are building a platform for success under you? If not, the Moabite curse might be operating. Search for ways you have invited the curse. What can you do to change the situation?

6. Describe clearly what sin brings on the Moabite curse and what repentance is needed to break the curse.

7. What change can you make in your life to intentionally earn more authority over the Moabite curse and to allow God to release into your life the blessing of more secure boundaries and more freedom to grow and build.

Curse 3.
Philistine Curse and Blessings of Truth

God intends that we use His truths to set people and all creation free, establishing the government of Jesus in the land. For this to happen, we must live a lifestyle of receiving and releasing truth so that God can continually give us more truths that we need to possess our birthrights.

Indication of the Curse

Do you repeatedly feel like you can get just so far with assembling a project or building a business or ministry, and you come up short because one key resource is missing that would make it all come together? This key resource might be people, buildings, money, skills, credentials, licenses, a platform to speak or any other tangible resource or favor. When we fail to seek new truths or withhold truths we have, we can invite the Philistine curse into our lives.

Legitimacy Lie

A person with the Teacher gift can more easily receive revelation or truth directly from God than can the other gifts. The legitimacy lie is "I am legitimate when I know something that you don't know."

Someone, for example, might keep the network passwords to herself so she alone controls who gets network access. Or we might refuse to expose fraud at work to keep our jobs. Jesus, however, used truth to set people free, and He was not afraid to speak truth to people who did not want to hear it.

One way to receive deeper truths is to commit to seek solutions for someone in deep pain. By embracing their pain and seeking God for a truth that will set them free, you are gaining authority over the Philistine curse and inviting the blessings of God into your own life. When you become life-giving in this way, be careful that the life you give empowers the other person and does not enable them.

Sins That Bring on the Curse

Sins that can bring on the curse are:

- We choose peace over truth.
- We withhold truth to gain power.
- We withhold truth to save a relationship.
- We refuse to deal with sin in our community or group for fear of embarrassing the leader or making someone angry.

Many of us have a deep-felt need to be accepted in community. People with the Teacher gift especially struggle in this area for the following reasons.

- People with the Teacher gift often see themselves as inadequate.
- Teachers typically can struggle to get along in community, especially with long-term relationships.
- Teachers tend to accept the lie that some people are better or more valuable than others.

Blessings and Earned Authority

Blessings that come when the curse is broken are supernatural strategies, truths and resources needed to complete our assignments. We can receive the revelation of deeper truths of who God is that we need to fix problems. Our life message emerges out of these truths of who God is. This message, based on the largest problem in our lives, is the key to possessing our birthright.

To gain authority over the curse, we must speak truth to whomever God directs us to speak truth to, even if it costs us the relationship, which it sometimes will. Often we must face the fear of man or the fear of failure. To do so, God might direct us to do something that appears foolish to ourselves or others. As we steward truth as God intends us to steward it, God can trust us with more truth, and we gain authority over the curse.

Shamgar and His Oxgoad

In Judges 3:31, we read that Shamgar used a cattle prod, a wooden stick, to kill 600 Philistines. Quite a feat! At that time, the Philistines controlled all the iron in the land, which prevented the Israelites from having iron weapons.

To dig a bit deeper in how the Philistine curse functions, let's compare how Abraham handled truth and relationships in Genesis 21 compared to how Issac handled similar situations in Genesis 26. Abraham had dug a well and the Philistines violently took the well from him. Abraham said to Abimelech, king of the Philistines, "I dug this well!" The Philistines greatly outnumbered Abraham's clan, but still he boldly spoke truth to power. The well was restored to Abraham and a treaty was made clearly establishing Abraham as the owner of the well.

In Genesis 26, we learn that Isaac redug the same well, but the Philistines drove him away and took over the well. Isaac accepted the violation, moved on and dug another well, only to have it happen again. Then Abimelech came to Isaac and claimed that he and his people had treated Isaac well! Isaac accepted these words and made a peace treaty with the Philistines.

For thought and discussion:

1. Read Genesis 21 and 26. Abraham had a different relationship with God than did his son Isaac. Describe how Abraham put truth over relationship and how Isaac put relationship over truth. Which is more righteous in God's eyes?

2. Gaslighting is when someone manipulates us into questioning reality. In Genesis, how did Abimelech gaslight Isaac? What had Isaac done to give Abimelech the open door to gaslight him?

3. Identify one fact in Isaac's life that might indicate the Philistine curse was operating.

4. God uses the foolishness of men to confront the wise and learned. To break the Philistine curse, God often asks us to do something foolish such as read Scripture each day rather than studying for a final exam so that our confidence is in God and not in our knowledge. If a friend were to tell you that this is what she plans to do, how would you advise her? What questions would you ask her?

5. Is there evidence that a key resource you need to move forward in life is missing? If so, search for clues for the Philistine curse operating. What can you do to fix the situation?

6. Describe clearly what sin brings on the Philistine curse and what repentance is needed to break the curse.

7. What change can you make in your life to intentionally earn more authority over the Philistine curse so you can build and refine your life message?

Curse 4.
Canaanite Curse and Blessings of Time

God wants to bless us with the time and space we need to develop our finest abilities so that we can reach fulfillment and possess our birthrights. For Him to do so, we must focus our time and efforts on His agenda and not ours.

Indication of the Curse

Are you forever busy, putting out fires and feeling exploited by your boss, your business or your church? Do you feel you have no time to do the really important things of life? The Canaanite curse might be at work. Of all the curses found in the Book of Judges, the Canaanite curse is probably most prevalent in the Body of Christ because of the current theology that it is acceptable for Christian leaders to exploit Christian volunteers and workers.

I was speaking with a pastor who asked one of his members to quit her job as a teacher and come work for the Christian school he was forming. The salary in the Christian school was much lower than the teacher's current salary. He said, "It's okay to ask her to work for less money because she's doing it for God."

Five indications the curse might be operating are:

- **Busy, busy, busy.** Those under the curse work hard under an endless workload but accomplish little of eternal value.

- **Denial and exploitation.** Someone is likely to be in denial, rejecting the reality of cause and effect, sowing and reaping. As a "master of spin," they are willing to put the extra burden on their followers for their own sin of over commitment. And they expect their followers to overlook their exploiting them.

- **Entitlement.** Someone might believe they deserve good "just because." They might expect to sow little and reap much, receive their spiritual inheritance without holiness, embrace too large a vision for the resources they have, or push their followers too hard.

- **Loyal devotion to a person or organization that is not life-giving to them.** Followers can have a false sense of loyalty and devotion to leaders exploiting them. They work hard for the leader or group, waiting for promises to promote or build a platform under them that never happens. They are continually trained for "some day." The leader or organization "depends" on them and they are never equipped and released.

- **Difficulty breaking free from sexual sin.** Pornography was involved in the sin of Ham, father of Canaan.

Legitimacy Lie

The foundational lie that invites the Canaanite curse is, "I am legitimate when people want and need to be with me or want to follow me." This fourth curse is aligned with the Exhorter gift, and the immature Exhorter is inclined to build their legitimacy on having a following.

Sins that Bring on the Curse

We or someone in our family exploited others in the family, or we caused another family member to sin. We felt better about our sin by using the excuse "everyone is doing it." We excuse our sin because good things are happening in other areas of our lives.

Blessings and Earned Authority

When the curse is broken, we are blessed with the time and opportunity to develop our potential of eternal value, including our personal giftings, anointings, birthrights and callings.

Authority over the curse is earned with a firm conviction that our legitimacy comes only from God Himself and no other source. We can say from the depth of our hearts, "I don't need people to affirm me. I don't need a following. I don't need success. I'm able to confront wrong. I'm willing to back away from all people, associations and organizations as God leads."

A higher level of authority over the curse comes when we are life-giving to people who are not in our sphere of responsibility. We can give them life in such a way that they are empowered and not enabled.

> The Exhorter tends to get things done by leaning on the favor of man. They must learn to depend on the favor of God.

Deborah and Barak Sang a Song Together

Barak was called by God in Judges 4 and 5 to defeat the Canaanites in the land. Authority over the Canaanite curse, of all the other curses, comes through knowing our true legitimacy is in God alone. In the story of Deborah and Barak, we can see how each walked in true legitimacy before God.

The legitimacy of Deborah as a female judge was *totally* dependent on God. She had no authority other than what God gave her. As a prophetess, she sent word to Barak that the Lord commanded him to take 10,000 men to a certain location and there God would deliver the Canaanites into his hands. Barak responded, "If you go with me, I will go; but if you don't go with me, I won't go." Deborah warned him that he would not get credit for the victory if he took a woman with him. Laying his reputation aside, Barak still wanted Deborah to go, and she did. As it turned out, Sisera, the commander of the Canaanite army, was killed by a woman, Jael, who used a tent peg to kill the man while he slept.

We can get insight into how the Canaanite curse came about by looking at the story of Noah and his family in Genesis 8 and 9. Noah was told by God to go into the ark, first the men, followed by the women. When it was time to leave the ark, God told him to come out by couples, with his wife beside him, followed by his sons with their wives beside them. Changing from God's old order to God's new order can be extremely challenging! We don't know why Noah did not obey God, but they left the ark following the old order.

Later, Noah was alone in the tent when Ham sinned against his father, resulting in the curse on Ham's son, Canaan, who would be exploited by his family. We might never know how the story might be different if Noah's wife had been invited into her place beside her husband.

For thought and discussion:

1. God had chosen Barak and set him up for success. How did Barak's attitude of allowing a woman to take credit for the victory demonstrate his sense of legitimacy?

2. The Canaanite curse causes family members to be exploited. When Jesus was on the earth, He walked out the victory over the curse by laying down His life for His followers, going in the opposite spirit to the curse. He also demonstrated His legitimacy was not dependent on the crowds following Him. Give one or two examples where leaders in your life have been life-giving to you or have done the right thing even when it cost them followers.

3. Do you feel that you are or have been exploited in a family, job or church situation? Or have you exploited others? What can you do about these situations?

4. Describe clearly what sin brings on the Canaanite curse and what repentance is needed to break the curse.

5. What change can you make in your life to intentionally earn more authority over the Canaanite curse to free up time to develop your finest abilities with eternal value?

Curse 5.
Midianite Curse and the Blessings of Accumulating Assets

To possess our birthrights, we need to accrue the capital, resources and assets needed to build. God wants to bless us to build and protect these assets, so they increase over time.

Indication of the Curse

Ever work hard to save up money or another asset and just as you were about to enjoy some success, your hard-earned asset was lost or deeply diminished? Then you go through the heart-breaking efforts to build again. If so the Midianite curse might be the reason.

Seasonal devouring is one way the curse operates. With seasonal devouring, the curse happens at the specific time when someone sinned. For example, every June unexpected bills come in, the car breaks down, the refrigerator fails, all devouring your resources.

A curse that devours during a certain season of time might be the Midianite curse or a curse on time. You learned about breaking curses on time in Chapter 3.

Legitimacy Lie

The legitimacy lie is, "I am legitimate when I can provide the resources you need." We feel legitimate when someone is dependent on us. The root of the legitimacy lie is to believe that our resources are ours to use as we see fit, rather than surrendering all to God and stewarding His resources as He leads.

Sins That Bring on the Curse

Two fundamental types of sin can bring on the curse:

- We choose comfort or the easy path over our calling. For example, a leader is unwilling to provide a clear command structure and does not confront problems in the organization.

- We do not confront sin, especially in our leaders, family members, or people to whom we feel we owe a debt of gratitude or feel loyal to.

Devouring happens when we see our protection or provision coming from some source other than God. The main issue is we want to own our lives and are not willing to steward for God the resources He entrusts to us.

Blessings and Earned Authority

The blessing that comes when the curse is broken is we can accrue the capital and other assets necessary to possess our birthrights. We earn authority over the curse when we pursue our callings, laying down our own agendas to do so. As we devote ourselves fully to God's calling on our lives, He is able to bless us with all the resources needed for that calling.

Gideon Chose His Own Way Rather Than God's Calling

In Judges 6-8, we learn Gideon was chosen by God to deliver Israel from the Midianites and to judge (govern) Israel. After he won the battle through the supernatural help of God, the nation asked Gideon to rule over them. He said, "I will not rule over you, nor will my son rule over you. The LORD will rule over you." Then he asked for gold, which he used to make an ephod (the garment of a priest). The Israelites worshipped the ephod, and it "became a snare to Gideon and his family." The word snare means "draws destruction to it."

Gideon refused to govern the nation but rather wanted to be a priest of the Lord, perhaps because his father, Joash, was a priest of the Canaanite gods Baal and Asherah. The Israelites knew it was illegal for Gideon to have an ephod, which belongs only to priests, and Gideon was not a Levite. But, because he had done so much good, they felt they owed him and could not confront his sin.

For thought and discussion:

1. Read Gideon's story in Judges 6-8. The Midianite curse is especially dangerous to the next generation. How did Gideon expose his children to the curse?

2. A pastor taught his congregation that the closer they walk with God, the more they will align with the pastor and his vision. Make up three scenarios where this teaching is true and three other scenarios where the teaching is dangerous and can lead the members of the church into the Midianite curse.

3. State your calling from God as clearly as you can. What efforts are you making today to walk out your calling or to prepare yourself for your calling?

4. If you have no idea what your calling is, ask three trusted friends or your mentor what they see in you that might indicate what God is calling you to. Describe your passion, what makes you angry, your talents and how you see God. What is it about God's character that you see that others don't see? This is a clear clue to your calling.

5. Describe clearly what sin brings on the Midianite curse and what repentance is needed to break the curse.

6. What lifestyle changes can you make to intentionally earn more authority over the Midianite curse to accrue the resources you need to possess your birthright?

Curse 6.
Jotham Curse and Blessings of Social Structures

God wants to bless us with life-giving social structures where life flows from leaders to their followers, which is a virtue of the Ruler gift. And then, leaders can raise up the next generation of leaders to be life-giving to their followers.

Indication of the Curse

Have you ever been in a group where entitlement, gossip, discontent, lawlessness, backbiting and betrayal are common and even expected? This could be because of the Jothan curse.

Indications of the curse are:

- Leadership is unstable or weak.
- General discontent and divisions often happen, usually through power plays rather than a disagreement over principles.
- Gossip is seen as normal and goes unchecked.
- Lawlessness and "bending the rules," such as regularly being late to work or overextending lunch hours is seen as socially acceptable and normal.
- Nepotism might be present, where favor is shown to relatives who don't merit it.
- Betrayal presents as attacks behind someone's back or forcing a righteous person out of the organization because of an offense. Someone leaves the company taking customer lists or trade secrets with them.
- The curse invites a covenant-breaking spirit. A church split or family breakup is sometimes caused by the Jotham curse in operation.

The Jothan curse often follows the Midianite curse. A family business, ministry or church where family members are on staff and the senior leader does not provide strong leadership is especially susceptible to these curses working hand in hand.

Legitimacy Lie

The legitimacy lie is "I am legitimate when I have an institution I can use for building." A similar legitimacy lie is "I am legitimate when I have a lot of people under my covering and in my ministry." Because the Ruler gift is designed by God to build life-giving structures, a person with this gift is especially susceptible to this lie.

People who have a wounded or corrupt attitude toward leadership can be especially susceptible to

this legitimacy lie. They might want to take over the organization because they don't honor or appreciate what the leaders have done for them.

Sins That Bring on the Curse

The two types of sins that invite the Jotham curse are ingratitude toward our leaders and lawlessness. We sin by harming those who have done us good.

Blessing and Earned Authority

When the curse is broken, we can experience the blessings of God to build life-giving social structures. With these social structures, we can raise up the next generation of healthy leaders.

We don't always need an institution to complete our calling. Jesus demonstrated what a life-giving structure can look like without an institution. He prepared eleven men to be leaders, was life-giving to many other people, and died on the cross. When He said, "It is finished," He announced He had finished the work that God called Him to do.

The blessings to possess our birthrights accrue like this:

1. When the Aramean curse is broken, the legal system works, and favor is given by God and man.
2. When the Moabite curse is broken, boundaries are secure.
3. When the Philistine curse is broken, we receive the truths we need to establish the government of God.
4. When the Canaanite curse is broken, we are able to develop our finest abilities.
5. When the Midianite curse is broken, we can accrue the capital we need to build.
6. When the Jotham curse is broken, we can build the social structures that release life into the culture and raise up the next generation of leaders.

We earn authority over the Jotham curse by continually learning to express gratitude toward God and people, especially to our leaders. We are extremely careful to watch our words, and we don't gossip about others in our organization or community.

Jotham and Betrayal from Within

In Judges 8 and 9, we read that after Gideon died, the nation did not know who was in charge because Gideon did not raise up leaders after him. Gideon had 70 sons by his many wives. In addition, his son, Abimelech, was the son of Gideon's concubine.

Abimelech took advantage of the weak governmental structure with no clear line of command and said to his town Shechem, "Do you really want 70 sons in charge? That's like no one in charge. Wouldn't you rather have me, your relative, be your leader?" The nation had also failed to show gratitude to Gideon or his family, making it possible for Abimelech to insight Shechem against the other sons. He hired incompetent (empty) men and used them to kill all the 70 sons except Jotham, the youngest, who escaped.

Later, when Abimelech was being crowned king, Jotham pronounced a curse on Abimelech and Shechem that they would destroy each other. God waited three years for Abimelech and Shechem to repent. When they did not, God allowed the curse to stand, and they destroyed each other. This destruction began when people stirred up discontent and began accusing each other.

For thought and discussion:

1. The components that bring on the Jotham curse and its resulting betrayal and destruction are 1) the legitimacy lie, 2) the sins of ingratitude toward leaders, 3) lawlessness, and 4) sedition. List these four components in the story of Abimelech and Shechem as told in Judges 8 and 9.

2. Take some time to consider who has invested in you within the past couple of weeks. Write a thank you letter, email, phone call or text to this person to say you noticed and you value what was done. How does a regular habit of gratitude toward your leaders protect you from the Jotham curse?

3. We all benefit from the generational blessings of our leaders and forefathers who have helped us get where we are today. Think about physical structures such as hospitals, schools, streets and public works built by previous generations and the taxes they paid. Consider spiritual blessings such as grandparents who prayed regularly or intercessors who pray for us today. List ten sources of generational blessings in your life. How can you express gratitude toward someone or group on this list?

4. In your discussion group, discuss holding each other accountable to avoid gossip. What statement can you make when you or another slip up and gossip? Can you introduce a code the entire group understands that brings a smile without an offense?

5. Do you see any evidence of the Jotham curse operating in your life? If so, can you trace the curse back to what you or your forefathers have done to bring on the curse? What can you do to change the situation?

6. Describe clearly what sins bring on the Jotham curse and what repentance is needed to break the curse.

7. What lifestyle changes can you make to intentionally earn more authority over the Jotham curse to build life-giving structures needed for you to possess your birthright?

Curse 7.
Ammonite Curse and Blessings of Possessing Your Birthright

God has a birthright for each of us, and He desires to bless us with everything we need to possess our birthrights. To receive our birthrights, we must have a blessing-based relationship with God, rather than a trade-based relationship.

Indication of the Curse

A couple has a passion to own their own business, but the husband takes too many risks and often chooses unreliable partners; therefore, the wife no longer trusts him to launch their next business. They remain barren in their birthright as entrepreneurs. The primary indicator the Ammonite curse is at work is barrenness. Other indicators of the curse in operation are:

- We take unnecessary risks, even to appear reckless to others.

- We tend to be surrounded by people without strong character. Scripture calls them "empty" people.

- Many times we cannot trust a boss or leader, which leads to our wanting to be in control. For this reason, we choose bosses or leaders who are weak.

Legitimacy Lie

The legitimacy lie is "I am legitimate when I have earned God's blessings or favor." This lie causes us to develop a trade-based relationship with God.

04

Sins That Bring on the Curse

In a blessing-based relationship, someone blesses the other without expecting payment or trade. In a trade-based relationship, it's tit for tat. I give you something and expect something in return. Sometimes the trade is unspoken such as when someone "does a favor" for us and then expects a favor in return. In Romans 8, God says to owe no man anything except to love one another. In a righteous relationship, there should be no unspoken expectation of debt when one helps the other.

In Genesis 12, God had a blessing-based relationship with Abraham so that Abraham could in turn bless many.

When we don't believe we deserve God's blessings without trading something back to Him in return, we can bring on the Ammonite curse.

Blessings and Earned Authority

God wants to bless us with His rest and His power to possess our birthrights without expecting anything in return.

To earn authority over this curse, we might first need to get healing for any lies we have believed about our unworthiness or God's lack of generosity or goodness. We must know that our past or current mistakes or failures do not prevent God from blessing us.

We gain earned authority over the Ammonite curse as we receive God's blessings with joy and thankfulness, savoring in His goodness and love for us and celebrating the goodness of God, especially His generosity.

John the Apostle learned how to do this. Jesus loved him even though Jesus called him the Son of Thunder and it was clear that John was a blamer and hard on others. John did not deserve that special love from Jesus, and yet he was able to receive it and grow into a larger person. Each of us need to learn to receive God's love in this way.

Jephthah and His Trade-based Relationship with God

In Judges 10-12, we read how the Israelites served other gods and, in doing so, called down yet another curse on themselves. God gave them into the hands of the Ammonites; they cried out to God, and He sent a deliverer, Jephthah.

Jephthah was a mighty warrior and the illegitimate son of his father. When his father died, his brothers drove Jephthah away so that he would not receive a share of the inheritance. Later, the city elders searched for Jephthah to bring him back to lead the fight against the Ammonites.

Jephthah had righteously stated that the land in dispute clearly belonged to the Israelites by the will and power of God. He declared the Ammonites were there illegally, and he petitioned God to settle the dispute (Judges 11:14-27). Then the Spirt of the Lord came upon Jephthah, and the battle was won.

The tragedy of the story is that Jephthah made a reckless and foolish vow to sacrifice whatever came out of his house when he came home in victory. And who should come out of the door first but his daughter, his only child!

For thought and discussion:

1. Read Judges 10-12. Jephthah was not able to accept the blessings of God and his birthright as Israel's leader and defender without trading something with God. List as many reasons as you can why this was so.

2. If you were Jephthah's friend, how might you advise him to make peace with God before he started the battle so that he would have confidence that God would come through for him without his having to trade with God?

3. In your own life, consider what, if anything, you believe you owe God. Sit with God and ask Him if, indeed, these are legal debts. How can you settle your accounts with God?

4. List three gifts or blessings that God has given you. Make a plan to celebrate and savor these gifts.

5. Do you see any evidence of the Ammonite curse operating in your life? If so, can you trace the curse back to what you or your forefathers have done to bring on the curse? What can you do to change the situation?

6. Describe clearly what sins bring on the Ammonite curse and what repentance is needed to break the curse.

7. What lifestyle changes can you make to intentionally earn more authority over the Ammonite curse so that God can release into your life the blessings needed to possess your birthright?

Concept 4.3
Curses on Land and Offices

To complete our discussion of curses in this chapter, let's briefly mention curses on land and offices. Recall from Chapter 2 that God made holy time, land, community, birthright and offices. When land is cursed, no matter how hard we try, we cannot receive God's blessings while on cursed land. For example, a business might work hard to apply the financial principles of Wisdom but still cannot thrive until the curse on the land is broken. In another situation, a family experiences many strange accidents in their new home that stop the day they break all curses on the land and house.

When you experience devouring and destruction in your life, try to determine if it is associated with the land you are on. For example, you experience destructive accidents. Do these accidents occur only when you're on that land or happen no matter where you are? If they are limited to this land, chances are you have discovered a curse on it.

Curses on an office can explain why a man is elected mayor of his city after having made many righteous promises, but as soon as he takes office his heart changes, and he reneges on many of these promises. He had stepped into an office that was defiled and cursed by those who had previously held the office. Other offices that might be defiled or cursed are the office of husband, wife, mother, father, mother-in-law, pastor, physician, teacher or boss.

For more information on breaking curses off time and land, see the album, "Tools for Cleansing Time & Land" by Arthur at **theSLG.com.** For more information on breaking curses off time, see the Spiritual Warfare album "Curses on Time" at **theSLG.com.**

For more information on breaking curses off of an office, see the album, "When Your Call is Blocked" by Arthur at **theSLG.com.**

SOLVING PROBLEMS

Recall that we solve problems in four steps: (1) Collect data, (2) look for patterns, (3) identify principles, and (4) apply these principles to new situations. In this chapter, we work on solving problems in relationships.

Problem 4.1 Using Reality Therapy for Problem Solving

William Glasser, a writer and psychiatrist, developed what he called choice theory and reality therapy. Although many topics are up for debate, we can learn much from him about solving problems in relationships.

He claimed that everyone has the right to choose for themselves and we cannot choose for another. When we try to force others to choose what we want, we destroy the relationship by destroying the other person's *right to choose*. On the other hand, by accepting a "live and let live" philosophy, we learn to get along with others.

Dr. Glasser identified seven deadly habits intended to control others, which can destroy relationships:

- Criticizing
- Blaming
- Complaining
- Nagging
- Threatening
- Punishing
- Bribing (rewarding to control)

He also identified seven caring habits that can build healthy relationships:

- Supporting
- Encouraging
- Listening
- Accepting
- Trusting
- Respecting
- Negotiating differences

According to Dr. Glasser, when a relationship goes bad, most likely someone was trying to control another person by making choices for them. He helped people see the reality of the picture they held in their heads that could only be satisfied if the other person could be controlled. His goal was to change the picture to a new picture that could still satisfy but allow the other person their choices.

Let's see how this plays out in a few situations.

- **Story 1.** Mary has a fear of going out of the house alone. She refuses to leave the house unless her daughter or husband Dan is with her. Sometimes she refuses to answer the phone when Dan calls from work to check on her, and this makes him leave work early. She believes they have a good marriage because Dan is an attentive and devoted husband.

- **Story 2.** Ann is 11-years-old, but still does not like to sleep alone. Most nights, she crawls into her sister Lucy's bed in the adjacent room even though Lucy gets angry and complains that Ann has yet one more time disturbed her sleep.

- **Story 3.** Jerry and Sam play together each afternoon after school. They often argue over which game they will play. Jerry likes football and Sam likes softball.
- **Story 4.** Karen volunteered to work in her church kitchen on Thursdays to feed the homeless. The other kitchen workers are unfriendly and don't accept her. She is thinking about quitting.
- **Story 5.** Allison leads an inner healing ministry and is training three new prayer ministers. Joe, one of the trainees, complains to Sally, another trainee, that Allison is not giving him enough freedom to use his skills as a counselor.
- **Story 6.** Jack runs a construction crew. Bill, a crewman, comes to work consistently late. Jack gets angry and shouts at Bill but does nothing more about the tardiness.

For each of the situations, answer these questions:

1. Who is exerting control?
2. How is trying to control damaging the relationship?
3. Which of the seven deadly habits, if any, are in play?
4. Who in the situation needs to change the picture of what they need to achieve satisfaction? What new picture might satisfy but not control the other person?
5. Which caring habit might help if it were introduced into the situation?

Now that you've applied Dr. Glasser's choice theory and reality therapy tools to a few situations, how did this change or help shape your view of what it is to walk in reality? Are you now more aware of cause and effect principles in relationships?

Problem 4.2 The Powerless Person Triangle

Believing the lie, "I am powerless or have few rights in community" can lead to relationships that fit in what is called the Powerless Person Triangle, sometimes called the Karpman Drama Triangle. See Figure 4-4.

In the triangle, we each have a default role of villain, hero or damsel in distress, although we can shift roles at any time to address the immediate emotion of powerlessness. Each person gets to feel powerful, but the root cause of feeling powerless is never dealt with. Similar to an alcoholic who feels powerful when they are drunk, denying the reality of powerlessness prevails.

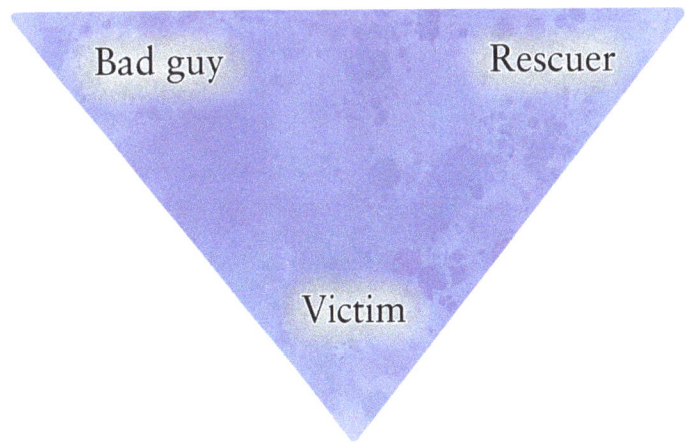

Figure 4-4 In the Powerless Person Triangle, each person stays in the triangle because they see themselves as powerless without the other members of the triangle

Follow these steps to learn how the triangle works:

1. Jane is stressed and depressed because her boyfriend broke up with her. To cheer her up, her mother Beth, drops her plans for the day and takes Jane shopping for some "retail therapy."

2. While shopping, Beth overcharges on her credit card to buy Jane a beautiful outfit.

3. Jane's father, Louis, comes home that evening in a rage over the text notice he received from the credit card company that their credit limit has been overextended yet one more time. In anger, he demands the new outfit be returned.

4. Jane yells at her dad that he doesn't love her and runs off to her room. Beth demands that Louis apologize to Jane. They argue while Jane sulks.

Discuss the family dynamics with your discussion partner and answer the following questions:

5. Who in the family is primarily playing the bad guy role? Rescuer? Victim?

6. Explain how each of the three family members are victims. How would you describe the powerlessness of each victim?

7. As the drama unfolded, how did roles switch?

For this family to get to the root causes of their powerlessness, answer the following:

8. Describe how the principle of reality could be applied to help each family member.

9. Describe how each family member could move from powerlessness to dominion by applying the principle of dominion.

10. Describe how the principle of truth could help each family member. Which core values discussed in Chapter 3 could each family member apply?

Problem 4.3 Synchronizing with Team Members

Have you ever thought someone on your team needed to know ___ to be a better person or team member, but you said nothing out of fear of ____? Where is the balance of accepting people where they are and helping them be better people? Here are three situations.

- **Story 1.** Eric leads a team and Charles refuses to accept his share of the responsibility. He always seems to have one more excuse why he is not the one to do a certain task.

- **Story 2.** Phil's daughter Janice is failing algebra. If she doesn't pass this course, she might have to repeat the 11th grade.

- **Story 3.** Hanna has a coworker, Alma, who is not focused at work because of trouble at home. Her husband is not working and refuses to look for a job, which is putting huge financial stress on the family budget.

For each story, answer these questions.

1. What fear might prevent Eric from discussing the situation with Charles? Phil with Janice? Hanna with Alma?

2. Assuming Eric has a good relationship and some earned authority with Charles, what strategy do you think he could use to help Charles? Phil help Janice? Hanna help Alma?

Problem 4.4 The Philistine Curse at Work

Clara founded a successful ministry that included a leadership team. As the ministry grew in visibility and size, the team claimed that Clara was in sin and had no right to run the ministry. Although she could not see her sin, she trusted her team and resigned from the ministry. Years later, she realized these mistakes were not "sin" and she should not have resigned. That's when she realized she had evoked the Philistine curse in her life, which explained why her new ministry was not prospering. How did Clara evoke this curse? What can she do now to earn authority over this curse?

Problem 4.5 Building a Business Should Not Be This Difficult

Harry is a successful businessman, but he has had to overcome many obstacles. He knows his business dealings should not be so difficult. When he asks God for insight, he is reminded of a family story.

In 1929, at the beginning of the Great Depression, Harry's grandfather co-signed a mortgage on his neighbor's farm. As the economy failed, both the neighbor and the grandfather lost their farms to pay the debt.

Answer the following questions:

1. Which curse is at work in Harry's family line?

2. What questions could someone ask Harry to uncover how he might be strengthening this curse?

3. What can Harry do to earn authority over this curse?

GROWTH PROJECT

These growth projects are designed to help you grow yourself and learn how to grow those you lead.

Growth Project 4.1 Parenting for Each Stage of Growth

Although we have one redemptive gift as our primary gift, we can express all seven, and good parenting requires we use all the gifts. For example, at the first stage of growth, belongingness, we need our parents to tell us and demonstrate to us we belong. The fathering Prophet gift sees and draws out of a child his or her design that expresses the light and love of God. A mothering Prophet delights in generous and tender giving to a child to solve the problem at hand. A mothering Prophet can bless the child's spirit, soul and body to come to rest, reminding the child's spirit that he or she was designed to align with and rest with God. Practically, a dad can gently hold, nourish and rock a child to sleep. All these are wonderful expressions of the Prophet gift in parents helping a child at an emotional level know they securely belong in the family.

In the following table, the stage and situation at that stage is listed. If you need help understanding each stage of growth, see the sections *Here We Grow* near the beginning of each chapter.

Situation	Stage of growth	Parenting redemptive gift	Immaturity
1	Belongingness	Prophet	At 8 months, I cannot go to sleep.
2	Know myself	Servant	At 3 years old, I want to play in the water.
3	Know myself	Servant	At 3 years old, I can't stand loud and sudden noises.
4	Moral standards	Teacher	At 6 years old, I lied to my mom.
5	Moral standards	Teacher	At 7 years old, I talked back to my dad.
6	Peer relationships	Exhorter	At 9 years old, I bicker with my older brother over who will go first to take a shower.
7	Peer relationships	Exhorter	At 11 years old, I went to the school dance, but no one asked me to dance.
8	Develop myself	Giver	I love piano, but I don't have the self-discipline to practice.
9	Fight and build	Ruler	I want to avoid eating sweets, but my friends just invited me for ice cream.
10	Become my own person	Mercy	I find myself getting angry and shouting at my children, just like my father did to me.

04

For each of the 10 situations, give some thought as to how each gift applies to each stage and each situation. Then describe how the gift might operate in this situation and what practically might work. Try to remember the good parenting you received as a child, or wished you had received.

Growth Project 4.2 Discovering Your Unique Treasures from the Journey

Do the following to examine your journey, which can help you discover your unique treasures put there by God.

1. Create a timeline for your life, labeling all the significant events on the timeline.

2. Look for patterns of blessings and troubles.

3. Look for any oddities in your journey. What doesn't fit?

4. Can you identify the treasures or design that God has put in you? For example, one person noticed that he had started multiple businesses over several decades and realized he was a serial entrepreneur.

5. Based on what you've done so far, can you identify a talent that God has given you that you might want to further develop?

6. What major problem do you see in your life that keeps repeating? How might this be a clue to your birthright?

7. Do you see any repeating cycles of devouring that might indicate a Midianite curse at work?

8. Do you see a pattern of emotional oddities that might indicate a cyclic trauma bond to time? Or perhaps a clue to your design?

Growth Project 4.3 Synchronizing in Community

Do you have a problem enjoying the joy of those in your close community, family, work or school? If so, follow these steps to work on synchronizing to others. Find the first step where there's a problem and start there.

1. Can you consistently observe details in others? Walk through a store or sit in a mall and watch people. Notice the details of their bodies and clothing.

2. Observe the emotions as expressed in body language. Is the person you're watching happy or sad?

3. Observe the emotions as expressed in body language. Identify their emotions using colorful and diverse words, such as "annoyed and bordering on outright anger."

4. Watch people who are enjoying themselves, such as athletes on TV, children playing in the park, adults playing a board game or people watching a funny movie. Can you laugh with them and enjoy their joy?

5. Can you enter into the fun time? Can you play a board game or sit with friends at a restaurant and enjoy your joy together as a group?

6. Can you sync with a group as you work together on a project?

When a group can synchronize as they work together, enjoying the synergy of the team, you are ready for corporate creativity to emerge!

SPIRIT PROJECT

The spirit projects are designed to enlarge your spirit, develop your spirit world and help you better synchronize with your spirit and with God.

Spirit Project 4.1
The Chronometer, the Compass and the Gyroscope

As you know from earlier chapters, we have the essence of God in us. Our spirits come from God and He has given us a spirit world. All of our humanity is designed by God to represent Him on the earth, to sync with Him and to express His nature. Three spiritual devices we are all designed to have in our spirit world are:

- The **chronometer** is a clock that is the essence of the Father and perfectly synchronizes with His time. With the help of the chronometer, we can synchronize our time to His time. When the chronometer is missing or damaged, our timing with God and His ways might be off.

- The **compass** gives us direction and is the essence of the Lord Jesus Christ. Have you ever heard someone say, "She doesn't have a moral compass?" They may not realize that this is actually a real device missing in her spirit world.

- The **gyroscope** gives us stability and keeps us oriented to the essence of Holy Spirit. In the physical, a gyroscope has a wheel within a wheel. See Figure 4-5. As the wheels spin, one axis within the gyroscope is not affected when the gyroscope tilts, which provides stability for planes, ships and race cars. I wonder whether the four wheels within wheels described in Ezekiel 1 were not four gyroscopes under the platform on which the throne rested.

In the physical world, a chronometer is an extremely accurate mechanical timepiece that can keep true time regardless of external forces, such as temperature and motion. This device was originally designed for ships to navigate oceans.

Figure 4-5 A gyroscope keeps objects oriented to a right horizontal and vertical axis or plane

Working with your spirit, do the following:

1. You or your partner ask your spirit to find and describe the chronometer, which might be in the air, on land or in the water. It might be small or massive. For example, Prophet might tell you the chronometer is beside the river on the north side and is about ten feet in diameter. When Prophet touches the chronometer, she can feel the presence of Father. As she leans against it, she can feel the essence of God's perfect timing filling her up. As she moves slowly around the chronometer, she can sense that time is being healed.

   Sometimes the chronometer is missing and there might be a false chronometer put there by the enemy to throw off the timing of God in your life. For example, Ruler found a chronometer at the bottom of the river, but the water is dark and murky. When Ruler commanded the chronometer to be seen as God sees it, it became a critter that he evicted. After the false chronometer was gone, Ruler invited Father to plant His chronometer in the land.

2. Ask your spirit to find and describe the compass. Sometimes the compass is embedded in the Cornerstone, which holds the essence of the Lord Jesus Christ. When the spirit needs direction, spirit can lay down on the compass or touch it to get direction from Jesus. For example, Ruler was missing. Prophet lay on the compass and rotated his body until he sensed he was pointing in the direction where Ruler could be found. People who were not taught right from wrong at the third stage of growth might be missing their spiritual compass. Our spirits can ask Jesus to come and place the compass in our spirit world.

3. Ask your spirit to find and describe the gyroscope. It might be small or massive, and its position is strategic. Not all gyroscopes look the same. My gyroscope was missing entirely, which makes sense when I consider how destabilized I was before healing. I saw the gyroscope as small and ineffective when Giver first asked Holy Spirit to place it in my spirit world. It took about two years for the gyroscope to grow to where I thought it might actually be useful to help keep me stable and oriented.

Then I received major healing and deliverance that got to the root of some severe childhood abuse. I had accepted the lie that I had no rights in community. When I rejected that lie, I watched as the gyroscope was turned right side up. It immediately grew and came alive! The plumbline of righteousness came down from the top all the way through, and the measuring line of justice formed the horizontal plane in the center of the gyroscope that now supports and orients my entire inner world. I have not destabilized since that day! Praise God for His gyroscope, righteousness and justice! I'm so grateful.

Spirit Project 4.2 Syncing with Others Begins in the Spirit

I was praying with a mom about her children who had been separated from her in a custody battle. I spoke to her spirit and asked, "Can you see the spirits of her children?" I was surprised when she said, "Oh, yes, they are right here. They sync with me."

When working with human spirits, never try to command, force or manipulate. The human spirit intuitively knows when it's not safe or wise to sync to another. Trust must develop first. More importantly, we never want to control the spirit of another.

For more information about the chronometer, compass and gyroscope, listen to Arthur's audio album, "Surviving but not Thriving" at **theSLG.com**.

When I was praying with another mom, the Mercy portion of her spirit told me about the beautiful gyroscope near the trees. Her children had great difficulty syncing to her, so I asked Mercy if she might invite their spirits to sync with her. She extended the invitation and they all rested on the gyroscope together. The mom reported it was easier for the children to sync with her for the next few days.

We are still learning so much about the spirit world, but if you're in a situation where children are having difficulty syncing with their parents, you might consider inviting their spirits to sync with the spirits of their parents.

However, be cautious. Sometimes a spirit knows it's not safe. I recall one spirit of a mom told me, "It's not yet safe to ask the daughter's spirit to sync." Mom needed to grow some first so that the child would be safe syncing with her.

Spirit Project 4.3 Learning to Sync with God

It is our joy to enjoy the joy of Father God! In Scripture, several Hebrew words are translated joy and have slightly different meanings. My favorite is *hedva* in this verse: "*The joy of Jehovah is your strength.*" *Hedva* means "joining joy." I love that thought. Joining joy with God gives us strength. We synchronize with Him in the most joyful way. Enjoying His joy is our joy!

Ask your spirit what it looks and feels like to experience joining joy with Father God! If your spirit finds it difficult to sync with God, most likely you have believed some lies about God that make you not trust Him enough to sync to Him. Ask your spirit what keeps him or her distant from God.

Spirit Project 4.4 Freeing Alien Human Spirits

An 8-year-old girl would hit other children without provocation. Discipline did not help, and we were pretty sure the critters had been evicted. Then we suspected an alien human spirit (AHS), which is a human spirit of another person (dead or alive) that does not belong in our spirit world.

The mom asked her daughter, "May I speak with your spirit?" And then she asked her spirit, "Was that someone else who hit your sister?"

The girl's spirit said, "Yes, there's a tall woman who hates her and hits her." The mom asked for the silver channel into eternity to be opened, and the girl watched as the tall woman walked down the channel toward a golden castle far away. The hitting stopped that day.

Most often, it's simple and easy to help an AHS find their way back to eternity. Suspect an AHS when:

- A person gets very sad when they should be celebrating or happy. Sometimes an AHS is grieving over not being able to live out their own life when the host person has a real life.

- When physical, emotional or behavioral issues defy solutions that work for others or cannot be explained by science, sometimes an AHS is the source of the problem.

- Extra weight that refuses to drop off is sometimes caused by an AHS.

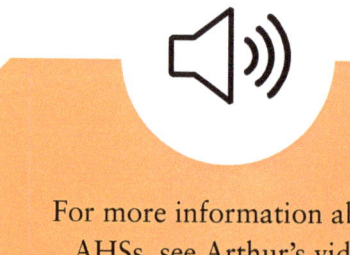

For more information about AHSs, see Arthur's video "Alien Human Spirits, Part 1" at **theSLG.com**.

Spirit Project 4.5 Spirit Warfare and Soul Warfare

The human spirit does warfare differently than the soul.
This is partly because the spirit is more aware that the victory is already won by Jesus and we are called to enforce the victory. In Ephesians 6, Paul describes our putting on the armor of God so that we can stand against the deceptions of the enemy. The armor is:

- The belt of truth, who is Jesus
- The breastplate of righteousness, who is Jesus
- The preparation of the gospel of peace, who is Jesus
- The shield of faith, who is Jesus
- The helmet of salvation, who is Jesus
- The sword of the Spirit, the Word of God, who is Jesus
- Praying at all times to Jesus

Intimacy with Jesus brings us to His dominion over the enemy. We stand in intimate victory with Jesus to enforce His victory.

So when we put on the armor, we are putting on Jesus. This reality is a wonderful picture of our dominion with Jesus made possible by our intimacy with Him. As we clothe ourselves in Jesus, the enemy sees Jesus and is terrified of us.

Here are some ways I've seen the human spirit do warfare.

- Servant slings his right arm out toward enemies in the far distance and releases a lightning bolt that takes out most of them. The others flee in terror.

- Giver and Ruler devise a hose to move water from the river of life to drown enemies down inside a deep pit in the inner world.

- Servant releases an east wind to drive out enemies encamped on a mountain.

- Prophet releases a laser light to drive out critters surrounding the soul.

Most of the time, the spirit simply says, "Go!" and they flee. But it's delightful to watch how creative the spirit can be and how much fun spirit can have when it's time to go into warfare mode.

CHAPTER
05 GROWING IN DEVELOPING MYSELF

"We steward well the relationships, gifts and talents Father has entrusted to us."

PRINCIPLE

Do you take good care of something, such as a lawn mower or evening gown, better when it is borrowed or when it belongs to you? Do you give it more care if you highly respect its owner? The better we know God, the more we are joyfully able to surrender all to Him and gratefully care for all He entrusts to us.

The Principle of Stewardship

To understand the **principle of stewardship**, let's begin with our life. Is my life my own to live as I choose, or does God own me and all that I have? Paul was talking about intimate sexual relationships when he reminded us that are bodies are gifts from God and we don't own them to use as we please.

> *Do you not know that your bodies are temples of the Holy Spirit, who is in you, whom you have received from God? You are not your own; you were bought at a price. Therefore, honor God with your bodies.*

1 Corinthians 6:19-20

Later, in this same letter to the Corinthians, Paul reminded them that he considered himself a slave to the Lord Jesus.

> *Were you a slave when you were called? Don't let it trouble you—although if you can gain your freedom, do so. For the one who was a slave when called to faith in the Lord is the Lord's freed person; similarly, the one who was free when called is Christ's slave. You were bought at a price; do not become slaves of human beings.*

1 Corinthians 7:21-23

Jesus purchased us from the kingdom of darkness by paying the highest possible price – His own life. Not only are we now owned by Him, we are also redeemed and made new creations by Him. We are like Him! The depth of what He did for us and gave to us is beyond understanding.

Paul said that even those who are slaves are actually free because of the depth and magnitude of freedom in Christ. How can Christ so set us this free even when living as a physical slave to another man? Only God can explain that to us! Pray that we all get it!

Everything He has given us belongs to Him. Everything. Our jobs, our homes, our cars, our children, our marriage, our money, our health, our hopes and our dreams. To surrender it to Him is to acknowledge what is true in the first place – it belongs to Him, it was always His, it does not belong to us, and we only steward it. To know that all belongs to Him is freedom indeed!

Spirit of Celebration

Sons of God celebrate their relationship with Father God and also celebrate when they know they have stewarded well what was entrusted. Slaves, on the other hand, might not see the resources entrusted to them because they don't see or trust the Giver of all good things. When we don't see the Giver or His gifts, we can become defiant and demanding, and we might accuse God of withholding good from us.

So they quarreled with Moses and said, "Give us water to drink." Moses replied, "Why do you quarrel with me? Why do you put the Lord to the test?"

Exodus 17:2

In this chapter, we explore what it means to be able and willing to steward the relationships and treasures He has given us.

HERE WE GROW

During the fifth stage of growth, that normally happens in the preteen and early teen years, we find great delight in developing our gifts and talents and establish a life-long commitment to developing ourselves.

Growth Stage 5. I Am Developing Myself

The fifth stage of growth, developing ourselves, requires that the second stage has already happened to some degree. Recall the second stage is when we discover ourselves and some of our preferences, talents and passions. Once we know that and are mature enough, we can make efforts to learn to play guitar, swim or whatever else we see inside us that we want to develop (see Figure 5-1).

Parents and mentors can help us by identifying what we really love to do and support us in learning to do it better. What should we develop or not develop?

Train up a child in the way he should go and when he is old, he will not depart from it.
Proverbs 22:6

Figure 5-1 We can't intentionally develop a talent unless we know what that talent is.

We all have unique designs from God, the way we should go, that lead us toward our unique fulfillment. It might take some trial and error to discover which talents or core abilities are worthy of development. Here are three principles to consider:

- **Fundamental skills we all need.** Some skills are fundamental to living life well and we all need to develop them, such as following directions, reading, writing, doing arithmetic, preparing our own food, keeping our things in order, getting along with peers, speaking well, and exhibiting good manners and etiquette in private and public settings. As Christ followers, we all need to learn spiritual fundamentals of hearing the voice of God and seeking relationship with Him through His Word. Parents and mentors are responsible for making sure children learn these and many other fundamental life skills.

- **We live life from our design.** In our preteen years, parents and mentors can encourage a child to develop their unique talents. We trust God that He has put in a person what they need for fulfillment, and that these talents are worth developing. Sometimes a child has many talents and it's impossible to develop them all. In these situations, wisdom is needed. However, the ultimate responsibility for a child to develop their talents is on the child, not the parent.

- **Don't struggle to develop a design we don't have.** Although there's some value in persevering through boredom and lack of progress, it's generally a waste of time and resources to require a child with no musical talent to take six years of piano lessons. And a child who has no interest or talent in gymnastics could better use their time learning to do something they love. Beyond the necessary basics, wisdom says to not force a child to struggle to develop a talent they don't have.

Both Mothering and Fathering are Needed

For a child to develop their innate abilities, we need a healthy balance of mothering and fathering in our lives.

- Someone in a mothering role (male or female) creates a safe environment and provides all the coaching and assistance needed. They are teaching the child to receive.

- Someone in a fathering role (male or female) provides opportunities for the child to develop or unpack their treasures. A father encourages a child to do the hard work, embrace the productive pain, accept responsibility and problem solve as needed. Sometimes the father may even remove what was given by the mother to help draw out inner strength in the child. See Figure 5-2.

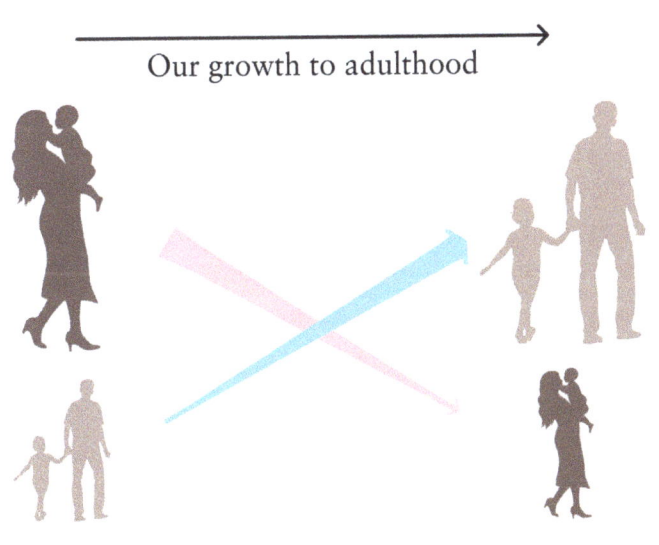

Our growth to adulthood

Figure 5-2 Regardless of which parent does it, as we grow, we need less mothering and more fathering

A single mom paid for piano lessons for her daughter, drove her to lessons, told her when it was time to practice and made sure she did the work. Was the mom mothering or fathering her daughter?

A single mom paid for piano lessons for her daughter and drove her to lessons. The daughter was responsible for her own practice and to remind mom when to take her to lessons. Was the mom mothering or fathering?

We Are Confident That We Can Add Value to an Organization

When we know some of our design and have developed some of our core abilities, we form personal goals and passionate plans to develop even more talents and abilities. We also are confident that when we join an organization, we will add value to it.

> Fulfillment and productivity flow when we know our unique design and are operating out of it. When we are skillfully operating out of our design, we are positioned for creativity. When an entire team is in this position, explosive creativity can result!

Recovering from This Missed Stage of Growth

Parents who don't understand the importance of developing the core design in their children might rely on mass schooling to develop their children. Mass schooling has its benefits, but when this schooling merely pushes a child through the system without attention to the child's unique design, the child is likely to grow up having never learned what is in their core design or how to develop it.

> Futility makes us feel we are useless and life is pointless. We recognize we should have more to offer, but we don't know how to find it or develop it.

Having missed this stage of growth, life might look like this.

- I have an excellent education, credentials and skills, but life is not fulfilling. This "something missing" feeling leads to futility and frustration.

- My job or work is boring and dull, and productivity is low. I find little fulfillment or joy in what I do.

- I don't have passionate plans for my future. I feel dead-ended in my career or job, and yet I don't know what's missing.

- I hope for and expect unending mothering. I love cruise ships – every need is met and there is nothing for me to do but receive.

- I will not embrace productive pain. Why should I bother because I don't believe it will take me anywhere.

- I settle for lack of fulfillment, and, therefore, I depend on external reward to find a reason to work hard. I might focus on affirmation from others, money or promotions at work.

> In a career, a person who does not know what treasures they have will be bored and long for retirement. Or they will focus on money or position. This last mindset can lead to the Jotham curse.

Remember it's never too late to grow up. To grow into this stage:

1. Look back at earlier stages of growth, especially stage two. Do I know what gives me pleasure and what I naturally do well without trying hard? The sweet spot is to find what I love to do that comes easy for me, which is coming out of my design.

2. Make a plan to develop this gift or talent and work the plan.

For earlier stages of growth, we need a community to help us, but we can independently work our way through this stage of growth.

CONCEPTS

In this part of the chapter, we discuss some concepts and skills for developing ourselves. We begin by contrasting Greek and Hebraic learning methods. One method leads to slavery and the other leads to sonship. Let's explore both.

Concept 5.1 Greek Learning

Greek learning is systematic, sequential, focused on content and driven by efficiency. The goal or product of Greek learning is cognitive knowledge and skills. Greek learning is used in traditional education and in many other learning environments. Let's see how it works in traditional education.

Teacher as Boss Leader

A teacher actively leads and controls the learning process and students are expected to passively follow and receive. The teacher assigns students the learning objectives, provides resources to learn the material and tests on the material. The mind is improved, and skills are learned.

The student is mostly a passive learner (see Figure 5-3), while the teacher is expected to keep the ball rolling by making decisions regarding topics to learn, learning objectives, curriculum, assignments of classwork and homework, assessment tools, evaluations, and depth and pace of learning and is responsible for student satisfaction, motivation and discipline and assigning grades to measure student progress.

To assign and assess the depth of learning, an educator normally uses the Bloom's Taxonomy model. See Figure 5-4.

Figure 5-3 The teacher is viewed as actively pouring into the student what the student passively receives

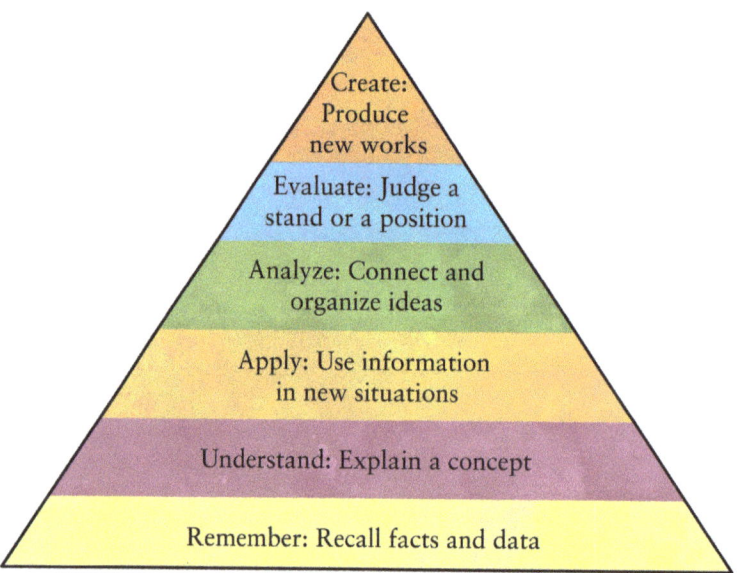

Figure 5-4 Blooms Taxonomy guides cognitive learning and creativity based on the accepted normal

Students as Followers and Slaves

When we consider how the teacher in traditional education is the engine and the student is expected to passively follow, it's shocking to realize how we are teaching our students to be good slaves who follow well the directives of those above us. The student is trained to

- Follow the structure and authority in the learning process as a passive learner.
- Learn the objectives for cognitive knowledge and skills and submit to the assessment.
- Stay within the confines of those who decide for us what and how we will learn.
- Use the accepted normal when judging the merits of positions, ideas and new works.
- Accept grades assigned to us by others to measure how well we are doing.

Focus on Mind and Body

With Greek learning:

- The mind is central to gathering and processing information and learning new academic and vocational skills.

- Knowledge and skills are more important than relationships.

- Focus is on what we can understand, how we see the world and what we can accomplish, which is the premise of humanism.

- The human spirit is largely ignored.

- The soul is taught to passively accept what others teach without questioning the premise of what is being taught.

- The result of being in a slave-structured institution as children taught with the Greek methods is we grow up to become **consumer learners**, seeking knowledge and skills prepackaged by others. See Figure 5-5.

Figure 5-5. The hungry consumer learner looks for prepackaged and finished learning products

Before we throw up our hands in exasperation at the realization that we have been raised as slaves to become consumer learners, let's turn our attention to how God intended that our children learn.

A friend, hungry to learn, read the entire manuscript of this book and then told me the book just didn't work for her. I asked her what she got from the Growth Projects. She said, "Oh, I didn't do any of the projects or answer the questions. I just read the book." She is a hungry, but passive consumer learner. To truly learn, we must actively engage with the content to make it our own.

Concept 5.2 Hebraic Learning

Hebraic learning is random, focused on context and process, and relationship driven. The goal of Hebraic learning is to develop the whole person, spirit, soul and body, who is able to live life to fulfillment in a life-giving family and community.

In Hebraic learning, cognitive knowledge and skills are learned, but they are not the primary focus, which is to build the whole person. Think of a playing field as a means to an end. For example, soccer (see Figure 5-6) can be a playing field toward the end goal of building a whole person. Soccer, without a doubt, requires active learning and uncovers a need to grow character, attitude and values. When there is a bump in the road, such as two players cannot get along, a wise coach will pull these two players off the field to address personal character issues. Playing good soccer cannot happen unless a person has good character.

Hebraic learning involves active learning in real life. Major differences in Greek learning in our traditional school systems and Hebraic learning in family and community are:

Responsibility for learning:

- Parents and students agree that they, not the school or the teachers, are responsible for the education of the student. Professional teachers and a school might be engaged to assist and support.

- A person is in charge of their own development and learning, which is called active learning.

- The human spirit is involved. As problems or failures arise, we invite our spirits to help the soul to troubleshoot the root cause of the problem and solve problems as we connect to God and His wisdom, using spirit tools and/or soul tools.

Figure 5-6 Soccer is the playing field that reveals the need to grow in spirit, soul and body

- Fathering teachers (parents, mentors and professional educators) build strong relationships with their students, model good character and work ethic and help students grow and build.

- Students are given as much autonomy as they can handle. The home or school provides learning resources, such as online curriculum, that students can study at their own pace.

- In a homeschool co-op or school setting, the atmosphere feels more like a synchronizing family than a formal classroom.

What is learned and how it's learned:

- Everyone agrees on basic cognitive skills all must learn, such as reading, writing, arithmetic, basic science, literature, history, clear thinking, and problem solving.

- Basic spiritual skills include life-giving connections and submission to the Trinity, including the ability to hear and follow the voice of God, Bible study and mediation, and being led by our human spirits.

- Teachers continually help a student mature through the stages of growth and unpack their design.

- As soon as a student has mastered the basic cognitive skills done by all, they learn skills that match up with their design.

- Everyone helps everyone. Older children help the younger ones. Teachers provide one-on-one mentoring, and they seldom lecture before a class. Students work in learning teams where they share the work and learn together.

- As situations arise, a person is required to learn and grow to meet the challenge at hand.

- Many real-life and pseudo-life problems and projects are solved and built by the students.

- As real-life problems or projects arise, students are motivated by a felt need, also called inquiry learning. The need to know is created by the project or problem at hand.

- When students are mature enough, they will take on the responsibility to develop skills in a trade, professional career or business owner.

How assessments and evaluations happen:

- <mark>Life itself becomes the assessment tool.</mark> Life brings many challenges, such as solving problems, helping others, time management, goal setting, selection of topics to study and projects to do, getting along with peers and leaders, and syncing in a family or work team. As challenges are faced and overcome, the student is considered successful.

- Students who believe they have mastered a challenge are responsible to demonstrate mastery to their parents and teachers. All agree the topic is mastered before they move forward to the next topic. Grade levels and grades (A, B, C, D or F) are optional.

- Everyone evaluates the quality of work. Students are taught how to evaluate their own work, and their evaluation of their own work is considered primary.

- When students graduate from this homeschool, co-op or intuitional school, they will have accomplished the first six stages of growth and moving into the seventh stage. They will be on track to develop vocational skills suitable to their design, and they will have an intimate relationship with God as His sons who can build His Kingdom.

Figure 5-7 shows the four-step process we have been using for creative problem solving throughout the book. How does this figure compare to Bloom's Taxonomy shown in Figure 5-4?

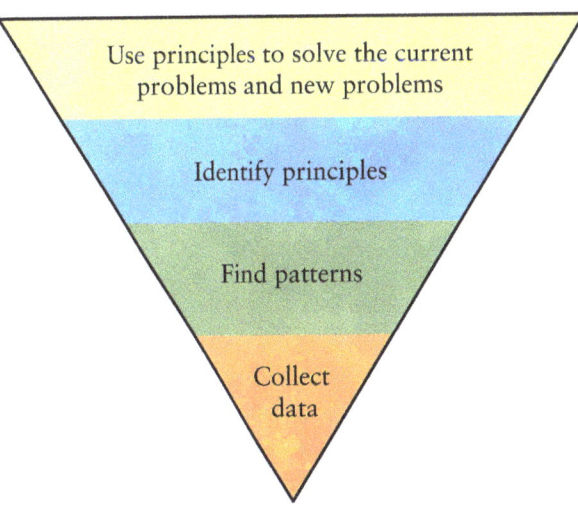

Figure 5-7 Four steps to creative problem solving

Teacher as Fathering Leader

The Hebraic teacher (parent, mentor, or professional educator) takes on a mothering role and quickly progresses to a fathering role as soon as possible. ==The fathering teacher is a friend, role model and mentor who cheers on and unpacks their students.== The process of learning is driven by the needs, hopes and dreams of the student in a life-giving community.

One of the most successful models for Hebraic learning is to homeschool while running a family business. Everyone in the family works and grows together (see Figure 5-8).

Figure 5-8 A family business is an effective way to raise children using Hebraic learning to grow slaves to sons who know how to build

In this book, we work to develop spirit, soul and body, using Hebraic learning methods. The random and cyclic nature of learning is the way this book was designed to be used, as you dip in and out of it to whatever you need to help you in the moment.

We learn about Hebraic (Hebrew) learning in the Scriptures. God used these methods to raise up the Israelites (Hebrews), and Jesus discipled His apostles.

We Learn Best When We Are Ready

I took my 10-year-old granddaughter, Cari, fishing. On the drive there, she told me that when her dad and uncle take her fishing, they try to teach her all kinds of things about fishing, but she just wanted to fish! I took note.

For about an hour, she enjoyed dropping her hook and bob into the shallow water, watching the small fish nibble at her bait. Then she walked over to where I was casting and tried to cast, tangling her line. As we untangled her line, I quietly asked, "Would you like me to show you how to cast?" As she nodded yes, I quickly showed her the motion, making sure she saw when to release the line. On her first try, she made a beautiful cast with great delight. She said, "I didn't understand when to release the line. I was doing it when the rod was behind me."

Her dad and uncle are way better fishermen and casters than I, and I'm sure they tried to teach her to cast with greater skill. But I honored her desire to not be taught until she was ready to learn and change.

For thought and discussion:

1. How do the terms "felt need" and "inquiry learning" fit in your understanding of how I taught Cari to cast?

2. Give an example of someone trying to teach you something you were not ready to learn.

3. How could that person have watched you, waiting for when you were ready?

4. What are some things we must teach new employees that they must learn whether they are ready or not?

A New School in Myanmar (Burma)

Recently, a group of us launched a new school in Yangon, Myanmar (formally Burma), with a lead teacher, two part-time teachers and 16 students in a one room building. We worked for months to build the culture, writing much of this book as we discussed, envisioned and planned the culture for our new school. Here are a few fundamental actions we decided to take and what happened during the first week:

- All parents, students and teachers signed agreements that parents and students are responsible for the education of the students and our school will support them.

- Each morning, students recited the creed in Chapter 1, which set the tone for the day.

- We set the goal for the first two weeks for everyone to know who they are as sons of God, hear the voice of God, and become a team who care for and support each other.

- By the end of the first week, all students were able to hear the voice of God. Figure 5-9 shows a picture 8-year-old Victor drew on the third day of school when he asked to see Jesus.

Figure 5-9 Jesus, the Tree of Life, and Adam and Eve as drawn by Victor

Notice in Victor's drawing the combination of imagination and revelation. Adam and Eve hiding behind bushes came from Sunday School curriculum, and Jesus as the Tree of Life came from revelation. Both can work together to grow us in our perceptions of God and His ways.

05

- Somehow this picture inspired Victor to ask his teacher, "May I write a book about me?" The question led to our idea to collect all the art students have drawn for a few months as we ask students to explore what their story with God will be. Next semester we plan to ask a team of older students to research what it will take to produce a bound book created by each student. This team of book publishers will be responsible for buying the publication equipment and teaching the younger students to use it. A school project was born by Victor's wonderful question!

- On Friday, another child asked his teacher, "Why doesn't everyone in the world know about this school?" So now we're thinking of a project to write a brochure about the school that will be used to recruit new students.

- Everyone works to only speak English in the classroom, and cognitive learning is accomplished by online American homeschool curriculum.

- We are creating projects to build cognitive skills and all kinds of other skills and growth. As we build a project and encounter a problem in relationships, attitude, or character, we stop the process and focus on addressing our ultimate product – the whole person.

- We have defined the product of our school as whole adults able to rebuild their nation. Our goals for the next two years are each person will be able to:

  - Get along with all classes and genders of people
  - Speak, listen, read and write fluent English
  - Think for themselves, without being told what to think
  - Solve problems in all kinds of playing fields

- Students assess themselves, supported by parents and teachers, as to which stage of growth they have achieved, and the skills needed to have a vocation in Myanmar. When all agree they have achieved their goals, they will graduate from our school, and we will have an enormous and magnificent celebration!

- In the meantime, we celebrate every student who achieves and those who keep persevering even when they have not yet met a benchmark.

- We are forming our first project designed to rebuild the nation. This year, older students are learning about the seven curses and blessings in the book of Judges and then will study the history of their nation, looking for evidence of these curses at work. Next year, our plan is to create strategies and projects to move in the opposite spirit of these curses to invite God's blessings into the nation. Then we plan to build businesses and other projects in Yangon to implement our plans. Our hope is that by the fourth or fifth year, our school will be running one or more successful businesses that will pay the monthly expenses. The school will be self-sustaining, and Yangon will be changed.

For thought and discussion:

1. How does our plan to rebuild the nation line up with the four steps to solve a problem?

2. In Chapter 3, we described the four ways people are motivated. How are these four motivators used in our school?

3. Create and describe a way you would teach Bible to the older students, ages 11 through 17.

4. Create and describe a way you would guide and/or train the 16 students in our school, ages 6 through 16, to help each other and become a team.

5. Dorothy homeschools her three children. She complained that they spent all day trying to learn a new math skill, when what they really needed was to discuss attitudes toward schoolwork. What advice would you give Dorothy about time management?

Concept 5.3 Thriving in Our Jobs and Careers: Stewardship

In our quest to develop ourselves, let's explore the personal growth and skills for building that can come through jobs, internships and volunteer programs we participate in. Even our role as a student can be considered a job.

How does the principle of stewardship apply to our jobs? Let's look for this principle in these verses:

> *Slaves, obey your earthly masters with respect and fear, and with sincerity of heart, just as you would obey Christ. Obey them not only to win their favor when their eye is on you, but as slaves of Christ, doing the will of God from your heart. Serve wholeheartedly, as if you were serving the Lord, not people, because you know that the Lord will reward each one for whatever good they do, whether they are slave or free.*
>
> *And masters, treat your slaves in the same way. Do not threaten them, since you know that he who is both their Master and yours is in heaven, and there is no favoritism with him.*

Ephesians 6:5–9

Figure 5-10 Who do you work for and who pays you? Your boss or Jesus?

Paul directed both slaves and masters to see themselves working for God. See Figure 5-10.

This principle of stewardship applies to both leaders and followers:

- **I serve God.** All that I do on the job is for God. I answer to Him for my attitudes and actions. He watches what I do even when my boss does not.

- **God is my provider.** "My God shall supply all your need, according to His riches in glory in Christ Jesus." Philippians 4:19

  A huge key to the principle of stewardship in employment is to disconnect our provision from our paychecks and disconnect our paychecks from our jobs. Our paychecks are not our provider or our provision. We serve God with our jobs and He provides well when we walk uprightly with Him. This truth alone will transform how we see our jobs.

- **Everything is Father filtered.** Even though I might serve a difficult boss in a difficult environment, I can thrive when I know this is God's assignment for me and He turns everything for good when I trust Him.

  For the LORD God is a sun and shield: the LORD will give grace and glory: no good thing will he withhold from them that walk uprightly. Psalm 84:11

- **We have to know we are sent.** If you believe God chose this job and sent you to it, you can rest that good will come from it. That's not to say one day you might find it necessary to fire your boss and move on to a different job.

Living for an Audience of One

Robert F. Kennedy Jr, a prominent American attorney, tells the story of his quest to know if God exists. Unsure, he decided to live his life for a season as though God was watching him all the time.

He told of rushing through an airport terminal late for a plane when he tossed chewing gum paper into a trash can as he ran. He noticed the paper fell on the floor. Under the premise that God was watching, he turned back, picked up the paper and threw it in the can. He made his plane and described that day as a turning point in his life. Things started to come together. Lots of things. And then he realized he was sensing and hearing God's direction for his life.

For thought and discussion:

1. How was Mr. Kennedy practicing the principle of stewardship in his quest to know if God exists?

2. Much of Kennedy's life has been devoted to protecting the environment, including simple things like not leaving trash on the floor. What might be a good guess as to his Trinitarian design? Explain your answer.

3. Kennedy reportedly made the statement, "Environmental work is spiritual work." How do you interpret that statement? If you were sitting with Kennedy, what three questions would you ask him to unpack that statement?

Concept 5.4
Thriving in Our Jobs and Careers: The Leader's Role

Whether we are a student leader or CEO of a large company, we are all called to lead knowing God is our leader and modeling His leadership style. We can be a boss leader, mothering leader or fathering leader. Jesus modeled both mothering leadership and fathering leadership.

Mothering leaders teach a son how to receive in an ever-changing environment, resourcing a son and teaching a son how to use these resources. Fathering leaders are responsible for teaching sons how to give and build. He generally does that by putting incremental degrees of responsibility on the son.

When fathered, will a son cave, whine, blame or try to take back rights taken from him, or will they grow into the new challenge? The father is responsible for leading this growth process.

Here are some guidelines to help a leader navigate teaching a son to give and build:

1. **Decide what and how much responsibility you will put on a son.**

   - **Design.** As best as possible, understand the design of a son. Try to assign tasks that align with what God ordained this son to be and do.

   - **Experience.** The idea is to stretch without overwhelming. Put on the son what is a reasonable challenge based on their current experiences.

   - **Character.** If a son is emotionally fragile or has obvious character flaws, address these wounds on the inside before putting unfair responsibilities on them.

> Recall that a slave is not interested in the values of their masters. Sons, however, know the values of their fathers and share these same values.

2. **Set expectations.**

It's up to the leader to explain their values to a son; a leader should not expect a follower to read their minds about what's important or how the follower will be evaluated. Explain your values in detail so the son understands what is important to you and what motivates you. Encourage the why questions which a follower must know before they understand your values. Set clear expectations as to how you will judge whether the son did well.

For example, when working on a project, it must be clear to all involved who is on point – the team leader who coordinates the entire project. All information must flow through this one person; otherwise, confusion can result. This communication flow can be a metric for evaluation.

3. **Mitigate risk using high or low insurance.**

Before a son earns trust, a leader must risk on a son and find out by observation where the strengths and weaknesses are. A leader can mitigate the degree of risk by the levels of insurance, which is the time and effort the leader must invest to supervise the son:

- **High insurance.** For a new hire, you need high insurance until the new hire has earned some trust. When you assign a task to a new hire, don't micromanage them, but do check in often to make sure the person is on task, not wasting time, not violating your values, and is following through with the expectations you have set. When checking in, the best way to lead is by asking questions such as, "Do you think you used your time wisely this afternoon? How would you evaluate your work on the project so far?"

- **Low insurance.** For a son who has already earned a great deal of your trust, you don't need to check up as often. You can allow the person to work more independently and with more freedom for creativity. Apply varying degrees of insurance for varying degrees of risk.

4. **Dialog and debrief at the end of the project or within a reasonable time period.**

This step is essential, and it's extremely important the son feels safe in the process. "Failure is normal and highly valued." If the project was a success, celebrate well. If the project was a failure, see it as an opportunity to learn and grow.

5. **Adjust the level of risk or trust based on what was learned.**

After the debriefing process, move forward with what was learned.

- If the son did well, trust is earned, more responsibility can be given, and lower insurance is appropriate.

- If the project was a failure, trust is lost, and higher insurance is needed.

  o If caused by lack of experience, more supervision is needed or projects assigned need to be scaled back. Is more training appropriate?

  o If caused by violating the son's design, try to find another place in the organization where they can better work in their design. Is there a way you can invest in the son to better discover their design?

  o If caused by a character flaw, suggest some resources to assist the person's transformation. Somone can offer, "May I walk with you through this?" Transformation requires embracing productive pain. If the person is not willing to embrace that pain, the leader eventually must enforce that responsibility. It is not okay long term to stay in a character flaw. If denial or refusal to face the pain prevails, perhaps the person doesn't fit in the organization.

Concept 5.5
Thriving in Our Jobs and Careers: The Maturing Son's Role

Are you a servant or a son? We are all in process somewhere on the many planks in the bridge that lead from a servant who struggles to sync with their leaders and God into a mature son able to give and build effectively and joyfully in community. When we sync with our leaders, we share their core values, and we use their authority as our own to build and create.

Here are a few reasons why it's important to sync to our leaders:

- **To honor and give glory to God.** As we embrace the values of our righteous leaders, we can better embrace God's values to honor and sync with Him.

- **To receive more authority.** The more we share our leaders' values, the more they trust us and can delegate their authority to us. The more authority we have, the more we can build and create and delegate that authority to those we lead.

- **To possess birthright.** As we learn to lead others, we can build a community that collectively can possess our birthrights.

Here are a few tips to help you sync with your leaders:

- **Make sure you understand what is expected of you.** If you don't know where you are going, you probably won't get there. Know what you are expected to do and how you will be evaluated on meeting those expectations. If you don't know, ask; don't guess.

- **Ask the why questions.** If a leader doesn't explain why you are expected to do something, it's your responsibility to ask. Slaves focus on outward behavior and are satisfied to obey their masters without knowing why. A son is motivated from the heart and needs to understand what motivates their leaders. To be a son, you must know and embrace the values of your leaders.

> A leader builds up their people by imparting their core values and delegating their authority.

> "The man who knows how will always have a job. The man who knows why will always be his boss." Ralph Waldo Emerson
>
> The point to this quote: Learn to ask the why questions.

- **Know why you are here.** Are you here for the paycheck, yourself or the Kingdom of God? When you know that you are motivated by love of God and His Kingdom, you are better positioned to joyfully flow in community and sync with leaders.

- **Everything is Father filtered.** Many of the greats in Scripture were required to serve ungodly people as their leaders. Father allowed that to happen to mature His sons. When you trust that God means you well and knew your chosen leader had flaws, you can settle in and grow where God wants you to grow. When you have grown to be a larger person because of this situation, God can move you on to bigger things.

- **Every problem is an opportunity to grow.** Allow the stretching. When things don't go as planned, expect to discuss what is wrong, how it went wrong, why it went wrong, and what we all need to do to make it better. Own your junk. Speak truth with compassion. Embrace productive pain. Develop a healthy model of reconciliation that you learned about in Chapter 3.

Will You Bet on Yourself?

Jill is in her twenties. She finished a couple of years of college before she ran out of money and went to work as a grocery store cashier. On the side, she coaches a softball team of middle school girls living in the inner city of her metropolitan area. Then she applied as a personal assistant to the CIO (Chief Information Officer) of a small company near where she lives.

After a couple of interviews, the CEO told her they were extremely skeptical she could handle the job with so little education and experience. And yet they were both impressed with her character, as she gave so passionately into the lives of these young, impoverished girls. The CEO offered her a 90-day probation and made it clear that she would be let go after 90 days if she failed the test. He explained she would be judged on two expectations: Prove she had good chemistry with the CIO and prove that she was a quick and independent learner.

For thought and discussion:

1. During the interview process, how did the CEO evaluate Jill as to design, experience and character?

2. What risk was the CEO taking? How did he mitigate that risk?

3. If you were the CIO, how would you lead Jill for the first 30 days? 60 days? 90 days on the job? For example, how would you supervise her? What tasks or projects might you assign her? What criteria would you use to evaluate her? How might the CIO help Jill feel safe when she is being evaluated?

4. If you were Jill, what would you focus on during the 90-day probation period?

"The Great Game of Business" by Jack Stack

In Chapter 2, you learned about Jack Stack. He saved a manufacturing plant from bankruptcy using an open book management structure where most employees were part owners in the company. Their new culture changed employee mindsets of "I'm just here to do a job and go home" to that of owners who were "here to make a contribution to our lives." They created a culture where people couldn't blame others for the situation they were in.

Some fundamental changes Jack made include:

- Build credibility by always telling the truth about scheduling, stock flow, cash flow, sales and everything financial. Tell the truth to employees, owners, bankers, vendors, customers, schedulers and anyone else who needed to know.

- Establish a win-win culture. Never take advantage of anyone and don't shortchange yourself or your people. Don't try to win by intimidation or boasting.

- Build confidence in other people. Leaders aren't perfect and don't always have the answers. Share your problems with those you lead and expect they will come up with solutions. Better to promote someone too early than not early enough.

- Teach the numbers. Let your people know everything you know about the company. Everyone routinely sees the balance sheet and income statement. More importantly, everyone knows exactly how their performance affects one or more items on these documents. They observe the effects of what they do. Jack called these documents the company's scoreboard and each person kept a scorecard, which showed how their performance affected the company scoreboard.

For thought and discussion:

1. We all need a way to observe and measure our success. In Jack's company, what was defined as success? What are some metrics that Jack used to measure success? What are some metrics that employees use to measure their success?

2. Many companies are built on a master/slave culture. Jack strived to build his company on a father/son culture. Describe how a company or other organization that you personally are familiar with is built on a master/slave culture.

3. For this company, describe three changes you would suggest to shift it toward a father/son culture. Which of the three changes would be easiest to implement? Why?

4. Someone once said, "No money, no ministry." Why should a church or other non-profit include money matters (donations or expenses) as at least one metric for success?

5. If you were to own your own company, would you use open book management where all employees and owners had full access to the income statement and balance sheet? Discuss with your discussion partners the pros and cons of open book management.

 Kahlil Gibran and His Teachers

Kahlil Gibran, an immigrant to the United States from Syria and world-famous artist and poet, considered his book of poetry, "The Prophet," his greatest work. My most favorite quote from this book is, "Even as the strings of a lute are alone though they quiver with the same music. Give your hearts, but not into each other's keeping. For only the hand of Life can contain your hearts."

Gibran lived in a poor area of Boston and attended public school, where his teachers noticed his unusual interest in art and theatre. They connected him to Fred Holland Day, an artist in his own right, who mentored Gibran and set him on a journey to fame.

For thought and discussion:

1. Public school teachers seldom have the time or energy to explore the design of their students. How fortunate for Gibran that these teachers did. Have you ever had a teacher who pointed out to you something about your design that you had not seen? Describe the impact of that event.

2. Have you ever seen an untapped design in another person? What can you do to help them see it and you affirm it?

3. According to the quote from Gibran, what is the danger in synchronizing so closely with another you lose yourself in the relationship?

We now turn our attention to how the spirit realm can obstruct or release us into our birthrights.

Concept 5.6 Who is Leviathan and Why Do We Care?

Imagine what you might have felt if you had been Isaiah on the day he said:

I saw the Lord, high and exalted, seated on a throne; and the train of his robe filled the temple. Above him were seraphim, each with six wings: With two wings they covered their faces, with two they covered their feet, and with two they were flying. And they were calling to one another:

"Holy, holy, holy is the Lord Almighty; the whole earth is full of his glory."

At the sound of their voices the doorposts and thresholds shook and the temple was filled with smoke.

"Woe to me!" I cried. "I am ruined! For I am a man of unclean lips, and I live among a people of unclean lips, and my eyes have seen the King, the Lord Almighty."

Isaiah 6:1-5

Isaiah had many experiences with God. Why did this one rattle him so much? Maybe it was because he saw a new facet of God he was not prepared to see. Maybe because he was standing at the threshold to the temple when it began to quake as the terrifying seraphim flew overhead, loudly worshipping God. Maybe the smoke? Maybe his conviction of his sins and that of his people? Maybe all of this shook him to his core.

Regardless, the solution to his terrible predicament came when a seraph touched him with fire:

Then one of the seraphim flew to me with a live coal in his hand, which he had taken with tongs from the altar.

With it he touched my mouth and said, "See, this has touched your lips; your guilt is taken away and your sin atoned for."

Then I heard the voice of the Lord saying, "Whom shall I send? And who will go for us?" And I said, "Here am I. Send me!"

Isaiah 6:6-8

After Isaiah was touched with fire, he was willing and ready to step into the new calling God offered him. The word seraph (singular of seraphim) means "fiery serpent," which fits with the nature of God as a "consuming fire." Hebrews 12:29

Anne Hamilton in her book "The Threshold Guardians & the Covenant Defender" makes a case that the fallen Leviathans, as fire breathing serpents described in Job 41 and Isaiah 27, were once seraphim guarding the throne room of God. Because the gifts and callings of God are irrevocable, even in their fallen state, they can still challenge us when we approach a season of entering into our birthrights and callings as Isaiah did in Isaiah 6.

To support Anne's position, we see in Numbers 21:6 where God sent seraphim to bite His people when they grew impatient that it was taking too long to enter into their birthright land and complained to God and Moses. To deal with the situation, God instructed Moses to make a seraph, and Moses made a snake and put it on a pole. (Most translations use the word snakes in this Scripture, but the literal translation is seraphim snakes.)

When Jesus spoke with Nicodemus in John 3, He compared Himself to a righteous seraph who would give life to His people:

> *Just as Moses lifted up the snake in the wilderness, so the Son of Man must be lifted up, that everyone who believes may have eternal life in him.*

John 3:14

The analogy further fits when you consider Jesus as the Passover Lamb where the Blood was placed on the doorposts and threshold to deliver us from death. When we eat Him as the Passover Lamb, we enter into a threshold covenant with Him, depending on Him for our everything.

In Arthur Burk's album "Joy Unstoppable" we hear about these same concepts.

- We need the seven righteous heads of Levithan to help us through the transitions into our callings and birthrights.

- When we attempt to step into our rightful birthrights but our hearts are not aligned with God's heart, the unrighteous seven heads of Levithan can challenge and hurt us. They twist and bring chaos to thrust us backwards so we cannot go forward across the thresholds into our birthrights. See Figure 5-11.

- With the help of the seven righteous heads, we are free to frolic with joy unstoppable in our relationships with the Trinity and in possessing our birthrights.

Figure 5-11 The negative heads of Leviathan can block or divert us from transitioning into our birthrights

So how do we cross over a threshold into our birthrights without evoking an unrighteous head of Leviathan? The delightful picture that Anne Hamilton paints for us is the bridegroom picking up his bride and carrying her over the threshold. In times of transitions into birthright, it's necessary that we go deeper into our intimate relationship with Jesus, our Bridegroom, becoming even more dependent on Him than before.

When He carries us over, we can be assured we are safe from Leviathan's attacks. ==This is a beautiful picture of merging together intimacy with Him with the dominion we need to build His Kingdom.==

Arthur talks about the joy of a child who never knew pain. It's a beautiful picture of frolicking in water that God intended for His beautiful creation, the righteous Leviathan.

Let's look at each of the seven unrighteous and righteous hands of Leviathan and what we can do to gain earned authority over an unrighteous head and invite the righteous head to help us. See Table 5-1. Remember that entering our birthrights is not a one-time event but a journey of growing in intimacy with God and building His Kingdom. As always, it's all about the King! David described it this way:

But God is my King from long ago; he brings salvation on the earth.

It was you who split open the sea by your power; you broke the heads of the monster in the waters.

It was you who crushed the heads of Leviathan and gave it as food to the creatures [people] of the desert.

Psalm 74:12-14

Table 5-1 Seven Heads of Leviathan

| Head | To Invite the Negative Head | | To Invite the Rightous Head | |
	Actions	Effects	Actions	Effects
1	We ignore God and His ways. We seek God but in a lazy way.	Darkness in our lives. We are invisible. We attract dark people.	We intentional seek God, His light and His ways.	Light is on our paths. We are visible. Righteous people see and notice us. We attract high quality people into our lives.
2	We use God's authority to help ourselves or others. Or we refuse to use God's authority and work in our own strength.	Weather works against us. We have problems with air (mold in the air or lung problems).	We use God's authority to bring glory to God and only for His purposes.	Weather cooperates with us. Air works with and for us.
3	We don't pursue truth and the life of God.	We age prematurely. Disease and other physical problems distract us. Our stuff wears out prematurely.	We focus on giving life to others. We seek life and revelation for ourselves and others.	We live to a good old age with healthy and active bodies. Our stuff lasts.
4	We exploit and use the time of others. We miss our appointments with God.	Time works against us. There is never enough time.	We sync to God in using our time and honor the time of others.	God syncs us to Him. Time works for us. We have extra time.
5	We consume resources without building beyond ourselves. Our bad parenting comes from not releasing our children to God. We can nurture in a wrong way and enable.	Sound works against us. Electronic equipment gives trouble. Communication is difficult and people don't hear our hearts. It's hard to hear God.	We find and use raw materials to build beyond ourselves. We practice 3 healthy levels of parenting.	We have good communication with people, and people hear our hearts. Sound works for us. Electronic equipment is reliable. We hear God's heart and will.

Head	To Invite the Negative Head		To Invite the Rightous Head	
	Actions	Effects	Actions	Effects
6	We accept lose-win, win-lose, and lose-lose situations as necessary and normal.	Institutional structures don't work for us. Transitions into new seasons are rough and hindered. Flow is hindered.	We are committed to win-win dealings with all people.	Institutional structures work with us and are life-giving. We have smooth transitions into new seasons. We have freedom to pursue our birthrights.
7	We depend on others to connect to God. We savor the spiritual experiences of others but don't pursue God for ourselves. We obey God but don't initiate or build past that.	We experience lack of spiritual vitality and little or no protection from spiritual defilement. We cannot unpack the spiritual treasures we have.	We pursue multiple ways to connect with God (land, nature, water, motion, Bible study, worship, work, fun). We seek more varied and in-depth experiences with God.	Nature cooperates with us as an onramp to heaven. We have wider experiences with God. We are able to enter and explore more of heaven.

For more information about the negative and righteous heads of Leviathan, listen to the audio album "Joy Unstoppable" by Arthur at **theSLG.com.**

With the help of the righteous heads of Leviathan, problems are solved as we get to know God better. Out of these experiences with God, we can develop our life messages that others need. As we help many know God in these ways, we find ourselves experiencing our birthrights. See Figure 5-12.

Our Birthright

Our Life Messages That Others Need

Our Experiences With God

Our Greatest Problems

Figure 5-12 Our birthrights emerge as our experiences with God develop into our life message

SOLVING PROBLEMS

Recall that problems are solved as we collect data, identify patterns and their underlying principles, and use these principles to solve current and future problems.

Problem 5.1
Larry and His Boss Leader

Larry has taken his first real job right out of high school. He decided to take a gap year before college and to find out whether he really wants to be a software engineer and to save a little money for college. His good grades and the CompTIA A+ certification he achieved in high school landed him an IT support job with a large corporation in his city.

The first day on the job, Larry realizes there will be no formal training and he is expected to train himself. On the second day, he messes up big time and causes the accounting department network to crash! He quickly turns to a co-worker with more experience who helps him get the network back up. During that hour, the rest of his team fields calls from accountants. As soon as the problem is resolved, Larry tells his manager what happened and how it was resolved. The following morning, his manager blames the entire situation on Larry in the staff meeting.

> When patterns you observe don't make sense, widen your perspective to consider some new principles, which might explain the patterns. Try filtering the data through the seven heads of Leviathan.

Answer the following questions:

1. After his manager spoke, all eyes turn to Larry, waiting to hear his response. If you were Larry, which principles would you use in your response? What would you say?

2. Recall that people are either takers, makers or breakers. Which do you think Larry is? His manager?

3. People on a team are either workers or blamers. The best leaders are workers who inspire and never blame. How could Larry's manager have been a fathering leader in this situation?

4. How can Larry use this first week on the job to gain earned authority over the first head of Leviathan? Over the second head of Leviathan? Over the sixth head of Leviathan?

5. How can Larry view what his manager did so that Larry can truly celebrate what happened?

Problem 5.2 Surrendering Our Finances to God

To separate our job from our paycheck, we can recognize that we work for King Jesus at whatever job He has assigned us. Whether dental hygienist, lawyer, assembly line worker, secretary, employee, self-employed or freelancer, the money we receive is not tied to our success in these areas when Jesus is our King and Provider.

Mary is a dental hygienist and works in a dental office using the equipment the dentist has provided and receives a salary-based income. When she finishes cleaning teeth, the patient pays the dental office for her services.

Answer the following questions:

1. As Mary's mentor, she complains to you that her current job does not make enough money, but she believes she has heard from God to stay there. How can you help Mary become a better steward of the income she receives as a dental hygienist?

2. Explain how separating the paycheck from the job makes us better stewards of both our money and our jobs.

3. How can you describe to Mary that Jesus is her provider? Remember the power of an inspiring story. Is there a story from your own life or elsewhere that can help?

4. How can Mary's pay structure be used to help Mary separate in her heart her provision from her job?

5. When we see our provision coming from our employers, how does this invite the negative fifth head of Leviathan?

Problem 5.3 When Does Parenting End?

The opposite of stewardship is a poverty mentality that causes us to hold tight to all we have. Often this can be seen in parenting. People want to own their kids and never really let them go. Healthy parenting can be described in three stages (see Figure 5-13):

- **Stage 1: Lots of mothering.** We provide raw materials and the finished product for our kids. For example, we buy the groceries, make their meals, and clean up the kitchen.

- **Stage 2: A mix of mothering and fathering.** We provide raw materials and expect our children to help produce what they need. For example, we pay for groceries and our kids prepare meals and clean up.

- **Stage 3: Lots of fathering.** We coach our children to gather their own raw materials to produce what they need. For example, our children get a part time job while in college so they can buy their own groceries and fix their own meals.

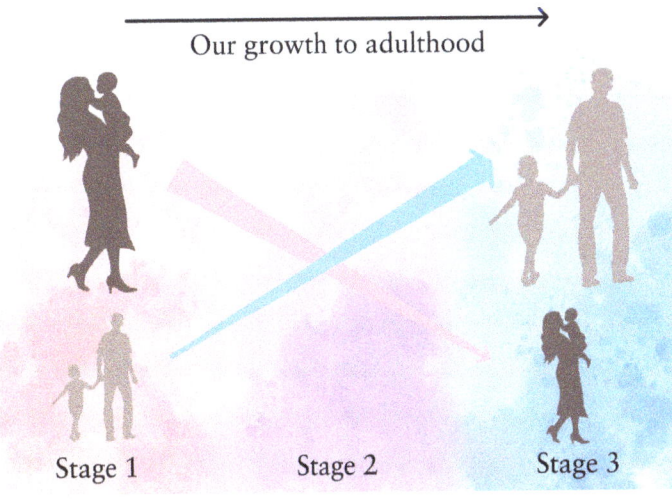

Figure 5-13 Healthy parenting can be viewed in three stages

Suzanna has four daughters and was divorced when the youngest was a baby. She generally has a fathering style of parenting and taught her older three daughters to care for themselves, take responsibility for their lives and work hard. However, she treated Jackie, her youngest, differently. Suzanna was still providing for Jackie up until she married at 30 years old and was still living in her mom's basement. The other daughters often muse how the youngest was raised by a different mother than the older three.

When Suzanna was searching her heart to understand, she realized she was able to trust God with the older three and easily allowed them to "leave the nest with ease and dignity," but she needed and wanted to keep her youngest for her own comfort.

Answer the following questions:

1. Why do you think Suzanne chose to hold Jackie so tightly? How could this situation explain why Suzanne and her oldest daughter have trouble communicating?

2. What can Suzanne's oldest daughter do in the spirit realm to improve her communication with her mom? In the physical realm?

3. Jackie married a man who is unable to provide for his family. What could be the patterns and principles involved in her life? How can Jackie and her husband move in the opposite spirit to better function as a healthy family?

4. How has Suzanne agreed with the poverty spirit? The victim spirit? What truths can she accept as her own to get out of agreement with each?

5. Of the seven stages of growth, which stages do you think Suzanne might need to work on? Why?

6. The older three daughters remember a happy childhood, but Jackie describes it as full of strife and trouble. Why might these siblings view childhood differently?

Problem 5.4 A Family Business and Dishonest Contractor

Olivia, an Exhorter, and John, a Ruler, own a construction business. Oliva serves as the CEO, architect and designer. She makes the final call on how the business operates. John runs the financial end of the business as the CFO. On a large residential renovation job, a subcontractor ran off with money paid up front, leaving the family business in big trouble. John wanted to break the contract with the house owner, but Olivia decided to honor their word to the owner and push through.

Answer the following questions:

1. Olivia works very hard 6 or 7 days a week as she wears many hats in the company, which is like her baby. Which patterns and principles do you see might affect the current situation and how Olivia runs the company?

2. Olivia decided the entire family should chip in to get the subcontractor's work done and still stay on budget and on schedule. Her teenage children started coming to the job site right after school each day and worked until late at night. Some weekends they also worked. The children complained bitterly about the arrangement but felt they had no choice. Which negative patterns and principles might affect these teens in the future? What can they do to go in the opposite spirit so they can be blessed by God?

3. What decisions can each family member make so that, in the future, God can bless their timelines?

4. What decisions can John and Olivia make so that they have better discernment as to which subcontractors to hire?

Problem 5.5 Alice in the Classroom

Alice teaches middle school science. She wants to make a gentle shift in the classroom culture to move from Greek learning to Hebraic and apply as many other principles in this book as she can.

Alice announces on the first day of school that she expects students to help other students and work in learning teams. She divides the class into learning teams of 3 or 4 students.

Answer the following questions:

1. What principles is Alice applying by requiring the students to work in learning teams? How does that foster Hebraic learning?

2. Student A told his team, "I don't care about you, and I don't want to help you." What can Alice say to help this student learn the new culture?

3. During the first week of school, Student B helped a weaker Student C and believes Student C can now do the work. Student C asked for more help, and Student B said, "That's on you, not me." How should Alice handle the situation when both students ask her to referee the situation?

4. One learning team tells another learning team, "If you excel, you make us look bad." Alice draws both teams together to discuss the comment. How can Alice lead the discussion?

5. One student who struggles academically commented privately to Alice, "I've never felt celebrated." How can Alice respond to this student? If you were Alice, how would you implement some protocols for celebration in the classroom?

6. Imagine every student in the classroom is wearing a sign in front that says, "Appreciate me" and one on the back that says, "Make me feel important." What can Alice do to build a culture that helps each student feel more appreciated or important without introducing a spirit of competition?

Problem 5.6 No Path Forward

Jerry purchased a commercial building and rented it to Terrance, who recommended an attorney to draw up the lease. Jerry had little experience with commercial leases and agreed to receive help from this attorney. Because repairs on the building consistently exceed the rental income, Jerry decided to sell the building. In trying to sell, he discovered the lease agreement gives full rights to the leaser and no rights to the landlord to expire or break the lease. The buyer of the building would be required to honor Terrance's lease, which means no buyer is interested in a building with such unsustainable terms.

Answer the following questions:

1. Jerry realized too late that he had made a lease agreement that gave him few rights. Which negative heads of Levithan might be in play? Why?

2. What questions might you ask Jerry to help him understand the principles involved and how he might have invited the negative heads of Levithan?

3. What can Jerry do to gain authority over these negative heads?

4. What patterns and principles might be in play with Terrance that might have a negative impact on his life?

Problem 5.7 Steward Our Children for God

In the American culture, most parents don't require their children to obey at first command and obedience generally follows a parent's raised voice or anger. Suppose you parent two children, four and seven years old, and you realize your children obey you only when you raise your voice in anger.

Answer the following questions:

1. What does it mean for your children to not be your own, but belong to Father God and you are stewarding them as His children and not yours?

2. Which head of Levithan might be at work in the family dynamics causing children to obey only to an angry voice?

3. How can you gain more authority to steward your children for God by cooperating with the righteous heads of Leviathan?

4. Practically, how can you shift family culture so there is more peace and joy in the family?

GROWTH PROJECT

These growth projects are designed to help us grow and learn how to grow others we lead by knowing God better.

Growth Project 5.1
Time Management with Lists and Rocks

When you first learn to accept responsibility to grow and develop yourself, some strategies for managing your priorities and time can help. One powerful yet simple strategy is to keep a to-do list.

Follow these steps to learn to use a to-do list to manage your time.

1. Make a list of all the things you currently have to do. Some items will be urgent, some important, and some nice to have. A few are both urgent and important.

2. Order the list from most important to least important.

3. At the beginning of each day, start with the urgent and important, which is called putting out fires. We all must put out a few fires each day.

4. If there's still any day left, start work on the most important item at the top of your list and work your way down.

Now let's add the rock in the jar to your time management strategy. If you put a large rock in a jar as in Figure 5-14, is the jar full? No, because you can add many small pebbles all the way to the top. Is the jar full now? No, not yet, because you can pour sand in the jar. Is the jar full now? No, because you can pour water into the jar. Is the jar full? Yes, there's nothing more that can fit in the jar.

Figure 5-14 The rock in the jar

What's the lesson from the jar? Your rock represents the most important thing you do today. Although some might see they can fill their day with many big and small things, the point to the story is we could never have put the big rock in the jar if all the other small things were already in it. If you don't know what your rock at the very beginning of the day is and don't get started on it by 10:00AM, you probably won't get to it that day.

Do the following to use this strategy.

1. At the very beginning of each day, take the time to sit with God and ask him, "What is my rock for today?" Most likely it will be something already on your to-do list, but it might not be.

2. You might still have to start your day with the necessary and urgent putting out fires, but start work on your rock as soon as possible. After you have the rock finished, then you can work on your to-do list.

3. If you are not able to get anything else done during the day other than the rock, you can be satisfied in knowing you have done what is important to God.

> "What is my rock for today?" is a son-mode question to ask God. A second question to consider asking God each day is, "What do You want to give me today?" That question is a bride-mode question. We are both brides of Christ and sons of God.

In a Kingdom-minded organization, teach and expect everyone to start their day by asking God what is my rock for the day. A fathering leader might make his or her rounds in the early morning asking each follower, "What is your rock for the day?" When everyone knows their rock, a sense of peace settles into what could be a chaotic day.

Growth Project 5.2
How Did Jesus Lead through Mothering or Fathering?

Go through the Gospel of Luke and list each time Jesus led someone. For example, He led his disciples to eat the last supper and the 70 to go peach and teach. For each incident listed, mark it as fathering leadership or mothering leadership. From your data and the patterns you identified, did Jesus do more mothering or fathering during His years of ministry?

Growth Project 5.3 Assessing Stages of Growth

When you interview someone for a position on a team or to be discipled or mentored, it helps to know where this person is in their stages to maturity and what holes they might have in growth stages not fully completed.

This project can help.

First, answer the 25 questions for yourself. Can you identify a need to grow in one of the stages? To practice your skill of assessing stages of growth, ask a friend for permission to interview them. The more people you interview, the better you get at interviewing.

Stage 1. Inner Strength and Personal Authority

Does the person have an internal strength that is not dependent on external community to stay strong and regulated? If not, the person might occasionally be emotionally wobbly and not grounded, which indicates a lack of belongingness, worth and competence that are needed to build legitimacy based solely on God's love for them.

Ask these questions. The first question is a throw away question designed to lead into the second question.

1. Have you ever seen a tragedy? How did you position yourself? For example, if you saw a car accident, did you drive away or immediately help?

2. Have you been in a tragedy? Who was there for you?

   Listen carefully to the answer. Is there a hint of helplessness, neediness, or building legitimacy on competence in handling tough situations? For example, a woman said she was in a car accident with her brother who was hurt, and she helped him because she was not hurt that much. That sounded good on the surface until a little probing revealed she was 3 years old at the time and had a broken right arm. This lady had built her legitimacy on competence.

Stage 2. Strong Pleasure Center

People with strong pleasure centers know what they like and don't like, which builds the ability to feel their way through a problem and use the intuitive process to make decisions. A leader without a strong pleasure center will get run over by strong team members.

These questions explore a person's pleasure center.

3. Where do you see yourself in 10 years?

4. Which job did you love the most in the past?

5. Describe the worst job you ever had.

6. Which position in this organization would you love the most?

7. Where would you like to go if you had three weeks of paid vacation?

   When describing the worst job, you're looking for the person knowing exactly what they don't like. However, if the person begins to blame and point fingers, they might be blamers and are likely to cause trouble in an organization.

Stage 3. Strong Moral Standards and a Working Reconciliation Model

With these questions, you are probing for a sense of what is morally right. Red flags are finger pointing and blaming. These red flags also indicate the person has no healthy reconciliation model when conflicts occur. A person with no path to peace and closure when mess-ups occur will not have freedom to admit fault or a path forward to grow.

As you ask these questions, listen carefully for blaming and finger pointing. The first question is a throw away question to encourage the conversation to stay positive.

8. Tell me about the best boss you ever had.

9. Now tell me about your worst boss.

10. Describe the worst team you ever worked with.

In this last question, you are probing for a healthy reconciliation model.

Stage 4. Strong Peer Relationships and Ability to Build Community

At this stage of growth, we learn to get along with and enjoy people in a social context without an agenda to produce or work. We enjoy others enjoying their joy. Leaders who cannot build community will end up allowing the dominant person to build the community of the team.

As you ask these questions, look for the person simply enjoying people.

11. Describe an event in a social context, such as a church group, community gathering, party or family event. Where are you in the group? What were you doing?

    Listen for answers that indicate the person is the center of fun, the center of conflict, just watching from the edge, or totally avoids social events that don't provide them work to do.

12. Describe your pets. Do you treat them like people or animals?

    Listen for using pets as substitutes for missing human connections in their life.

13. Do you name things, such as your car, gun or computer?

    Listen for too much of that, which indicates a lack of human connections.

14. Describe your hobbies.

    Listen for hobbies that build relationships vs. hobbies in isolation. No hobbies might indicate a weak pleasure center.

Stage 5. Ability to Develop the Treasures Within

This fifth stage of growth leads to fulfillment, creativity and value added to the organization. A person who does not know about the treasures inside them does not know who they are.

With these two questions, you're looking for knowledge of the treasures and a plan to develop them.

15. What unpacked potential is within you?

16. What would it take to unpack that?

Stage 6. Ability to Build and to Fight for Values That Matter

When you ask these questions about building and fighting, remember you need to know why the person can fight. Is it for a personal offense or high standards? If the fighting is for a personal offense, the person might be a taker or breaker. If they cannot build or fight for principles, they will not add much value to an organization and will simply do as they are told.

As you ask these questions, listen for a maker, breaker or taker.

17. Describe your best building projects that brought the most gratification.

    Listen for stage 5 of growth. Did the project bring money or position or did it bring real fulfillment?

18. Which building project was the most difficult? Why?

19. If you had all the resources you needed, what would you build?

    Listen carefully. If the person doesn't have a project in mind, they are not a builder or maker.

These next three questions are about fighting for values that matter. If a person has risked an important relationship or job to stand on principle, this person has character worth celebrating!

20. Have you ever had to stand on principle and confront somebody that risked the relationship?

21. When have you won?

22. How did you rebuild the relationship after winning a hard fight?

    With this last question, listen for a breaker or maker. A breaker will win but not be concerned about the relationship. A maker will win and, as quickly as possible, work to rebuild a fragile relationship.

Stage 7. Legitimacy as an Adult Who Thinks for Themselves

A mature adult has laid aside voices in the past they disagree with. When we are still listening to the voices of our past, we will not be able to embrace new personal or corporate visions. On a team, a person might not be able to embrace the values of the team leader when the leader has different values from previous leaders.

With these questions, look for the person still listening to the voices of the past they disagree with or have not even considered which values people in their past have embraced:

23. Who were those who shaped the way you see life and had much influence over you?

24. What recordings or thoughts from them are still playing in your mind?

25. Do you agree with that voice?

For each person you interview, write a short summary of their strong and weak areas of growth and recommend what a leader could do to nurture or coach this person to grow in the weak areas.

To learn more about identifying missing or wounded areas of our growth, listen to Arthur's audio album "An MRI of Fathering" at **theSLG.com.**

SPIRIT PROJECT

These spirit projects are designed to unpack our spirits and build out our spirit worlds.

Spirit Project 5.1
Inviting Our Spirits into Conversations

Now that you have gotten to know your spirit and how the seven portions of your spirit relate to the Trinity, let's invite our spirits to help us in daily life.

Be intentional about developing these habits:

1. As you pray, ask your spirit to help. What does your spirit see that God wants you to ask for?

2. As you go about your daily activities, invite your spirit to help. "Spirit, will you help me with this project? What do you see that I don't see?"

3. Each night, before you go to sleep, invite your spirit to work on a solution to a problem on your job, in your studies, or in your family. Present the problem to your spirit and invite your spirit to look for solutions. When you first wake up, take some time to sit with spirit and ask what came forth during the night. This is one of my personal favorite ways to solve problems.

4. When in conversation, invite your spirit and the spirit of the person you are talking with to participate. It takes a little practice to go with the flow of following your spirit like this, but so much fun to do!

5. When working on a project, such as writing a book or preparing dinner, invite your spirit to lead. This too takes practice but is well worth the effort. Even as I write this, Teacher is thrilled to get the opportunity to say to you, the reader, that your spirit was designed by God to help and lead you, just as Holy Spirit helps and leads your spirit.

Spirit Project 5.2 Missing Portions of the Spirit

Sometimes a portion of our spirit is missing. Here is what happened with a lady we will call Deborah.

1. Deborah's friend was working with her spirit to make sure all seven portions were present. He asked, "Mercy, may I speak with you?" There was silence. Prophet was best able to engage at the time, so he asked, "Prophet, do you know where Mercy is?" Prophet didn't know.

2. The friend explained to Prophet how the compass could help find Mercy. He asked Prophet to lie down on the compass and rotate around it, sensing for the compass to point Prophet in the direction of Mercy. As Prophet did so, he felt Mercy when his body pointed north.

3. Prophet decided to ask Servant to help him explore the north and together that discovered Mercy captured inside a massive granite mountain.

4. Prophet and Servant returned to the other portions and the six of them talked about strategies to rescue Mercy. Giver was certain they needed to ask Jesus for help.

5. Jesus came, took them all to the mountain, and showed them how to open a massive door in the side of the mountain, drive out the critters guarding Mercy and set her free.

6. They took Mercy to the Spring of Conception to refresh her in the life-giving water there.

Do the following:

In this project, you can work directly with your spirit or ask a trusted friend to talk with your spirit.

1. Invite each portion of the spirit, one at a time, to engage with you. If one is missing, do the other portions know anything that might help?

2. If not, ask your spirit to take inventory of the resources you have so far in your spirit world as the spirit consults God which one to use first. So far in this book, we have talked about these spiritual assets and resources that might help:

   - Portions of the spirit and their gifts and tools (for example, Servant and his or her lightning bolts)
   - Chronometer
   - Compass
   - Gyroscope
   - Our authority over evil
   - Courts of heaven
   - Spring of Conception
   - River of Life
   - Plumbline of Righteousness
   - Measuring Line of Justice
   - Holiness to cleanse defilement off time, land, community, birthright and offices
   - Water baptism
   - Blood of Jesus and our Blood Covenant with Him
   - Our most powerful sources of all, Father God, Jesus, and Holy Spirit
   - The power and authority of the Word of God

3. Use the resource God highlights to begin to locate and rescue the missing portion. If you get stuck, ask a friend with more experience to help you find the next step. If you don't have such a friend, ask the Member of the Trinity you relate to best to help you.

You might be thinking why don't we just ask God to find the missing portion and bring him or her back. When we are young and immature children of God, He cares for us in this way. He is great at mothering His little ones and meeting their every need. But in this book, we are working hard to grow up to become sons of God who can build His Kingdom. In this fifth stage of growth, we are expected to learn to unpack the treasures within us. Father God finds much pleasure in coaching us to use the tools and resources we have to build our inside Kingdom world. He moves from mothering us to fathering us as we mature.

Spirit Project 5.3 Healing a Wounded Spirit

Is it possible that our spirit needs healing? Yes.

The Lord is close to the brokenhearted and saves those who are crushed in spirit.

Psalm 34:18

May God himself, the God of peace, sanctify you through and through. May your whole spirit, soul and body be kept blameless at the coming of our Lord Jesus Christ. The one who calls you is faithful, and he will do it.

I Thessalonians 5:23-24

The human spirit can be stabbed, vexed by critters, covered in shame, have missing parts, contain implants put there by the enemy, and even be replaced by synthetic spirits posing as a portion of our spirit. Here is a protocol you can follow to ask Jesus to heal a wounded or afflicted spirit.

In this example, we show what is possible. Prophet is helping Ruler get free.

1. Ask Ruler to stand so that Prophet can see him. Ask Prophet to stand in front of Ruler and report what he sees.

2. Invite Jesus to stand behind Ruler and shine His Shekinah glory into and through Ruler, like an X-ray to reveal whatever is there that needs attention. Here are a few possibilities:

   - Ruler has an iron band around his neck enslaving him.

   - A terrified critter is trying to hide from Jesus.

   - Stab wounds are in Ruler's back and a knife is sticking out of Ruler's side from past betrayals.

   - Ruler's right arm is missing.

   - There is an iron cross inside Ruler from his head to his feet.

3. If Prophet doesn't know what to do next, he can ask Jesus for help. Jesus can remove critters and devices, restore missing body parts, or explain to the spirit team what to do.

   In the case of the iron cross, it became clear that Ruler was not genuine. We asked Jesus to remove Ruler if Ruler was a synthetic, and Ruler immediately disappeared. (The next step was to find the missing, genuine Ruler.)

4. After a time of healing, the spirit portion needs rest and renewal in the presence of God. Sometimes, Jesus will take this portion of the spirit with Him to stay with Him for a season.

Spirit Project 5.4 Building the Seven Pillars of Wisdom

Wisdom has built her house; she has set up its seven pillars.

Proverbs 9:1

One of the most life-changing experiences for me was building the seven pillars of Wisdom in my spirit world. I had such a victim mentality that I had little wisdom and no clue how to protect myself and stay grounded in a relationship. The seven pillars of Wisdom are built under the surface layer of our spirit world and bring stability to our lives. Principles come alive in the seven pillars and our spirits can draw wisdom from them. Here is a brief overview of the process. It took me more than a year to complete it, but most people, who are not as damaged as I was, can do so in a much shorter time.

Do the following:

1. Ask your spirit to go toward the west and look for access down into the layer under the surface. This second layer is the domain of Holy Spirit and can look like another beautiful inviting world, or, as mine was at first, dark and small. It all depends on the degree of wisdom in our lives and our relationship with Holy Spirit.

2. Some or all of the pillars might already be built, and it might take some time to locate each one. The seven pillars are built on the principles of Wisdom:

   - Prophet aligns with the pillar of Design
   - Servant aligns with the pillar of Authority or Dominion
   - Teacher aligns with the pillar of Truth or Responsibility
   - Exhorter aligns with the pillar of Reality
   - Giver aligns with the pillar of Awe or Stewardship
   - Ruler aligns with the pillar of Freedom
   - Mercy aligns with the pillar of Fulfillment

3. Encourage one of the portions of your spirit to locate their pillar and inspect it with the help of Holy Spirit. Is it where it needs to be? Is it functioning as God intends? Is it life giving? Can the portion of the spirit aligned with his or her pillar draw life from it?

To help you see what is possible, here is one report from a dear friend who is grounded and strong in spirit describing two of her pillars of Wisdom:

Prophet wrote, "The pillar of design is a vibrant, fruitful living tree. I can't see the top; mostly I see the trunk. It was designed to grow and flourish, give life to all around it, and is made from the same light shining in me. It gives much shade, fruit, strong branches to swing from, a home for many animals and shade for other plants. Leaves move and make sound in the breeze. The most magnificent tree! Trees in the natural are reminiscent of it. It also nurtures the earth and the air. I, Prophet, can rest against it, eat its fruit, hang a swing on it, and enjoy the animals, breeze, and aroma, not to mention I'm a tree hugger. I can take a branch with me as a staff wherever I go. The design of this tree is a stunning picture of God's design for all He has made, including me."

A few days later, my friend wrote:

Today, Teacher is making more progress on finding her pillar. She sees the ceiling is not low on level two - it is high like the sky. I cannot see the top or the bottom of the pillar. The floor Teacher is walking on is glass, but this dimension goes below the glass, like the roots of Prophet's tree column. The pillar of responsibility looks like it is made of glass like the floor. It's clear so Teacher can see truth clearly with nothing in the way obstructing the view of truth. It's glasslike but more precious, unbreakable, perfectly sturdy, strong and reliable. It took a few days for Teacher to find the pillar, and for me to feel comfortable about which gender she is. Prophet and Servant came with her, and I asked God to show me as things really are, which is how I saw the ceiling is not low at all -- I can't even see one now. Teacher loves to know and discover truth and share it. She is very responsible to do that and is strong in me, as responsibility and truth are strong.

"I love the God who loves
to celebrate!"

"Rejoice in the Lord always; again I will say, rejoice."
Philippians 4:4

CHAPTER 06 GROWING IN FREEDOM AND LEADERSHIP

"We are free to build the government
of God together."

PRINCIPLE

Life-giving structures are created when leaders at the top release core values and authority to ride downhill together to all in their organization.

The Principle of Freedom

Sons of God are charged by God to govern the earth. When the government of God is implemented on the earth, leaders establish principles and core values that build a culture designed for their followers to be free to become all that God designed them to be. This is the **principle of freedom** in action. As individuals, we each need to be free on the inside and have the authority on the outside to live out our design, passions and dreams in a community that embraces freedom for all.

When people live out of their designs and passions in a community working toward a common goal, synchronization (moving together in harmony) happens, which leads to synergy. Synergy produces a combined effect that is greater than the sum of what each individual can produce alone. We call this creativity. When creativity is used for good, value is added to the community. Creative synergy flows beautifully and is fun, alive, freeing and energizing.

In a culture where synergy flows well, individuals are encouraged and supported to freely express their uniqueness. On the other hand, slaves are not so free because they don't expect or value synchronization or synergy and don't trust others well enough to synchronize to them, especially when times get tough. They can become demanding and defiant and feel entitled.

Notice in the following verses the people trusted God and Moses enough to be led into the wilderness, but when times got tough, they began to question the goodness and faithfulness of God and the competence of Moses. They were not willing to endure the hard times with the good times and stay the course to breakthrough.

They camped at Rephidim, but there was no water
for the people to drink. So they quarreled with
Moses and said, "Give us water to drink."

Moses replied, "Why do you quarrel with me?
Why do you put the LORD to the test?"

But the people were thirsty for water there, and they grumbled
against Moses. They said, "Why did you bring us up out of Egypt
to make us and our children and livestock die of thirst?"
Exodus 17:2-3

And he called the place Massah [temptation]
and Meribah [contention]
because the Israelites quarreled and because they
tested the Lord saying,
"Is the Lord among us or not?"
Exodus 17:7

Freedom starts on the inside and is based on our intimate relationship with God. The better we know God, the more freedom we have. In this chapter, we cover some principles for getting free on the inside, how to grow as a fathering leader who grows those they lead, and then how to build culture and social structures that bring freedom to those we lead.

"Exhorters build dreams. Rulers build culture."
Arthur Burk

During the sixth stage of growth, we learn to stand up for what is right and build something beyond ourselves. This level of maturity normally happens in the late teen years.

HERE WE GROW

Growth Stage 6. I Can Stand Up for What Is Right and Build

To stand our ground for what is right in the face of opposition:

> Jesus didn't confront the highly oppressive Roman government or argue with the Greeks. He did create some extreme confrontations with the religious leaders of His day (such as healing on the Sabbath), which ultimately led to His crucifixion. For His apostles, He purposely built strong relationships by sometimes confronting and sometimes allowing issues to slide.

- We need to be very clear about our principles and values. Is this value worth fighting for? Is this value worth losing a relationship?

- We need to be very clear who is our enemy. Someone once said if the enemy has an ID card in his pocket, he is not the enemy. In community, our enemies are not people – our enemies are ideas, concepts and wrong values.

- We need to be very clear on the real issue.

  ○ **Is the issue a personal offense?** Perhaps we first need to deal with our own offense and then decide whether we still have an issue worth fighting for.

  ○ **Is the issue a high standard?** Once we've determined the real issue and it's a high standard we will not compromise, we need to consider our options. Do we withdraw from the conflict or take a stand?

- Is it necessary to take a stand?

  ○ At the very least, we must all refuse to be run over or abused by team members or family members.

  ○ Should we walk away? We can read in the Gospels how Jesus walked away from many conflicts and purposely created others. Jesus embraced high standards, but He was very selective when to take a stand and when to walk away.

When I cannot stand up for what is right, life might look like this:

- I get steamrolled by family members, team members, bosses, neighbors or anyone else.

- I comply with others even when I cringe at what I'm saying or doing.

- I don't confront others when they're wrong. I'm a very nice person. Ugh!

- I'm ineffective as a leader because stronger team members talk over me and push their ideas on the team.

Here are some ways to take a stand on principle:

- Love never fails. When we stand on principle as an act of loving others who are in the wrong, we might lose the relationship, but we can do so with a clear conscience.

- Choose your words carefully. Don't accuse. Listen well. Stay on topic. Consider the mindset and design of your opponent. Don't allow the confrontation to bleed over into other issues. Stay calm and control your emotions.

> A fighter who is not also a builder can do great damage in community. They tend to be takers and not makers and will create a dog-eat-dog competitive and aggressive environment.

- Commit to doing the minimum amount of damage. When you have won the fight, switch gears quickly to immediately bring dignity and reconciliation to all parties involved.

- Do your best to quickly rebuild community after a fight.

Building Something Beyond Ourselves

Building happens when people on a team creatively build something that did not yet exist. Building something requires (1) skills, (2) resources and (3) opportunity.

The process of building goes something like this:

1. **I have a dream.** I have in mind what I want to build and I'm preparing myself to build. I'm acquiring the skills and resources I know I will need when the opportunity presents itself.

2. **I need people to build with me.** A team is a resource. I need a team who shares my values and knows how to build. Such a team collectively creates a great work environment where people participate, are inclusive, and work collaboratively. As you form a team, be sure the skill of a team member matches up with the person's design as best you can. Gino Wickman in his book *Traction* said it well: "You want the right people in the right seat."

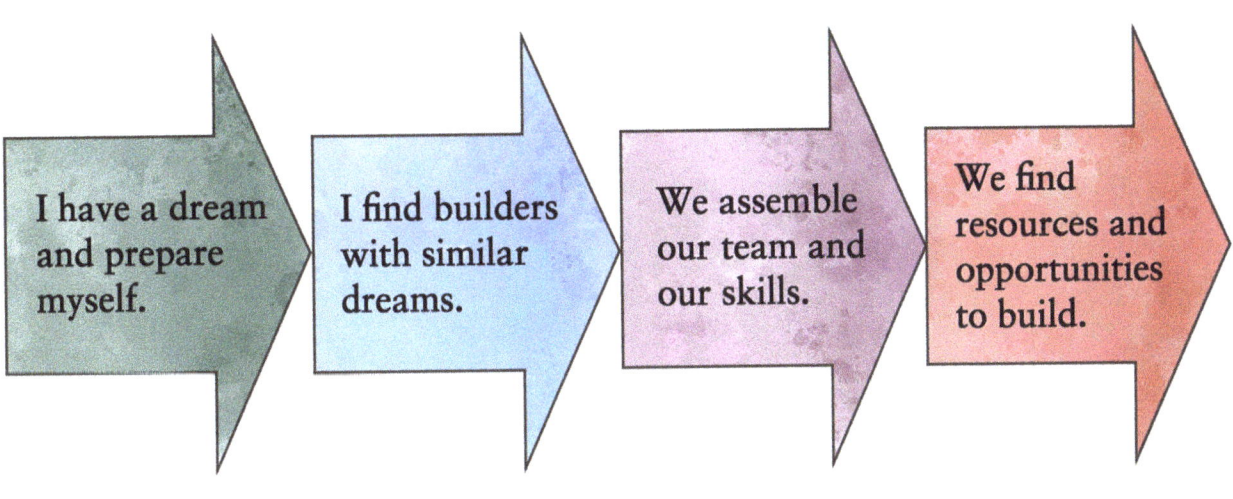

Figure 6-1 The process of preparing to build

3. **We need skills.** When the team recognizes a skill we don't have, we have two options. We can bring someone new to the team or develop the skill with someone already on the team.

4. **We see resources and opportunities.** Most people spell opportunity as M-O-N-E-Y. However, Jesus teaches us that opportunity is more about building something with the little entrusted to us. As God spoke to Moses when he was faced with a major building project, "Look at what is in your hand." Most of us overlook available resources and opportunities because they look small or insignificant. See Figure 6-1.

When I Don't Know How to Build

Most schools, public and private, don't teach their students to build, which is a great weakness of our current educational systems. In addition, many of us grew up in families who did not teach us to build.

When this developmental stage of growth is not completed:

- At work or school, I will obey, do as I'm told, and more-or-less act like a servant.

- I might have an idea or a dream, but I expect it to happen easily without embracing the necessary productive pain or hard work. I might even blame God for not bringing opportunities I believe He has assigned me.

- I might talk big, but I won't act on what I say.

To Grow into This Stage

The good news is, just as with the fifth stage of growth, most people can teach themselves to build. Here's a path forward to become a builder and to teach others to build:

1. **Start with ourselves.** In the last chapter, we learned about developing ourselves. Now take the next step and create a team around you of people able and willing to help you learn to build. Ask the team for assignments and tasks that will teach you to build. For example, if you want to build your own business, find a

mentor who has built a successful business and ask them to give you four or five assignments to improve your business skills.

2. **Build another person.** Invest your time, skills and resources to build up a child, a friend or someone who simply needs your help.

3. **Have fun building.** A creative way to teach building to teens is to set up a scavenger hunt with a particular building project in mind. Have teams go through the neighborhood, city or school asking friends and neighbors for this or that needed to build the assignment. Assemble the project over pizza!

4. **Be intentional.** Build something for a friend, child, school or non-profit. Design your building project to require that you learn a new building skill. For example, if you recognize a skill you need is time management, put the project on a timeline that requires you to better manage your time.

CONCEPTS

In this part of the chapter, we discuss how to be transformed by applying the moral laws of God, how to become a fathering leader and how to build beyond ourselves.

Concept 6.1 Freedom from the Inside Out

Freedom begins on the inside. It is based on intimacy with God and how well we know Him. Moral laws are principles given by Father God to protect our relationship with Him so that He can make His abiding home in us.

> *Jesus replied, "Anyone who loves me will obey my teaching. My Father will love them, and we will come to them and make our home with them.*
> John 14:23

Listed below are a few key moral laws. When these laws are violated, God is prevented from setting us free and blessing us with His presence and goodness.

To learn more about forgiveness, listen to the video "Forgiveness" at **FromHisTable.com.**

Moral Law 1. Forgiveness

Key Scriptures about forgiveness are Matthew 18:21-38 and Luke 6:27-42. Unforgiveness is demanding another give back what he or she has taken and maintaining a separation until the score is settled. Clues we have not forgiven include

Figure 6-2 Jesus waits to help us forgive in our hearts the one who owes us

replaying the story in our heads, resentment, bitterness, offense, separation, not choosing the presence of the other, gossip or revenge. When we find ourselves thinking, "If only he had not …" or "If only they had …" or "If only I had not …" we know there is unforgiveness.

Forgiveness comes when we relieve others or ourselves of the debt owed. We stop seeing others or ourselves as the one who must cough up the goods before we can be whole, well, happy, successful or free.

When we realize that Jesus is offering to meet our needs (see Figure 6-2), only then can we release our demands and ask Jesus to satisfy these unmet needs. Then we can have the grace to end the separation, be reconciled to ourselves or others and receive ourselves or others back into our hearts.

Forgiveness begins with a decision and happens in our hearts. Holy Spirit can be counted on to change our hearts when we ask Him to help. We know we have forgiven when we feel love and compassion toward the one who hurt us.

> A stronghold of the mind is the way we think. It can be so familiar we don't recognize it until others point it out to us.

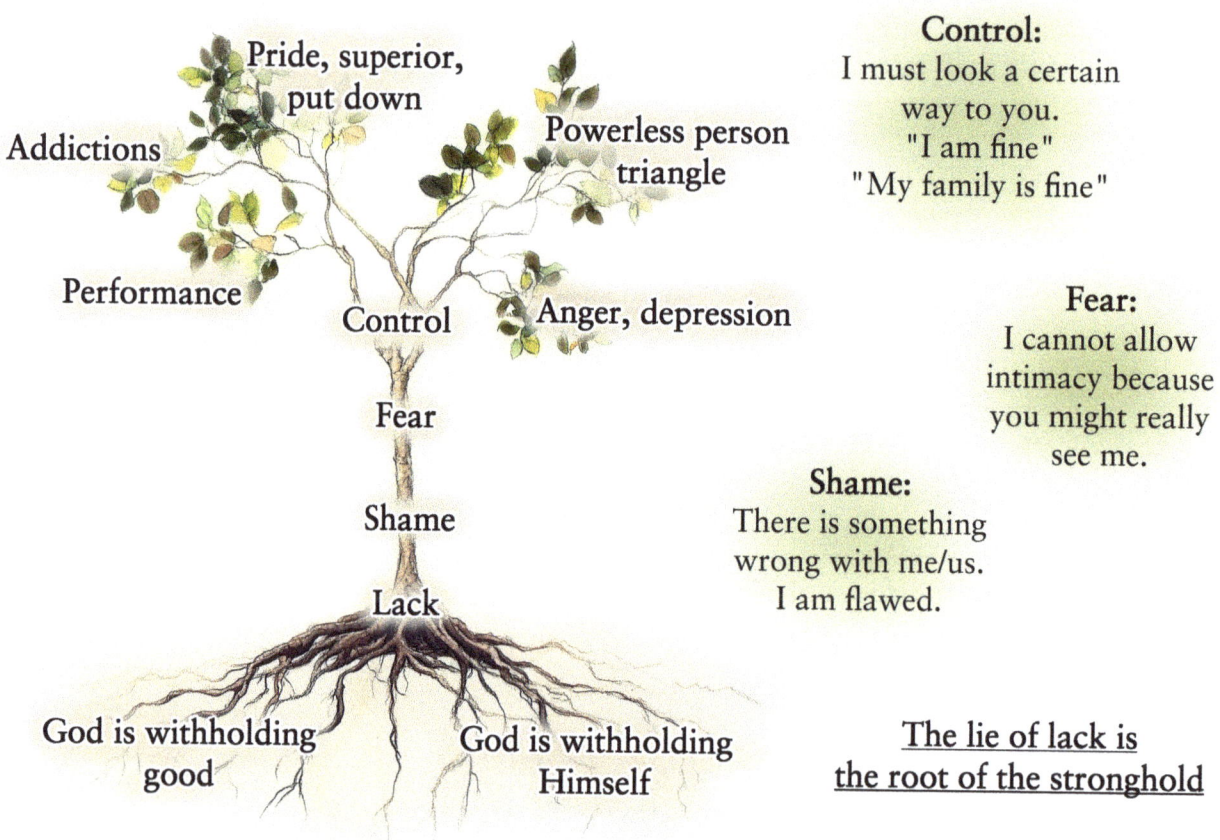

Figure 6-3. The shame, fear, and control stronghold of the mind

Moral Law 2. Live as a Victim or a King

God designed us to walk in dominion and wants us to build our lives rather than allow life to dominate us. All victim thinking is rooted in a poverty mindset: there is not enough for me or others I care for. Victim thinking makes us believe *we are not enough*, and that thinking can invite a victim spirit (critter) that brings victimization our way.

When Eve decided God might be withholding good from her, she considered He might even be withholding Himself from her. This double lie led her to believe she needed to *do something to be more like God*, even though God had made her in His image.

Eve agreed with shame when she decided she was lacking in her core self. This decision led her to sin because she forgot who she was, and her relationship with Adam and God were massively damaged. Agreeing with the lie of shame can lead to "the shame, fear, and control stronghold." See Figure 6-3.

To get free of this stronghold, we must change our thinking to believe that God is always giving us His best (Psalm 84), and He has created us in His image so that we are like Him. Because we are like Him, there is nothing we need to do to be more like Him or to receive His unconditional and ever-present love. This truth takes us back to belongingness discussed in Chapter 1.

God sees each of us as a king, able to make our own choices as to how our lives go. As kings (sovereign ones), we make our sovereign decisions regarding our lives. God promises He will enforce our decisions to choose life.

Moral Law 3. Judgements and Offenses

When we sit in judgement, we are taking a seat that belongs only to Father God and we receive the same sentence we doled out to another. See Luke 6:37-38. These judgements can be at work in our lives long after we have forgotten the judgements we made. We are dependent on Holy Spirit to show us where we have judged others.

The good news is Jesus has redeemed us, having become a curse for us. Jesus did not come to judge the world, but to save it. If you see a negative pattern that persists in your life, look for judgements made, especially against our parents. For example, I judged my mother to be weak, unable to protect me. One day I realized I had become a weak mother, unable to protect my children. I had become just like the one I had judged.

> Are we as Christians the standard bearers of righteousness or the carriers of unconditional love? It's Holy Spirit's job to convict another person of sin. Not our job!

Moral Law 4. Lies We Believe and Vows We Make

When we believe a lie, we give it power over our lives. When we make an inner vow, we set the course of our lives to follow that vow.

When my father abused me as child, I believed lies and made vows.

Lies:

- I am not worth protecting.
- Fathers cannot be trusted.
- I did something wrong.
- There's something wrong with me.
- I am forever broken.
- I am a victim.

Vows:

- I will never trust a father or a pastor again.

> Jesus is the Word, and when I take communion, I am eating the Word that became flesh in Jesus and in me. We can select Scriptures that contain the truths we need and regularly consume them in communion services until they become life in us.

- I don't need fathers. Just like an orphan, I will take care of myself.
- Because there's something wrong with me, I will never let others see me for who I really am.
- I will hide behind a mask of controlling everything you see about me.

It was not so much what happened to me that imprisoned me but how I responded to what happened that turned the course of my life toward captivity, until truth came:

> *Then you will know the truth, and the truth will set you free.*
> John 8:32

Lies do have power, but truth has more power. Here are some truths that I embraced and literally consumed.

- Jesus in me is my hope of glory.
- I am redeemed.
- I am worthy because He is worthy.
- Father God is safe and He protects me.
- Abuse does not define who I am.
- When I forgive, my life is restored back to Father God and He meets my every need.

Moral Law 5. Jealousy, Control and Exploitation

Jealousy is based on poverty thinking that if another person has something I want or need, I cannot have it because there is not enough of this good thing to go around.

Control is based on the same poverty thinking that unless I control another person, my needs will not be met.

Exploitation then occurs when I decide that I must be a taker for my needs to be met.

All these lies are based on the thought that God is withholding good from me or God is withholding Himself. The truth that sets us free is God is more than enough for me. When this truth is life to us, we are free to bless others and give others the freedom to choose their own paths.

Moral Law 6. Sexual Sin

> *"You have heard that it was said, 'You shall not commit adultery.'*
> *But I tell you that anyone who looks at a woman lustfully has already committed adultery with her in his heart.*
> Matthew 5:27-28

Sexual addictions can be complex and are always rooted in unmet need for love that only God can give. This deep love shortage is likely to have come from not receiving love as a child. A person who is not firmly rooted in God's love often searches for love in defiling ways. This defilement has grave consequences that include confusion and chaos as well as destruction of our spirit worlds and land.

The solution is to turn our hearts toward Father God for Him to fill us to overflowing with His love. When our needs for love are met by God alone and our love tanks are spilling over with His love, we can love others out of the overflow. We no longer need to "give to get" love.

Moral Law 7. Agreement or Participation in the Occult

Our God is a jealous God, and He wants to be our *only* supernatural source. He wants to be our all in all. We are forbidden to seek any source other than Him. That includes asking advice from the other world or from the dead, fortunetelling, witchcraft, and casting curses on another. We are supernatural beings who are covered with the Blood of Jesus, made pure by Him, and we seek no other supernatural help other than what is under the Lordship of Jesus Christ.

Invite Your Spirit to Help

When we disobey the moral laws of God, we can wound our souls, defile our minds and hearts, invite critters to use us, and defile our land, our spirits and spirit worlds. When we repent (change our mind and ways) after disobeying a moral law, we should be sure to ask our spirit if there is a critter present that needs to be evicted. Our spirit is most happy to clean up our inside world and evict any critters that were attached to the sin. Because we are in a Blood Covenant relationship with the Lord Jesus Christ and are one with Him, true repentance is joyful, fulfilling and easy.

> "Get your happy back and then you can lead."
> Author unknown

Concept 6.2 Becoming a Fathering Leader

Here are some characteristics that distinguish a boss leader from a fathering leader.

Change Myself Before Asking Others to Change

A boss leader focuses on the performance of others. A fathering leader, however, knows the only person they can control is themselves. God made it clear to Ezekiel that he needed to receive for himself first before he could help his people:

> *And He saith unto me, `Son of man, all My words, that I speak unto thee, receive with thy heart, and with thine ears hear."*
> Ezekiel 3:10

Change the System Before the Individual

A fathering leader understands that if one person fails, the problem is rarely the one person. To blame only one is a form of scapegoating. At least part of the problem must be borne by the system. Where did the system fail that didn't provide this person the support they needed? A fathering leader understands a person always performs better when support is built into the system.

Look for Solutions Before Accountability

When mistakes happen, a boss leader finds someone to blame, which in business is politely called accountability. A fathering leader doesn't see it necessary to point fingers but is more focused on finding solutions to the problem.

Building a School Culture from Our Design

In our new school in Myanmar, Gergler is the lead teacher and Khin Khin is her assistant teacher. Gergler, with the Ruler gift, has done a superb job bringing order and structure to the daily routine, curriculum and school policies. But after a couple of months, it became evident that some social problems among the students were not being given adequate attention. As we talked, we realized that it had been assumed that Gergler would handle any problems in the school, including social problems. But that was not Gergler's design, and it didn't come naturally for her to deal with this type problem.

Khin Khin, with the Teacher gift, however, is designed by God to be the reconciler and healer on the team. After Khin Khin was given the responsibility to address social issues, the school is back on track.

For thought and discussion:

1. Do you know someone who is great at creating structures and getting things done but not so good at resolving social issues on their team? Could that person be a Ruler?

2. Do you know someone who is not keen on structure but is very sensitive to the feelings and social needs of others? Could that person be a Teacher?

Give Support Before Rewards

Rewards and punishments are fundamentally used to manipulate and control people. A fathering leader, on the other hand, will focus on providing the underlying support each team member needs and is quick to ask their team what type of support is needed. Fathering leaders love to affirm and celebrate in healthy ways.

Best Boss Ever

Charlie was my best boss ever. He would make an assignment, provide the resources and set expectations for deliverables, which happened every few weeks. Each morning, he made his rounds to the cubicles of each team member. I recall with pleasure him sticking his head around the corner with a smile, saying, "Anything you need today?"

"Nope, I'm right on schedule and doing well!" If I came to him with a problem, his most frequent response was, "Is there another resource you need?" Charlie trusted me and I trusted him, and together we got the job done.

For thought and discussion:

1. Who is the best authority figure you ever had? Can you identify why?

2. Who is someone you lead? Describe how you support this person.

3. How do you celebrate their successes?

Use Self-Assessments Before Evaluations

A boss leader devotes time to evaluating their followers and providing recommendations for improvement. A fathering leader coaches followers to assess and evaluate themselves. They are skilled at asking questions to guide a person to set honorable and measurable goals and objectives for themselves.

"Daktar, Diplomat in Bangladesh" by Viggo Olsen

Dr. Viggo Olson, known to his friends as Daktar, devoted his life to building the first hospital in Bangladesh. His book tells about his adventures as family man, missionary, doctor and businessman in this war-torn underdeveloped nation.

One story that demonstrates his leadership style is when a border war broke out near their hospital between Bangladesh and India. Because of the seriousness of the threat, Dr. Olson gathered all pertinent information and then met with the medical missionaries and their families. The group decided that each family would make its own decision to leave the nation or stay. He then made a trip to the American embassy and received their blessing for the families who decided to stay.

The families who decided to stay were able to help many people during this dangerous time. Doing so gained them great favor in the eyes of the local and national governments for their steadfast help and support. Dr. Olson's loving and humble leadership helped establish the culture of the hospital and mission, as he delegated authority and trained local medical personnel to run the hospital.

For thought and discussion:

1. How did Dr. Olson delegate authority?

2. How did he exhibit skilled diplomacy?

3. Describe how he lived as a fathering leader.

Monkey Management in a School Structure

Ariel has a calling from God to build Christian schools, and her first year building her first school was stressful and overwhelming. Teachers had problems with the curriculum, students couldn't seem to learn, and parents were concerned their children were not succeeding. Everyone looked to Ariel for solutions. She arrived early and stayed late, putting out fires between teaching four classes, but still could not find time in the day to solve underlying problems at their root.

Then she learned about the book *The One Minute Manager Meets the Monkey* by Kenneth Blanchard. Here are some key principles from the book.

- Leaders delegate responsibility, entrusting their followers to solve problems. (Downward-leaping monkeys land on the one closest to the problem.)

- When followers bring a problem to a leader, leaders will not accept it but will teach, empower and support. (I won't accept your upward-leaping monkey, but I'm happy to teach you how to feed it.)

- Every problem has only one owner. (Make clear who owns the monkey.)

- Leaders supervise problems owned by followers. (Every downward-leaping monkey deserves to be insured with a round-trip ticket.)

- Leaders with fewer monkeys can spend more time helping their people.

- Ensure that the right things get done in the right time by the right people. (Some monkeys need to be humanely euthanized, and others need better food or other resources.)

In her second school year, Ariel decided to apply some of the principles of monkey management. A mentor asked her to list in order the people who seemed the most overwhelmed. She responded, "First me, then the teachers, then the students and then the parents. But I told the parents not to worry because we were taking care of it. I don't want the parents to worry."

Figure 6-4 shows the situation where Ariel has too many monkeys on her back.

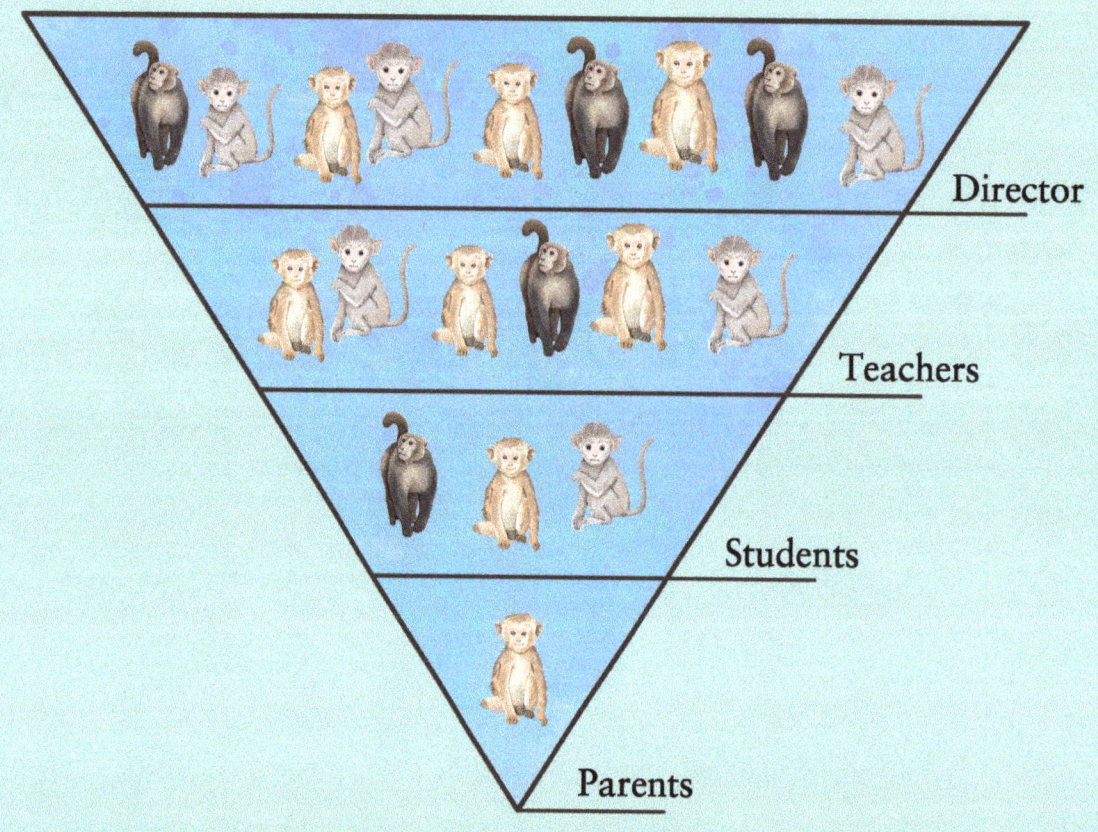

Director

Teachers

Students

Parents

Figure 6-4 The structure of responsibility shows too many monkeys at the top

For thought and discussion:

1. How might Ariel be empowering the negative sixth head of Leviathan?

2. How could Ariel reorganize her priorities so as not to empower the negative sixth head and invite the righteous sixth head of Leviathan?

3. How might Ariel have a distorted view of rights and responsibilities?

4. How might one or more of the seven curses on community and birthright be at work?

5. Assuming you have identified a possible curse, what can Ariel do to move in the opposite spirit?

6. Her mentor asked could the older children help the younger ones. She responded, "Well, I guess they could, but I don't really want to ask. They need to be spending their time learning." Do you agree or disagree with Ariel? Explain your answer.

7. In the Myanmar school you learned about in Chapter 5, parents and students sign an agreement that they are primarily responsible for the education of their children and teachers are there to assist. How might a similar position help Ariel get some monkeys off her back and onto their rightful owners?

06

> "Leaders become great, not because of their power, but because of their ability to empower others."
>
> John Maxwell

One Person Changed a Cruel Tradition

Around 400 A.D., Telemachus, a monk from Asia (modern day Turkey), felt led by God to go to Rome without knowing why. He found himself in the crowds at the Coliseum watching two gladiators fighting. Appalled, he rushed down into the stadium to get between them, shouting, "In the name of Christ, forbear!" One of the gladiators ran a sword through him, and he died.

As the crowd watched what happened and Telemachus lying dead in a pool of blood, silence fell and they all left one by one. Three days later, because of what Telemachus had done, the Emperor decreed an end to the gladiator games. The story of brave Telemachus that ended a cruel tradition is recorded in *The Ecclesiastical History* by Theodore Cyrus of Syria (393-457 A.D.).

For thought and discussion:

1. When all others are in agreement, it's difficult to stand alone for what is right. Describe the right that Telemachus stood for.

2. In our current culture, what cruelty do you see? Try to be as specific as you can to get at the core problem that transcends many situations in the current culture.

3. What is the principle that goes in the opposite spirit of this cruelty?

4. What might be an act of bravery that would take a stand for this right? List three or four more ideas.

Concept 6.3 Seven Stages of Building

The seven stages of growth align with the seven stages of building so that we can build beyond ourselves to benefit those in our sphere of influence. Building requires skills, resources and opportunity. Let's get the big picture of each stage.

Building Stage 1. Build Our Personal Authority on True Legitimacy

To build beyond ourselves we need a community. To fit into this community, we need to know our personal authority, which is based on knowing that God sent us there because of His love for the community. For God so loved this community that He gave you and me to it. When we truly know this, we can stand up for what is right, build well without fear, and see God in those we lead.

Building Stage 2. Identify Resources

Slaves cannot see raw resources but rather expect others to provide the finished products they need. Sons not only see raw resources but can visualize how to use them for building. Sons know their resources match up with their design and calling. Sometimes a raw resource is a person who needs cleaning up and building up to become a builder. (Think of David building up his mighty men who came to him as broken outcasts.) Some of our greatest resources are our earned authority from a difficult journey coupled with the favor of God.

Building Stage 3. Build on a Foundation of Righteousness

Our righteous core values are the foundation on which we build. Even the throne of God is founded on righteousness and justice.

Building Stage 4. Build a Working Model

With personal authority in community, resources and righteous core values in place, we are ready to build a working model of our vision. Our vision is birthed from our core passions and abilities, based on our design.

Building Stage 5. Establish Authenticity in All We Do

Authenticity happens in an organization when we are committed to change, which takes us incrementally closer to our vision. It's remarkable how many people and organizations have a vision but keep going for years without ever achieving it or even making significant progress in that direction. Sustained change is expected, verified and measured against the standards of our core vision and values.

Building Stage 6. Build Life-Giving Social Structures

The social structures we build in a team or business can take life or give life to those on the team. When structures are life-giving and produce freedom, followers are free and encouraged to operate out of and develop their designs, which takes them forward into their own birthright and calling.

Building Stage 7. Create a Culture for God to Enjoy

The sweet spot for the vision being built emerges when structures and systems align and everyone enjoys working with and syncing with others. Synergy and creativity emerge. This life-giving culture represents God both inside and outside the community.

Concept 6.4 Creating Life-giving Structures in Business

In this part of the chapter, we look at steps that provide a foundation for people to grow and build their business. The steps are designed for a business that already exists. Even if you don't own or lead a business, know that the principles discussed here can apply to any community of people who desire to grow and build.

Step 1. Clarify the Vision

Make the vision clear for everyone involved. Even when people have a vision that comes from God, it can still be difficult to articulate it. The following steps can help.

1. **Core values.** Gather your key leaders and identify your **core values.** The lead visionary can start the process, and everyone has opportunity to contribute. For our company, our core values are to honor God, value people and build with excellence.

2. **Core focus.** Define your **core focus** (core passion), which is your reason for being. Keep working on the core focus until you have only one, and this focus should fit in any industry. For our company, our core focus is to provide resources for people to grow and build out of their God-given design.

3. **Core niche.** Identify your **core niche,** which is the people you serve and what you do for them. Our core niche is Christ-centered individuals and groups who desire to grow and build.

> *"He who chases two rabbits catches neither."*
> Author unknown

4. **Targets.** Write **targets and plans** to include your ten-year target, your three-year picture of what you want the business to look like, your one-year plan, and your quarterly plan.

5. **Rocks and issues.** Define your **rocks** (priorities) **and your issues** (problems you need to solve).

6. **Marketing plan.** Write your **marketing plan,** which consists of:

> Many of the strategies presented here come from two books: *Traction* by Gino Wickman and *The Great Game of Business* by Jack Stack. If you own your own business or hope to one day, I highly recommend both books.

> If you are starting a new business, an excellent free resource to help with strategies and a business plan is My Own Business Institute at myownbusiness.org.

- **Your target market.** As part of your marketing plan, try to zoom in on your target market as accurately as you can. To do that, ask your leaders these questions.
  - Where are our customers located?
  - What are their characteristics?
  - How do they think?
  - What do they need?
  - What do they appreciate?
- **Your three unique attributes.** Ask yourself, your leaders, staff and customers what they like about your business and what matters most to them.
- **Your proven process.** This is best done in a one-page visual with text scattered through it to help people understand the process. This one-page visual is the very best marketing tool you can provide your sales team. A company's proven process will generally have three to seven steps. For example, for this book, our proven process to grow people is the seven stages of growth and the principles involved with each stage (see Figure 6-5).

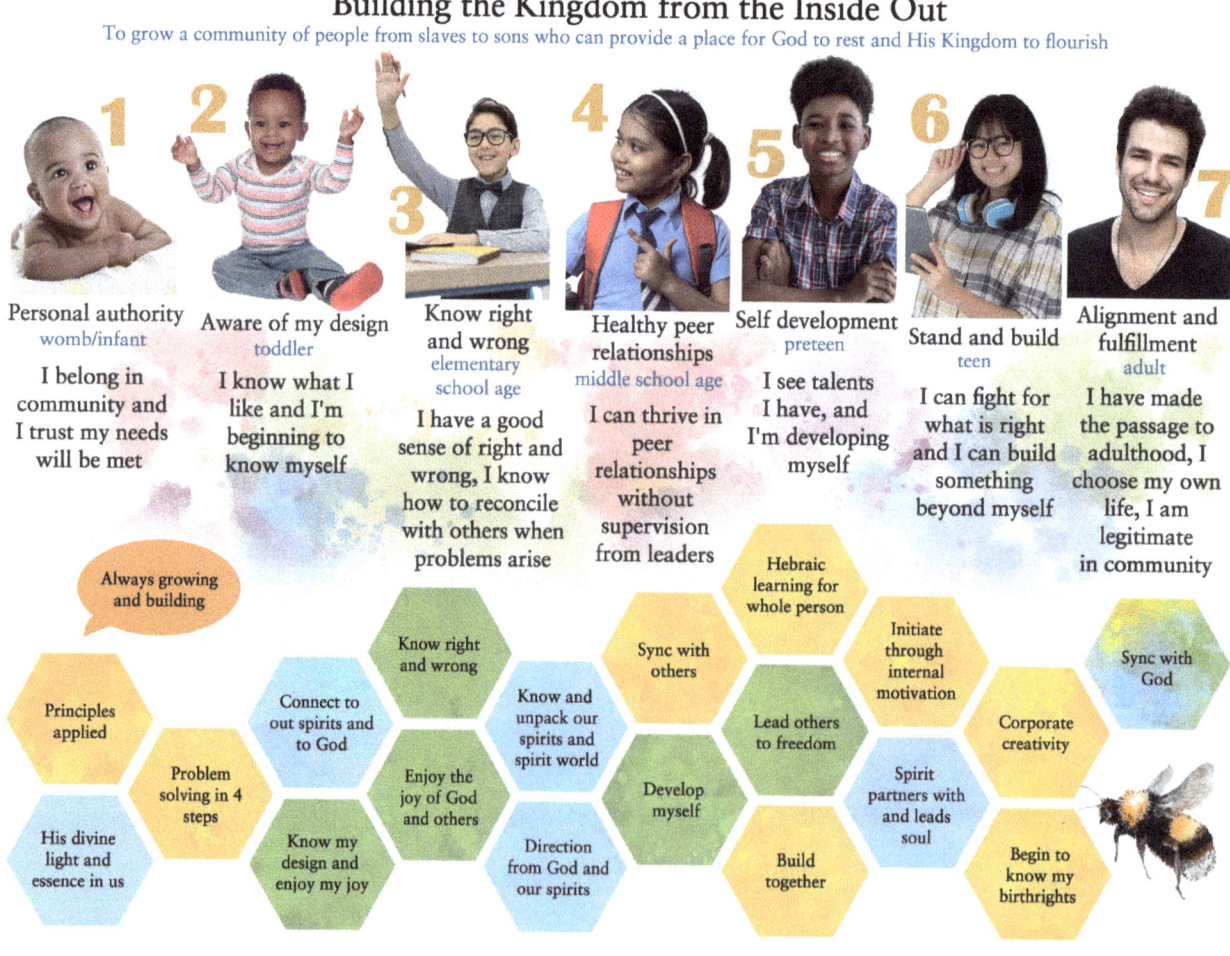

Figure 6-5 Our proven process to grow people who build beyond themselves [canva]

- **Your customer guarantee.** Once you've established this guarantee as something your customers can count on, everyone in the organization must commit to it and deliver as promised.

You should be able to write your **vision statement** from your core values, core focus, core niche and other items you've gathered in this vision process. If you can't, go back and look for what needs changing. Put all your vision components in a vision document that is shared with everyone in your organization. A sample format is shown in Figure 6-6.

Top Hat Roofing Vision

To bring truth, professionalism, and dependability to the roofing industry.

Core Values	1. Be the best we can be 2. Satisfy out customers 3. Provide master craftmanship	Three-Year Picture		
Core Focus	**Our passion:** To provide excellent customer service and master craftmanship **Our niche:** Residential and commercial roofing in the Atlanta area	Future date: December 31, 2028 Gross income: $800,000 Measurables: 135 repaired		
10 Year Target	$5 million in revenue with a 15% net margin	What does it look like:		
Marketing Strategy	**Target market:** 1. Residential roofing repair in Acworth 2. Townhouse flat roofs in Acworth **Three uniques:** 1. Our experiences in roofing manufacturing 2. Our 30 years in the roofing industry 3. Our superior expertise in roof repairs **Proven process:** Our products, techniques, and customer service assure customer satisfaction	• 10 roof jobs contracted per month • All jobs completed within estimated time commitments • All roofers trained on latest techniques		

Figure 6-6 Vision components for one company

Make a sincere effort to allow everyone to give feedback. Be vulnerable enough to realize you might be off and need to revise your vision components. Our vision statement for this book is:

To provide resources for people to grow from the inside out and to build big and well so that we can become God's inheritance, a place for Him to rest and His Kingdom to flourish here in the earth.

"People need to hear the vision seven times before they really hear it for the first time."
Gino Wickman

Step 2. Get the Right People in the Right Seats

The right people in your organization are those that share your core values and core focus. Whenever you interview someone, have prepared your core values and core focus speech. How do you know someone shares your values and passion? In a job interview, you might not discern everything you wanted to know. This is why a probation period is so important. As you get to know someone, you can observe how they relate to their job and people. Here are traits we look for in people we include in our organization.

1. Do the right thing. Stand up for rightness even when it costs you something.

2. Grow and be willing to embrace the necessary productive pain.

3. Build for the common good.

4. Respect others, especially those who mess up or don't fit social norms.

5. Commit to explore and develop your God-given design.

6. Respect authority.

7. Have fun.

Once we agree on our core values, we don't assume that is always so. People change. When problems arise with people, ask do they still embrace our core values? If not, they might fit better in other organizations that align with their current values.

The right seats in an organization are depicted in an organizational chart. Figure 6-7 shows a possible org chart. Many organizations are built on product facing, customer facing and finance facing components, which are also depicted in this structure.

One clue that a person might not still align with your core values is when they bring a monkey to their leader and refuse to take it back!

To make sure the right person gets in the right seat, ask three things.

- **Do they get it?** Does the person understand the job, what's required, and how the job fits in the organization?

- **Do they want it?** Will they genuinely like the job? Do they have a passion for the job? If someone accepts a job they don't really want, the sparkle and joy won't be there.

Executive Director
Plan, lead, coordinate, execute

Product Development	Sales and Marketing	Finances
Internal operations	Customer facing	Budget, accounting, HR

- **Does it fit their design and skills?** Will the person be operating primarily out of their design? Do their professional skills, knowledge, and social skills match up with the demands of the job?

A person can fill more than one seat (work two jobs), but don't make the mistake of putting two people in the same seat. One temptation for a leader who needs to fill two seats is to hire a new person to take one of those seats but keep the other seat. When you delegate authority, you have to let go.

Step 3. Collect and Analyze Data with Scorecards and Scoreboards

One of the core values we discussed in Chapter 3 is to value verifiable, measurable and sustained change. In general, anything we do that is monitored and measured improves. Here are two tools to measure success.

- **Scoreboard.** A scoreboard uses a few key numbers to monitor and measure what your organization is doing. The goal of a scoreboard is to collect data to measure success and reveal where adjustments can be made for improvements.

- **Scorecard.** A scorecard monitors and measures what individuals do in your organization. When a scoreboard and scorecard are designed well, every person in your organization has a number that is reflected on the scoreboard. Collectively, everyone knows how everyone affects the success of the organization.

> *Scorecards and scoreboards create a transparency in an organization that fosters authenticity and change.*

Here's a simple example of how measuring success in this way might bring positive change.

1. A ministry of five people runs a free mobile food pantry in a large city. The purpose of the food truck ministry is to bring people to a saving knowledge of the Lord Jesus Christ.

2. Each staff member keeps a record of hours worked, when and where they shared the Gospel with a client and whether they accepted Christ. Each Friday, their scorecard is given to the ministry leader.

3. Each month, the leader reports the data on a scoreboard at a staff meeting. Everyone can see how many decisions for Christ were made, when and where it happened, and who presented the Gospel. Then they spend some time discussing who is getting the most success and why, the best days, time of day and locations in the city that get the best results, and how the team can improve to get better results.

4. Each quarter, the leader reports to the food truck patrons the success of the ministry. The patrons can then use this to measure the cost of food and labor for each decision for Christ achieved.

Step 4. Have a Plan for Addressing Issues

Every organization has problems that need solutions. When you build a culture on trust, honesty, empathy and transparency, people have the freedom to openly talk about problems and find solutions.

Suppose leaders meet each quarter to work on their traction plan as shown in Figure 6-8. They restate and revise their one-year plan, identify their rocks (priorities) for the quarter, and make their issues list (problems). For this to happen, your culture must establish that bringing a list of problems to a meeting is both desirable and normal.

Traction

One Year Plan	Rocks	Issue List
Future date: Revenue: Measurables: Goals for the year:	Future date: Revenue: Measurables: Rocks for the quarter: |	What
	What	Who
1		
2		
3		
4		
5						What
---	---
1	
2	
3	
4	
5		

Figure 6-8 By openly identifying problems or issues, leaders can address one problem after the next without condemnation or shame.

Then solve one problem at a time. First decide which team owns the problem. (Remember, leaders high in an organization don't accept upward-leaping monkeys.) The team who owns the problem gathers to solve it. The process can look like this.

1. **Identify the real issue.** Don't be afraid to talk about the elephant in the room or speak up knowing others might not agree. A team must trust one another to make uncomfortable discussions possible. Everyone has a voice.

2. **Everyone contends for the greater good.** For this to happen, there can be no competition in the team. All the work done to build and synchronize a team for the common good pays off here.

3. **Don't go on tangents.** Keep the discussion focused on solving the issue at hand. Don't allow the discussion to go on endlessly. A decision needs to be made, and a wrong decision is better than no decision at all.

4. **Someone with authority makes the final decision.** Everyone is involved in finding a solution, but decisions by consensus don't usually work. In the end, the team leader must decide what happens. And don't forget that problems are solved in the four steps of collecting data, looking for patterns, and identifying and applying principles.

06

Step 5. Document and Follow Processes

To bring excellence into your organization, focus on consistent processes.

1. Identify your core processes that are mission critical for your organization to succeed.

2. Decide who owns a core process.

3. Have the owner document the process. Others can help.

4. Make sure everyone understands and follows this documented process.

Let's take the example of the food truck ministry. Suppose Joe, a staffer, has a proven success rate of helping people make decisions for Christ, far beyond the success rates of other staff. The entire team wants to be successful and decides that Joe should own this core process. Joe explains and documents his process, and everyone understands and follows it. As a result, the success rates of the entire team rise and the ministry and the clients they serve enjoy more success.

Step 6. Getting Traction

After your vision and structures are in place, you're ready to get traction. For that to happen, three things can help.

- Everyone knows their own rocks and the rocks of others.

- Meetings are concise and effective.

- Communication is good.

I love meetings led by people who keep us on target, move swiftly from one agenda item to the next and end on time. That's possible when the leader understands what's needed, is prepared, is a good communicator, is not a wimp, and everyone in the meeting is committed to the common good.

It's not necessary to document every detail of a process. Documenting just enough high-level details, maybe about 20% of it, should be enough to get great results.

Marcus and Narissa Whitman in Oregon Country

Marcus and Narissa Whitman shared a passion to evangelize the native Cayuse tribe of Oregon country, west of the Rocky Mountains. In fact, it's reported that Narissa only married Marcus because her denomination's missionary board refused to send out a woman who was not married. The mission began in 1836, and the couple paid dearly for their efforts. Three years into the mission, their only child, two-year-old Alice, drowned in the Walla Walla river near their cabin.

By 1842, it was clear the Whitmans had failed to convert the Cayuse to Christianity. In an altercation with a Cayuse chief, the chief demanded they pay for the land on which they had built the mission. Twice the chief slapped Marcus, knocking him to the ground, as his hat flew into the mud. Each time Marcus recovered, placing his muddy hat back on his head, and finally said to the chief, "When we came to this place, you promised me that you and the Cayuse people would be our friends and that we could live here. I made no promise to pay for this land then, and I still cannot promise. But you have acted shamefully today… Do you want us to leave?"

The chief knew he had been shamed in front of his followers. How could he continue to harass a man who would stand up to him without fighting him. To do so would only increase his shame in the eyes of his followers. The chief walked off without another word.

In 1847, a group of Cayuse murdered Marcus and Narissa along with several other missionaries. Let history be our judge. Although the Whitmans did not make many converts, they were solely responsible for thousands of Americans moving to the Oregon territory and settling there and ultimately for the United States to annex this northwest territory.

For thought and discussion:

1. The Whitmans defined their mission as evangelism and measured their success by the number of converts. How would you define and measure their success?

2. Why is it important to make regular efforts to reevaluate what is success and how is it measured?

3. Why is it important to collect data regarding success as verifiable, measurable, sustained change?

SOLVING PROBLEMS

Remember that we solve problems by collecting data, looking for patterns, identifying principles from the patterns, and applying these principles to new situations. In this chapter, you learn how to solve problems that occur when leading and building.

Problem 6.1 Grace to Forgive Ourselves and Others

Consider forgiveness as a contract made in the heavenly realms that God can use to bless us. It's important to search our hearts for those we still need to forgive. Do you find yourself replaying in your mind an offense or hurt and what you could have said? Do you think "If only he had not ..." or "Why can't she see...?"

To forgive, you can try the following steps.

1. Tell God what happened. Be as specific as you can.

2. Speak forgiveness. Release the person from any debt they owe you.

3. Bless the other person from your heart. Ask God to bless him or her.

4. You might need to go ask the other person to forgive you for holding unforgiveness in your heart. Or maybe you can talk to their spirit and let them know you've forgiven them.

5. Ask God to bless you and restore to you whatever the other person took.

Forgiving ourselves can be more difficult than forgiving others. I imagined myself standing in front of myself, such as in front of a mirror. When I did that, I looked all wounded and beat up and I realized this is what I had done to myself. I found myself asking me to forgive me for being so hard on me. Then the Scripture came to mind, "Do not call anything impure that God has made clean." Acts 10:15. I spoke tenderly to myself, trying to comfort the one I had hurt. I promised me I would not be so hard on me from that day forward.

1. Do you need to forgive yourself? If so, try imaging yourself standing in front of you. Have the conversation with yourself that can reconcile you to you.

2. Bless yourself truly from the heart. Ask God to bless you.

Problem 6.2 A Power Struggle or Authority in Action

Recall the powerless person triangle described in Chapter 4 and shown in Figure 6-9.

Here are some action steps to earn the authority we need to step out of the triangle into living a power-filled life. Present to God each step, one by one. Ask Him what truth He wants to tell you about this step in your life. Then ask Him what can you do to grow in this area.

1. **I take responsibility for my life.** After we have forgiven ourselves and others, we are free to take responsibility or ownership for our lives.

2. **I surrender my life to Jesus.** Now that I am responsible for and own my life, I can surrender that ownership to Jesus. My life is no longer my own; Jesus owns me and I belong to Him.

3. **I will go for the roots.** No one can change me except God and me working together. I purpose to go for the root causes of shame, fear and control. The root of shame is gone when I know that God is with me and providing all good things.

4. **I will change my actions.** I will learn to feed my own spirit and follow Holy Spirit. I will no longer blame or enable others.

5. **I am not a victim or your rescuer.** I repent of seeing myself as a victim in need of a rescuer. I repent of being your rescuer. I repent of controlling others with my needs or allowing the needs of others to control me.

6. **I choose life.** I will no longer depend on circumstances or people to make me happy and free. Father God gives me the right to choose, and I choose life.

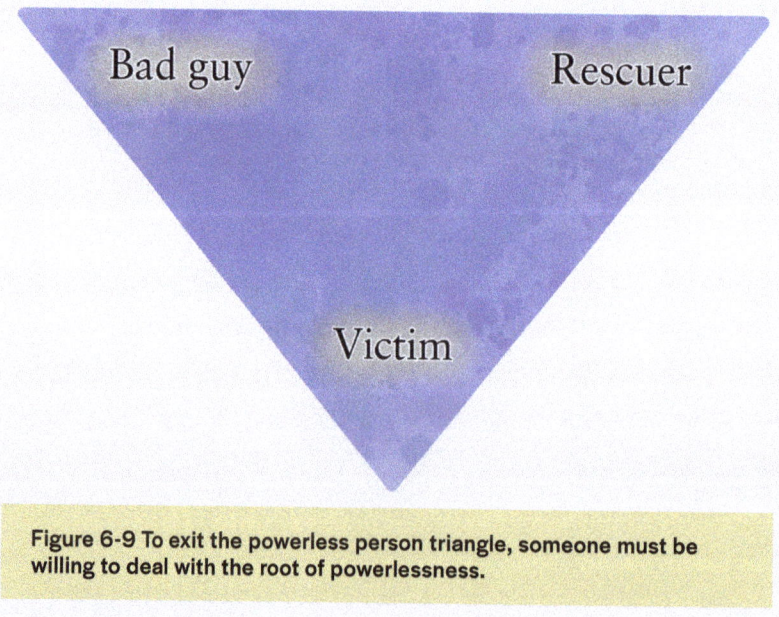

Figure 6-9 To exit the powerless person triangle, someone must be willing to deal with the root of powerlessness.

Problem 6.3 Monkey Management

A leader needs to periodically evaluate whether they are carrying some monkeys that don't belong to them.

Here's one helpful way to do this:

1. Make a list of all your current responsibilities, problems to solve and things to do.

2. Look through the list for monkeys that would be better served delegated to those you lead. Make a plan to hand off these monkeys.

3. Look for monkeys on your list that you have allowed to upward leap and return them to their rightful owners.

4. Sort everything else on your list into monkeys that fit your design and those that do not. We all must do some things that don't fit our design but the goal is to work at least 60% of the time in our God-given design. What can you do to move toward your design?

5. Prioritize your list and work top down. Ask God for the rock each day. Work the rock and go home satisfied.

Problem 6.4 Hiring the Right Leader

Suppose you are responsible for interviewing and hiring a Director of Operations for a small company. A core value of your company is that everyone is a worker and not a blamer. Here are the principles involved.

- **A person is fundamentally a worker or a blamer.** Debbie, the CEO, walks across the parking lot on the way into work and sees a piece of trash on the pavement. A blamer will wonder who is not doing their job and make a note to talk to the maintenance staff. A worker picks up the piece and tosses it in the trash can at the front door without another thought.

- **A leader must first be a worker and second be a leader.** By definition, leaders are people who have followers, and we lead by example. A leader who is willing to do whatever it takes and is able to inspire people to do the same will have many followers. Paul said, "I worked harder than any of you." 1 Corinthians 15:10

- **Followers must feel safe with their leader.** So here is where trust comes in. Debbie can work hard and lead by example, but if she criticizes David, head of maintenance, in front of the leadership team, trust is eroded with the entire team. Debbie can recover some trust at the next team meeting by admitting she was wrong in what she said and apologizing to David in front of the team.

If you were Debbie, what would you do to handle the problem of trash in the parking lot?

Make up questions you can ask an applicant for the Director of Operations job that can help determine whether the applicant is a worker or a blamer and whether the applicant can inspire people.

HERE WE GROW

These growth projects are designed to help us and those we lead to grow as builders.

Growth Project 6.1 Verifiable, Measurable, Sustained Change

Look back at Chapter 3 and reread the section "We Value Verifiable, Measurable, Sustained Change." Some organizations don't define success well enough to measure it. It's been said that if you don't know where you are going, you won't know when you have arrived.

You can use the following five activities to help explore how an organization can define and measure success.

Do the following:

1. Working with a partner or small group, examine a balance sheet and income statement for a business. Describe the purpose of each. If these financial terms are not familiar to you, google them and look for simple explanations.

2. On the income statement, identify the gross profit, net profit and profit margin so that everyone in the group understands and knows how to find or calculate each of these values from an income statement.

3. To develop your own scoreboard for yourself, your family, a church, a school or a business you hope to own one day, list the metrics you will use to measure success. For example, a family can measure success by its income (gross profit), amount saved each month (income less expenses, or net profit), or amount saved as a percentage of income (profit margin). Success can also be measured in other ways than money. For example, you can measure the success of a family by how many chapters of the Bible are read at family devotions each week or the number of evenings the family voted to have good conversations or play board games rather than screen time.

4. In Chapter 3, you developed a list of core values for yourself or your organization. Values should drive how you measure success. Compare the metrics on your scoreboard to your list of values. Do you need to adjust either the values or your metrics so that your metrics for success reflect your values?

5. Share your scoreboard with your family or other organization. In one week, report back to the group your success as verifiable, measurable, sustained change. How did your scoreboard function for you? Do you need to make some adjustments?

Growth Project 6.2 Evaluate How an Organization Measures Success

Evaluating how an organization defines and measures success can help you grow in wisdom and insight for your own organization. Select a ministry, school or business where you have access to staff or owners and can ask them questions about how they define and measure success.

Here are some steps to help:

1. Ask staff and owners how the organization measures its success. Be aware that some organizations don't measure their success. For these organizations, just asking the question can help the organization gain insight on how to improve.

2. Ask the staff and owners whether they believe their current scoreboard measures what actually should be measured. Is something missing? Is something too ambiguous? Is something inappropriately measured?

3. Discuss with staff and owners how the scoreboard might be better designed.

4. Do the people you interviewed see how their actions directly reflect one or more metric on the scoreboard? If they don't see they directly affect the scores, make some suggestions as to how to solve that problem using scorecards for each individual.

5. Discuss what you learned in this project with your discussion partner or group. If you were the owner or overseer of this organization, what would you change about how success is measured?

SPIRIT PROJECT

These spirit projects are designed to unpack our spirits and build out our spirit worlds, improving our relationships with the Trinity.

Spirit Project 6.1 The Trinity in Our Hearts

When we invite Jesus into our hearts or talk about His living in our hearts, we seldom stop to think what this might look like in the spirit realm. Arthur teaches about our four hearts: our spiritual heart, emotional heart, cognitive heart and physical heart. In the spirit, the inside is larger than the outside. We can look into our spiritual hearts and see whole worlds or dimensions open to us. The heart and the entire cardiovascular system represent the work of Jesus Christ.

The heart has four chambers (see Figure 6-10) with specific blood flow patterns.

1. Blood flowing from the body enters into the right atrium, the first chamber. This chamber aligns with Father God. The blood flowing into the right chamber contains carbon dioxide given off by body cells.

2. Blood then flows to the right ventricle. This chamber aligns with the Lord Jesus Christ. The right ventricle pumps blood into the lungs where carbon dioxide is removed and oxygen is added.

3. Blood flowing from the lungs enters the left atrium, the third chamber. This chamber aligns with Holy Spirit. The blood is full of life-giving breath or oxygen.

4. Blood flows into the left ventricle and is pumped back into the body. This chamber is where the Kingdom of God originates in our spiritual hearts.

Father God and joining joy

Holy Spirit and calm joy

Jesus Christ and dancing, leaping joy

Kingdom of God and exuberant, celebrating joy

Figure 6-10 Our hearts have four chambers that align with Father, Jesus, Holy Spirit and the Kingdom of God

The spiritual heart is described as the innermost center of anything, including our spiritual life, feelings, will, thoughts and even our intellect. The condition of our hearts is described in Scripture to be central to our walk with God, and we are encouraged and warned to prepare our hearts to walk uprightly with God.

And he did evil, because he prepared not
his heart to seek the LORD.
2 Chronicles 12:14

Consider these Scriptures to help you visualize what your spiritual heart might look like and how it might function.

*Jesus answered and said unto him If a man love me,
he will keep my words: and my Father will love him, and
we will come unto him, and make our abode with him.*
John 14:23

*Even the Spirit of truth; whom the world cannot receive,
because it seeth him not neither knoweth him: but ye know
him; for he dwelleth with you, and shall be in you*
John 14:17

*And when he was demanded of the Pharisees, when the kingdom of
God should come, he answered them and said, The kingdom of God
cometh not with observation. Neither shall they say, Lo here! or, lo
there! for, behold, the kingdom of God is within you.*
Luke 17:20-21

*For the kingdom of God is not meat and drink, but
righteousness, and peace, and joy in the Holy Spirit.*
Romans 14:17

> Moving from visitations of God to becoming a resting place for God is marked with great abiding joy.

When people first begin walking with God and partnering with their human spirits, they might experience Father, Jesus and Holy Spirit coming to visit them in the spirit realm, and they might go to visit Father in the heavenly realms. For example, in Chapter 2, you learned how to go into the courts of heaven to cleanse generational bloodlines. It's awesome when God can come to us and we can go to Him on a regular basis. However, our walk with God can go to a whole new level when we provide a place for God to abide (make His permanent resting place) with us.

The Exhorter portion of the spirit has primary responsibility for the heart, and Servant is primarily responsible for the pericardium, the sac filled with fluid that surrounds and protects the heart. Following are steps your spirit can use to prepare your heart as a place for each Member of the Trinity to abide with you. Your spirit might change the order of the steps.

Do the following:

1. Cleanse the pericardium. Ask Servant to look at the pericardium and make sure all the fluid inside is cleansed of any critters or defilement. If you have had a hard heart in the past, Servant might find stones or even critters that need removing. As always, when the spirit needs help with a task, other portions of the spirit can help, and you can always invite the Trinity to help you.

2. Invite Jesus to send a heavenly being of His choosing to surround the heart with His protection and love.

3. Ask Exhorter to examine the right atrium and prepare it as a place for Father God to abide. When Exhorter says the place is prepared, invite Father God to come to dwell in your heart. When Father abides with us, we experience a new kind of joy, which I call "joining joy." It's the joy of assurance that Father is always with us and will never leave us. When we experience joining joy with Him, fragments of an orphan heart that still remain will surely dissipate over time.

4. In my experience, it works well to turn next to the left atrium, the abiding place of Holy Spirit. For people who have been deeply wounded, this chamber might be occupied by a spirit of chaos. (Holy Spirit brings order, which is the opposite of chaos.) When Exhorter is satisfied the chamber is prepared, invite Holy Spirit to take His place. When Holy Spirit abides in our hearts, He plants the seeds of the fruit of the Spirit and these fruits begin to manifest in our lives. The joy we experience as a fruit of the Spirit is a calm joy that results from His order.

5. Ask Exhorter to prepare the right ventricle as the location to enthrone Jesus in our hearts. Father and Holy Spirit will work with your spirit to prepare this place. For me personally, Exhorter built Mt. Zion in the right ventricle as the place for Jesus to be enthroned.

6. When your spirit agrees it is time to invite Jesus to take His seat in our hearts, heaven will participate in a magnificent ceremony. A heavenly being will be assigned to usher in the King and you will be forever changed! The joy this enthroning brings is a jumping, leaping, dancing joy of seeing the King take His throne in us! This is beyond words!

When each Member of the Trinity is abiding in your heart, the lyrics of this old children's song take on a whole new meaning:

"I've got the joy, joy, joy, joy down in my heart, down in my heart, down in my heart. I've got the joy, joy, joy, joy down in my heart to stay!"

Watch for other fruit of the Spirit to grow from the left ventricle, the chamber of the Kingdom of God.

Spirit Project 6.2 Our Spiritual Lungs

The lungs remove carbon dioxide from our blood and infuse oxygen into it. The lungs have five lobes, three on the right and two on the left (see Figure 6-11), and these five lobes align with spirit, soul, body, birthright and offices.

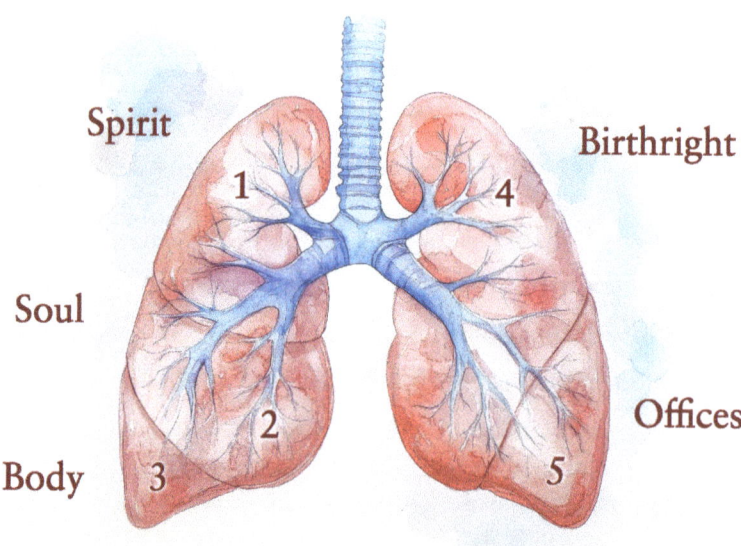

Figure 6-11   Our lungs have five lobes that align with spirit, soul, body, birthright and offices

Our lungs and the entire pulmonary system represent the work of Holy Spirit, and the Giver portion of our spirit is primarily responsible for the lungs. Adam and Eve were created with true legitimacy because they were created like God, in His image, and they walked in close fellowship with God, representing Him on the earth. But with the fall, legitimacy was replaced with shame. It is the work of Holy Spirit to restore us back to true legitimacy as God's children, created in His image, walking in close fellowship with Him, and representing Him.

> *For those who are led by the Spirit of God are the children of God. The Spirit you received does not make you slaves, so that you live in fear again; rather, the Spirit you received brought about your adoption to sonship. And by him we cry, "Abba, Father." The Spirit himself testifies with our spirit that we are God's children. Now if we are children, then we are heirs—heirs of God and co-heirs with Christ, if indeed we share in his sufferings in order that we may also share in his glory.*
> Romans 8:14-17

You can explore how this work of Holy Spirit aligns with the work of the lungs.

Do the following:

1. The Giver portion of your spirit is adept at helping the soul experience sonship. As a son of God, we are created in His image. Ask Giver to show you the upper right lobe of the lung and show you how Holy Spirit is or has released legitimacy as a son of God to your spirit. When I did that, I saw how my spirit came from the womb of Holy Spirit, born of Him. It was a holy moment of awe. What do you see or sense?

2. Ask Giver to show you the middle right lobe, aligned with your soul. How does Holy Spirit give legitimacy to your soul? What do you see or sense?

3. Ask Giver to take you to the lower right lobe, aligned with your body. What do you see or sense?

4. Ask Giver to show you the upper left lobe, aligned with your birthright. What do you see or sense? Can you get a better view or understanding of your birthright by looking into this lobe?

5. Ask Giver to show you the lower left lobe. Do you see one of your offices that you have not seen before?

6. How does what you have seen in the five lobes align with the work of Holy Spirit described in Romans 8:14-17?

Spirit Project 6.3 Spirit, Soul and Body Alignment

In this book, we have made efforts to build a bridge for the soul and spirit to engage and communicate (see Figure 6-12) and for the spirit to give life to the soul and body. To better appreciate how God wants to bring salvation to spirit, soul and body, let's explore how we are like God in spirit, soul and body. Knowing this can help us see how glorious we really are and help us synchronize our spirit, soul and body to God.

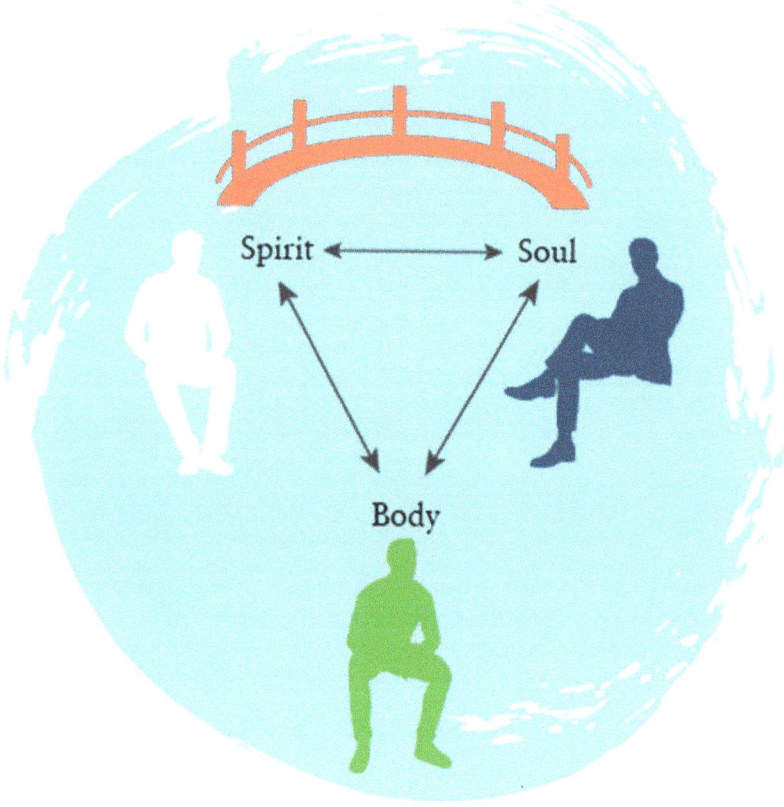

Figure 6-12 The spirit can engage with soul and body to bring life to both

Similar to our having a spirit, soul and body, God has a spirit, soul and body.

God is Spirit, and His worshipers must worship Him in spirit and in truth.
John 4:24

Behold my servant, whom I have chosen; my beloved, in whom my soul is well pleased: I will put my spirit upon him, and he shall shew judgment to the Gentiles.
Matthew 12:18

Now is my soul troubled; and what shall I say? Father, save me from this hour: but for this cause came I unto this hour.
John 12:27

He seeing this before spake of the resurrection of Christ, that his soul was not left in hell, neither his flesh did see corruption.
Acts 2:31

Now ye are the body of Christ, and members in particular.
1 Corinthians 12:27

Ask God these questions:

1. Father God, how is my spirit like You?

2. Father God, how is my soul like Your soul?

3. Holy Spirit, how is my spirit like You?

4. Holy Spirit, how is my soul like Your soul?

5. Jesus, how is my spirit like You?

6. Jesus, how is my soul like Your soul?

7. Jesus, how is my body like Your Body?

"I am in awe of the God who wants us to build with Him"

"For every house is builded by some man; but he that built all things is God." Hebrews 3:4

CHAPTER
07 GROWING IN FULFILLMENT AND JOY

"We are enjoying all Father has given us, living to the fullest."

07

PRINCIPLE

Some have described fulfillment as the sense of knowing they are in the right time and space, with the right team and right resources, doing the things they were designed to do. Glory!

The Principle of Fulfillment

Father God offers to each of us the **principle of fulfillment** so that we can fully live our lives at peace with ourselves, our families and our communities, doing the works God designed for us to do. Many seek happiness. Happiness is good, but we truly are not happy unless we are fulfilled.

The one key to the principle of fulfillment is how well we know God. The better we know God and His ways, the more we love Him, the better our lives work, and the better we can build His Kingdom. Sons are continually moving toward God, but slaves are content with a second-hand relationship with God.

When the people saw the thunder and lightning and heard the trumpet and saw the mountain in smoke, they trembled with fear. They stayed at a distance and said to Moses, "Speak to us yourself and we will listen. But do not have God speak to us or we will die."

Exodus 20:18-19

This decision to step back from God when His people didn't like what they saw and heard was the core decision that kept them out of the promised land and their fulfillment. When we perceive that God has done something we don't like or understand, or life in general disappoints us, we each have a decision to make. Will we step back from Him or toward Him? As we step toward God, grow and build, we experience the passion, joy, fire and purpose rise up as a wellspring of life.

When I first met Father God as a good Father, I still did not know what might happen to that relationship when I messed up. A few weeks later, I sinned mightily against a brother. I could not bring myself to turn to Father God for days after that. Then one day, I decided, no matter what would happen, I needed to see whether God would receive me. I immediately saw a vision. I was a little girl hiding behind my Father's open bedroom door, afraid to go in (see Figure 7-1). As soon as I peaked around the door, I saw my good Father smiling and waiting patiently for me (see Figure 7-2). Father is always ready to receive us, even when we are at our worst.

Figure 7-1 Will Father receive me?

Figure 7-2 Our good Father waits patiently for us to choose Him

The more we know God, the more of God we express in all we do. When a community does this, we create a culture that represents Him well and the community thrives. Can you imagine what it would be like to live in a culture that Father God Himself has created? He creates an atmosphere of love - truly on earth as it is in heaven.

HERE WE GROW

In the seventh stage of growth, we accept full responsibility for our lives and learn to partner with God to follow Him and His ways.

Growth Stage 7.
I Have Made the Passage to Adulthood; I Choose My Own Life

Therefore shall a man leave his father and his mother, and shall cleave unto his wife: and they shall be one flesh.

Genesis 3:24

This Scripture speaks of leaving (departing from) and cleaving (chasing after or pursuing). Leaving and cleaving can apply to a man and his wife, and we can also apply it to leaving all those who have invested in us to cleave to Jesus, becoming one with Him.

Parents, pastors and other leaders must recognize when this growth stage happens in our lives. I recall my friend, Gwynn, telling me about her pastors, who had reparented her, hearing the words from God, "Release Gwynn, full grown." As they prayed over her and released her from their care, she made the passage to adulthood. They released the responsibility to grow her up, but still remained her friends, encouragers and advisors. She accepted full responsibility for her life and no longer felt it necessary to accept their advice or emotional support – for that she turned to God.

This seventh stage of growth to adulthood normally happens in our late teens or early twenties. In this stage we embrace a new culture or build our own. To do that, we must evaluate the culture we are currently experiencing and compare it to the one Jesus offered when He said, "The Kingdom of God is at hand." People of His day embraced it, ran from it, ignored it or viciously attacked it. Each adult must decide for themselves.

Recall that culture is built on core values we all agree to. As children, we seldom think to evaluate the values of our parents or our community. We rarely reject a family value or embrace a new value our family does not accept. But as adults, we must do that. With the seventh stage of growth, we carefully evaluate the set of values we were raised with, reject some and choose others as our own. As we build a new set of values within us, we are stepping into adulthood.

> "The best day of your life and mine is when we take full responsibility for our attitudes. That is the day we really grow up." John C. Maxwell

When this growth stage is not reached:

1. I might still be listening to negative voices in my head from parents, teachers or previous bosses saying things like:

   o You'll never be able to do this.

   o This is the way we treat those who offend us.

   o Our family will always be poor.

   o You're not pretty enough, funny enough or smart enough.

   o When someone makes us angry, we have the right to yell, accuse or swear.

2. I make decisions or choose relationships based on what my family, church, pastors or other leaders believe.

3. I base my legitimacy on fitting into community or accept other legitimacy lies to help me feel valued by God and others.

Take a moment to reflect on how you might have grown as you worked your way through this textbook.

1. In Chapter 1, we discuss how our identity and legitimacy are based on the essence of God in us and the good fruit and good works He has called us to do. What changes have you made about being and doing?

2. In Chapter 2, we learn about our Trinitarian design, redemptive gifts and our spirit. Are you making progress exploring your design and your spirit?

3. In Chapter 3, we discuss many core values. Which values are you embracing as your own? What old values have you rejected?

4. In Chapter 4, we discuss getting along with peers and the obstacles to overcome that might interfere with our thriving in community. Have you chosen or are you building a life-giving community?

5. In Chapter 5, you learn strategies to develop yourself. Are you working on a project to develop a talent or gift you have?

6. In Chapter 6, you learn about building and leading? Are you building yourself? Building those you lead?

7. In this chapter, you learn about alignment and rest. What does it mean to be aligned with God, yourself and others?

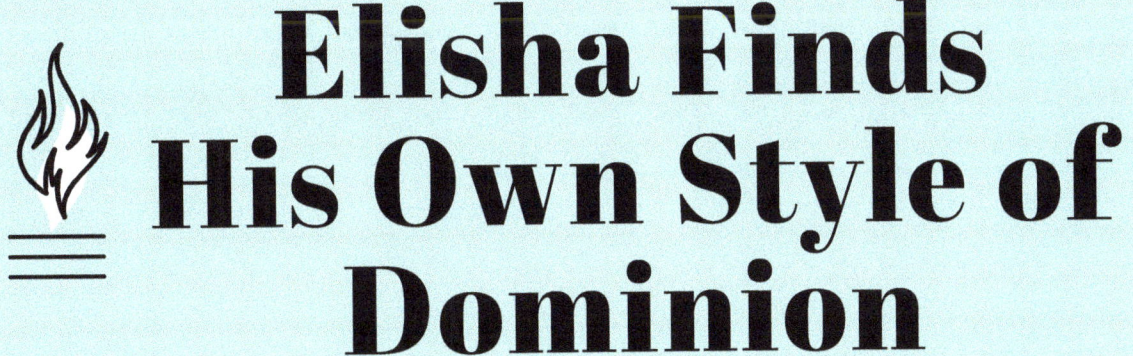

Elisha Finds His Own Style of Dominion

In the first 13 chapters of 2 Kings, we read about Elisha, who appears to have carried the Giver gift and was mentored by Elijah. Both Elijah and Elisha stood in the office of Prophet to Israel. Elijah, with the redemptive gift of Prophet, did not do community well.

When Elisha first stepped into the office of Prophet to Israel, right after the ascension of Elijah, it appears that Elisha was still listening to Elijah's harsh voice still in his head. When a group of boys mocked Elisha for his baldness, he called down a curse on them and they were mauled by two bears.

Later, however, in 2 Kings 6, we read how Elisha was able to resolve an act of war and aggression against Israel without violence. When the Aramean army came, Elisha prayed they be struck with blindness. He then led them right into Israel's capital and instructed the king to treat them kindly, solving the problem without bloodshed and ending the conflict.

> Remember that the office of Prophet is different than the redemptive gift of Prophet. The office of Prophet is a ministry appointment made by God for a specific assignment, and the redemptive gift of Prophet is a personality type we are born with and is part of our spiritual DNA.

For thought and discussion:

1. Who is someone you admire who has mentored or fathered you in some way? List three good qualities in this person you admire.

2. What is one character trait or mindset in this person that you chose not to embrace as your own? Have you seen yourself acting in this way, even though you really don't want to think or act this way?

3. What positive action can you take to change your thoughts or actions?

CONCEPTS

Throughout this book, we have been growing our spirits and souls and exploring our design, life message and birthrights. Let's connect some dots and tie all this together under alignment with God.

Concept 7.1 Alignment of Spirit, Soul, and Body

In Chapter 2, we introduced the idea that we are like a tree made of spirit, soul and body.

> *Blessed is the man that walketh not in the counsel of the ungodly, nor standeth in the way of sinners, nor sitteth in the seat of the scornful.*
>
> *But his delight is in the law of the LORD; and in his law doth he meditate day and night.*
>
> *And he shall be like a tree planted by the rivers of water, that bringeth forth his fruit in his season; his leaf also shall not wither; and whatsoever he doeth shall prosper [succeed].*
>
> Psalm 1:1-3

I have seen myself as a tree of life with the portions of my spirit making up the tree and myself (soul) as blossoms on the tree drawing others into the life I offer. See Figure 7-3.

Figure 7-3 Seven portions of the spirit and soul as a tree of life

As a tree of life, I want to build a place for God and others to rest in abundance, as Jesus described:

Another parable put he forth unto them, saying, The kingdom of heaven is like to a grain of mustard seed, which a man took, and sowed in his field: Which indeed is the least of all seeds: but when it is grown, it is the greatest among herbs, and becometh a tree, so that the birds of the air come and lodge in the branches thereof.

Matthew 13:32-33

For me to be fully whole, my spirit must fully connect to God and function to heal and grow my soul and make my body well and fit. Each portion of my spirit has a job to do.

1. Prophets use design and the awe of God to build vision and solve problems.

2. Servants use authority and freedom to build solid foundations to raise up leaders. Servants free and cleanse the spirit, soul and body.

3. Teachers use truth and responsibility to be life-giving and to heal and reconcile people. Teachers heal and reconcile the spirit, soul and body.

4. Exhorters use their hunger for God and relationship with God to support and model the corporate mission of community, uniting people in a common cause to know God better.

5. Givers use resources to build access to God and community so people can become one with God. Givers resource the spirit, soul and body.

6. Rulers use organic structures to build culture to bring life to community and beyond.

7. Mercys use fulfillment and alignment to build sustainable ecosystems.

Joy is an inside job. Joy abides in my heart when my spirit, soul and body are aligned with Him.

True Legitimacy Comes from Alignment with God

True legitimacy is knowing that we are holy ones, imperishable, citizens of heaven, chosen and sent. We are in the right time and place, with the right people, doing the right works God sent us to do.

1. **Time.** Our times and seasons are holy to God. We have been sent to earth at the right time and are synchronized with His timing.

2. **Land.** We are living and working on land that is holy to God, set apart for God's purposes in us and through us.

3. **Community.** God placed us in holy families of His choosing. We live in holy communities set apart for His Kingdom work.

4. **Birthright.** God has assigned to us holy birthrights. We have come to this time, space and community with appointed assignments for which we are designed and equipped to accomplish for His glory. At the heart of each birthright we experience and know God in one more way that others need.

5. **Offices.** God has ordained that we stand in the offices He created to represent Him with His authority in the spiritual and physical realms. From these offices, we release the heart and will of God on the earth.

To walk with God in this way, we must:

- Be reconciled to our spirit, soul and body.
- Be reconciled to Father, Son and Holy Spirit.
- Be reconciled to our design and our past.
- Be reconciled to our birthrights and offices.

Concept 7.2 Alignment in Community

I was designed by God to bring alignment in community. My passion for this arose when I was standing in a classroom teaching a group of computer science students about an algorithm to solve a system of equations. (If you'd like to know about this mathematical algorithm, email me and I'll send it to you.) Here are the spiritual truths hidden in the algorithm downloaded in that moment:

- Absolute alignment and rest in community this side of eternity is not possible, but we can come close to rest here in the physical realm.

- God uses community to bring us to rest as "iron sharpens iron."

- God chooses people for a holy community based on His wisdom and plans, not ours.

- The more difficult people in community (the ones despised and spoken against) hold the more important keys to our coming to rest. Jesus was despised by many and seen as a difficult person:

> *And Simeon blessed them, and said unto Mary his mother, Behold, this child is set for the fall and rising again of many in Israel; and for a sign which shall be spoken against;*
>
> *Yea, a sword shall pierce through thy own soul also,) that the thoughts of many hearts may be revealed.*
>
> Luke 2:34-35

Over the years since that day, I've watched the cause and effects of these principles. I'm also a student of revival, and I've especially observed how they function when God initiates a revival. Let's look at two scenarios, one negative and one positive. The first example shows what can happen when a revival is sparked, and the principles are violated.

1. God brings a group of people together from various economic, racial and cultural backgrounds.

2. He gives a very special anointing to one person in the group, someone who is not favored or highly valued by the group. When we are not loved or valued, God delights to compensate by putting His glory in this low place:

> *For thus saith the high and lofty One that inhabiteth eternity, whose name is Holy; I dwell in the high and holy place, with him also that is of a contrite and humble spirit, to revive the spirit of the humble, and to revive the heart of the contrite ones.*
>
> Isaiah 57:15

3. This person enjoys the attention of the group for a season because of the special gift from God. Their need to be legitimized by the group diverts them from receiving their true legitimacy from God alone.

4. The person messes up. This failure might be the result of unhealthy admiration from people, not enough personal devotion toward God, character issues or just because they are socially awkward and don't know how to handle the favor they are receiving.

5. Strong leaders might step in to "oversee" this person, trying to fix the problem while protecting the special anointed gift. If the person doesn't yield to the oversight (control), the leaders might drive the person away, or, at the least, shut them down. The special gift may or may not remain in the group for a season. The revival dies before it's fully birthed and firmly established in the group.

Here's what can happen when we embrace God's principles to come to alignment and rest.

1. God brings a group of people together from various economic, racial and cultural backgrounds, and everyone recognizes each person has dignity and value in the group.

2. When someone messes up, regardless of what anointing or spiritual gift they carry, loving and mature people walk with this person to help them overcome social awkwardness, character flaws or brokenness.

3. The entire group benefits from accepting the productive pain of embracing difficult people on a journey to wholeness.

Every one of us, at one time or another, will become the "difficult person" in a group. No matter if we are the newcomer or the senior leader, we all have internal issues to overcome, and eventually our messes show up. By design, God intends that communities don't judge their fallen leaders or difficult newcomers, but rather see these events as opportunities for everyone in the group to grow and come to rest.

Dignity for All of Us

Kristen works as the lead behavioral specialist in a public elementary school. The key to her success is bringing dignity to everyone in the school, including her assistants, the principal, the classroom teachers, and every student. She delights to seek out the most rejected and find a way to bring them dignity. One day she was called in to help Jake, who had disrupted the entire class yet one more time. As she and Jake talked, she realized he was very creative and also painfully aware of the mess he had caused.

She turned his attention to two boys fighting on the other side of the room and asked him how he would solve that problem. Jake explained that one boy was a natural leader and the other boy didn't like being controlled. As Kristen and Jake talked, he made up a game for the entire class to play where leaders could lead without controlling and everyone could have fun.

For thought and discussion:

1. How did Kristen give dignity to Jake by asking him about the two boys fighting?
2. How did Kristen leverage Jake's design to bring him dignity?
3. The classroom teacher wanted Kristen to remove Jake from the room, but Kristen tried to find a way for Jake to be included. If you were Kristen, how could you bring more dignity to the classroom teacher?

Aligned with Those We Admire

People who don't know their legitimacy often try to find it by identifying with admired leaders. This legitimacy by association happened often in Scripture and usually ended badly (an example is the man of God from Judah in I Kings 13). On my own journey to legitimacy, I have fallen into that trap several times. Here are the principles that can help us align righteously with our anointed and magnetic leaders:

- We might think we need this person in our lives to possess our birthright, but this mindset is a form of idolatry. We can trust the Lord Jesus Christ to meet ALL our needs in Him and Him alone. Surrender to Jesus with whom, when and how we walk with others.

- Your leader might be highly anointed and of fine character, but he or she is also human with flaws, faults and weaknesses. "Why do you call me good? No one is good except God alone." We can admire a leader and express gratitude for all they have done for us, but don't put that person on a pedestal. No one other than God belongs there and this is also idolatry.

- Guard your heart against an emotional attachment to a leader. When you find yourself in that place, remember Ecclesiastes 3:2, "a time to plant and a time to uproot." If you are planted too close to this person, in their shade, you cannot have direct access to the sunlight. Uproot yourself and plant yourself again where you have room to grow to maturity, rooted in your own direct relationship with God. You don't want to vicariously live a second-hand relationship with God through this leader.

We can learn from and receive life from our leaders, but we also need to align properly with them as equals before God, each of us secure and legitimate in our own relationship with God.

Many fallen leaders who were put on pedestals by their followers found themselves stoned as soon as they fell off it. From the pedestal to the pit! So not right!

God has no grandchildren or second born. In Christ, Father God relates to us all as His firstborn. At a deeply felt level, we must each know we are His favorite!

Concept 7.3 Becoming a Resting Place for God

The seventh stage of growth equates to the Mercy gift and the seventh day of creation, where God rested. What does it look like for God to rest with us and in us?

A Place to Lay His Head

A worship event in Atlanta, GA, became life altering for me when I asked Holy Spirit if He would take me into the heavenlies so I could worship from heaven to earth. I heard Him say, "It's more exciting here in the earth!" As I was pondering that thought, Jesus rode in on His white horse and asked, "Want to come for a ride?" In a moment, we were riding across the sky into China. The horse landed in the lobby of an institution. We left the horse in the lobby and walked down a hallway into a large room filled with baby cribs. Jesus walked up to one bed and laid His hand on a baby and whispered quietly, "She will be with Me in a few days." I knew then she was very sick and would die soon.

Then He said, "I want to show you why I come here often." He took me into a cleaning closet where a woman sat on the floor against the wall praying. He sat on the floor beside her and lay His head on her chest. It was clear that He was drinking deeply from the love given to Him by this woman. Then He stood up and said, "I want you to tell her story around the world." Immediately, I was back in the worship center in Atlanta.

My head was spinning with what had just happened! Never had I ever thought Jesus needed love from us. And was it even possible He has mothers on the earth? He immediately gave me two Scriptures to quiet my fears and begin the confirmation of these ideas.

Jesus replied, "Foxes have dens and birds of the air have nests, but the Son of Man has no place to lay His head."

Matthew 8:20

But Jesus replied, "Who is My mother, and who are My brothers?" Pointing to His disciples, He said, "Here are My mother and My brothers. For whoever does the will of My Father in heaven is My brother and sister and mother."

Matthew 12:48–50

Then later, I realized another Scripture that describes what this woman was doing for Jesus:

The King will reply, "Truly I tell you, whatever you did for one of the least of these brothers and sisters of mine, you did for me."

Matthew 25:40

In the following Scriptures, Jesus said He is providing a place for us to rest and asks that you and I also provide Him and His Father a place to rest.

My Father's house has many rooms [permanent abode]; if that were not so, would I have told you that I am going there to prepare a place for you?

John 14:2

Jesus replied, "Anyone who loves me will obey my teaching. My Father will love them, and we will come to them and make our home [permanent abode] with them.

John 14:23

For thought and discussion:

1. I told the story to a church in Thailand. The translator told me later that another woman from the United States had told the very same story, and Jesus had initially given her the very same two verses, instructing her to tell the story over the world. Why is it so important that God allowed me to know He had sent two people to tell the story of the woman in China?

2. Why is it reasonable to assume the Chinese cleaning lady held these babies in her arms and loved on them?

3. In providing a place for these babies to rest in her arms, how was she providing a place for God to abide with her?

4. Who do you know who might be classified as "one of the least" that you can love? Sometimes people who see themselves as important and in control are actually among the "least of these." At other times, it's a despised one who has no idea how to be a true loving friend.

5. In John 14, the same Greek word is translated rooms in verse 2 and home in verse 23, and means a permanent abiding place. In the last chapter, you learned how you can offer your heart as a permanent abiding place for Father, Jesus and Holy Spirit. Do you think the Scriptures in John 14 correlate to God dwelling in our hearts? Why or why not?

6. The seventh stage of fathering is Mercy fathering where a father demonstrates to a son his own coming to rest toward his son. How might a father do this in practical ways? How does Father God do this for us?

Becoming His Inheritance

In Exodus 32-34, the Israelites had worshipped the golden calf and Moses tried to save them from God's judgement. After he failed to save them, he told God that he wanted to know God better. God gave Moses a new glimpse of His goodness.

And the LORD descended in a cloud, stood with him there, and proclaimed His name, the LORD. Then the LORD passed in front of Moses and called out:

"The LORD, the LORD God, is compassionate and gracious, slow to anger, abounding in loving devotion and faithfulness, maintaining loving devotion to a thousand generations, forgiving iniquity, transgression, and sin. Yet He will by no means leave the guilty unpunished; He will visit the iniquity of the fathers on their children and grandchildren to the third and fourth generations."

Moses immediately bowed down to the ground and worshiped. "O Lord," he said, "if I have indeed found favor in Your sight, my Lord, please go with us. Although this is a stiff-necked people, forgive our iniquity and sin, and take us as Your inheritance."

Exodus 34:5-9

We can read how God saw inheritance in the book of Joshua. Collecting several verses into one statement, we see an inheritance is an undisturbed place of rest, free from our enemies, where we can raise our young and our cattle can roam free.

For thought and discussion:

1. Dream big on this one. In your own life, what would it look like for God to rest in you?

2. I once heard of a support group that met regularly. A seer happened to walk by the building while the group was meeting and saw many demons hanging out around the building. Later, she asked the leader of the group why all the demons around the building. The leader told her it was probably because she did not allow demons who followed members of the group to come into the building. How do you think it would feel to walk into a home where no enemies of God are allowed to enter?

07

3. What are some things you can do so that God can rest, free from His enemies, in your home and family?

4. Describe what your home and family might look like when you position it to be a place where God is free to raise His children there.

5. The expression of cattle roaming freely is a picture of freedom and prosperity in a big way. What might it look like in your life for God to be able to prosper in His own big way?

Concept 7.4 Find a New Way to Connect with and Worship God

Remember from Chapter 5 that the seventh righteous head of Levithan can help us possess our birthrights when we find new ways to connect with God and worship Him. Figure 7-4 shows a way to look at birthright as a merging of intimacy with God that produces much fruit and building His Kingdom as a place for others to rest.

Consider these components shown in the figure:

- People know us by our fruit. The fruit of the Spirit is foremost in all we are and do.

- We are like a tree planted by the waters that gives fruit in its season.

- As Jesus spoke, we are like trees that provide a place for birds and others to rest in our branches.

- All that we build with Him is progressive and valuable, from the most humble cottage to a tower of strength and refuge.

- The Kingdom we build is life giving to many who can find rest, protection and comfort.

- We worship God in intimacy with Him and others, giving dignity, worth and victory to all who come to us.

Figure 7-4 The fruit of the Spirit can lead us to merging intimacy with God and building His Kingdom from the inside out

SOLVING PROBLEMS

Recall that we solve problems by collecting data, finding patterns in the data, identifying principles in the patterns and using these principles to solve similar problems.

Problem 7.1 Unable to Rest

Sally is a high achiever. She's always worked hard at home, in school and in her career. Her passion is to build God's Kingdom, and she leaves no stone unturned to make that happen. Sally grew up in a highly abusive home where women and girls were treated as less than men and boys. The men in the family were served by the women, and the men made all decisions. Sally knows she needs to learn to rest and have more fun in life. She has come to you for advice.

Do the following:

1. List three principles that involve the fractals of two that could apply to Sally's inability to rest.

2. Which stages of growth do you think Sally might still need to mature in? Explain your answer.

3. What upside-down and backward thinking might Sally believe about herself?

4. How would you advise Sally to help her find more rest and fun in life? List 3 to 5 principles she might begin to apply in her life.

Problem 7.2 Managing Conflicts

I lived my life trying to avoid or resolve conflicts until a mentor pointed out to me that Jesus often initiated conflicts. I read through one of the Gospels and was amazed the many times I read where Jesus purposefully started a conflict. Follow these steps to learn what Jesus wanted from conflicts and how He managed them.

Do the following:

1. Read through one of the four Gospels, making a list of each time Jesus was in a conflict. List the reference, who was involved, the conflict and the outcome of the conflict.

2. Analyze the data, looking for patterns. Here are some questions to use to uncover some possible patterns.

   a. What was the purpose of the conflict? Was Jesus trying to build relationship or did He have a different objective?

   b. Was the conflict with the religious leaders, the crowds, His disciples or another group?

   c. Did He share information or withhold information? To whom did He consistently give information?

   d. What was the outcome of the conflict?

3. List as many principles as you can find in your list regarding conflict management. For example, one principle is that conflicts can be helpful for growth and transformation.

4. Are there any situations in your life where you can apply these principles?

Problem 7.3. Driven from Community

Think of a situation where you or another were driven from a social community, such as a church group, club or family. Based on the community alignment model presented in the chapter, answer these questions.

Answer the following questions:

1. What were the events that led to the person leaving the community?

2. What productive pain could have been embraced that might have kept the community together?

3. Was it beneficial for the one who left the community? Did it do harm to this person?

4. Was it beneficial for the community for the person to leave? Did it do harm to the community?

5. What could have been done differently to improve the outcome?

6. How did poor communication keep healthy reconciliation from happening? What could have been done to improve communication?

7. What are some principles that were applied or violated in this situation?

GROWTH PROJECT

These projects are designed to help us grow and help us grow those we lead.

Growth Project 7.1 Reconcile to Ourselves and God

The word *reconcile* means to coexist consistently and in harmony with another. If we are not reconciled, it means we are incompatible or opposed to the other. God said He made a covenant of life and peace with Levi so that they could walk together.

> *My covenant was with him of life and peace; and I gave them to him for the fear wherewith he feared me, and was afraid before my name.*
>
> *The law of truth was in his mouth, and iniquity was not found in his lips: he walked with me in peace and equity, and did turn many away from iniquity.*
>
> John 10:27-28

When we make covenant with someone, we become one with them. God and Levi walked in peace and equity. They were one and they walked reconciled and in alignment. Use the following directions to gain an understanding of your level of reconciliation with God.

Do the following:

1. Consider how you might not be reconciled to God. Here are some questions that might start the conversation with God.

   a. God, what truth do you want me to know about my connection with You?

   b. God, what truth do you want me to know about my walk with You?

2. For each Member of the Trinity, ask questions to grow in walking with the Father, Son and Holy Spirit.

   a. Father, is there any lie I have believed about You? What is the truth about that lie?

   b. Jesus, is there any lie I have believed about You? What is the truth about that lie?

   c. Holy Spirit, is there any lie I have believed about You? What is the truth about that lie?

3. As you mediate on each answer, ask God how you can reconcile with Him and better walk as one with Him.

Think of reconciling to ourselves as making peace with and becoming one with ourselves.

Consider these questions:

1. Is there any way you have rejected your spirit leading you? If so, how can you reconcile to your spirit?

2. Is there any way you resent or disrespect your soul, your mind or your heart? If so, how can you reconcile with each area?

3. Is there any way you have rejected or disrespected your body? How can you reconcile that inequity?

4. Is there anything in your design you disrespect? How can you reconcile to your design?

5. Is there any way you have despised your past? How can you celebrate your past and reconcile to it?

6. Is there any way you have disrespected your birthright? How can you reconcile?

Growth Project 7.2
Connecting Your Name, Your Identity and Your Birthright

For most of us, it takes years to grow into our legitimacy, our identity and our birthrights. God leads us through this growth and one way He does that is calling us out by our names.

The gatekeeper opens the gate for him, and the sheep listen to his voice.

He calls his own sheep by name and leads them out.

John 10:3

When God gives us a name, He offers the grace to grow into that name.

07

Do the following:

1. Do you know the meanings of your given name and last name? Based on these meanings, can you craft together a name God has given you? For me, my name is Norma Jean Andrews. My parents had no idea it means "a courageous model of God's love and grace," but Father God knew that.

2. What personal and private name has God called you? Sometimes that's a mystery to solve. Jamie Winship tells the story of one lady, whom God often calls, "My criminal." She didn't understand why until He led her into a powerful ministry to inmates in a maximum-security prison. God often calls me, "My child." At first, I thought He was reminding me that I needed to grow up. But now I see He wants me to see myself as His offspring and help others see themselves the same way - divine beings with the DNA of God in our blood.

3. The names that God has given you can help you see your unique identity built on both who you are and what God-size problem He has called you to solve. As best you know now, state your unique name, identity and birthright, as one coming from God to represent Him on the earth, as only you can.

We all expect to refine our understanding of our identity and birthright many times. And often God will give us a new name as He transitions us into our birthrights.

Growth Project 7.3 Redemptive Gifts of Business

This book is not intended as a tell-all comprehensive work to grow and build, but rather a launching pad for each of us to prepare ourselves to possess our birthright. Look at the last two rows in The Big Picture table at the beginning of this book. Perhaps in these rows you can find more clues about your birthright.

When someone has a vision for a business, that business will have imprinted on it the DNA of the visionary, including the redemptive gift of the visionary. As you read through the following business descriptions, look for clues where you might fit.

- **Prophet business.** A Prophet visionary will envision a business that offers new ideas and paradigms for their customers and staff. Prophet businesses tend to be on the cutting edge with their products and services.

- **Servant business.** A Servant visionary focuses on raising up leaders and invests much in the training and education of its leaders.

- **Teacher business.** A Teacher visionary focuses on excellence and strives to get all the details right. A Teacher business does not stop short until completion and perfection is attained.

- **Exhorter business.** An Exhorter visionary is passionate about their vision, and an Exhorter business can rock the world with creative culture-changing ideas.

- **Giver business.** A Giver visionary and business provides access. Think of McDonalds. This was the first business to offer drive-through services, which allowed for easy access to their food.

- **Ruler business.** A Ruler visionary and business build structures and provide a high level of mothering and fathering.

- **Mercy business.** A Mercy visionary will build a business on a powerful ecosystem where the atmosphere created draws in their customers. Think Starbucks.

To learn more about the redemptive gifts of businesses, listen to the series of albums "Social DNA of Business" by Arthur at *theSLG.com*.

Growth Project 7.4
The Seven Mountains of Culture

God gave to Bill Bright of Campus Crusade and Loren Cunningham of Youth with a Mission the concepts of the "seven mountains of culture." He explained to them that this was a strategy to disciple a nation. He said if the Kingdom of God could prevail in each of these seven areas of a culture, an entire nation could be discipled. The seven mountains of culture are: media, religion, education, family, celebration, government and economy, as shown in the last row of The Big Picture table at the beginning of this book.

Can you see how each of these seven mountains relates to the seven redemptive gifts? Do you agree or disagree with the order that I have them arranged in the table? Explain your answer.

SPIRIT PROJECT

This spirit projects are designed to help develop your relationship with your spirit and the spirit world.

Spirit Project 7.1 Learn from Your Spirit

Our spirits have much to give us and it's wonderful when we have a close enough relationship with our spirits so that we can learn from them.

Follow these general guidelines to learn from your spirit:

1. Acknowledge to God and your spirit that you want to learn from your spirit. Ask Holy Spirit and your spirit to teach you what you need to know.

2. When you're learning from someone, you look to them for direction, wisdom and guidance. Get in the habit of asking your spirit for help whenever you make a decision, try to solve a problem, build, create, or do anything else. You are unlikely to get direction or wisdom from your spirit if you don't ask.

I'm not suggesting that you choose a relationship with your human spirit over a relationship with God. Your soul needs to know God as much as your spirit does.

3. When you are doing anything from reading your Bible to washing dishes, ask your spirit to come to the front and help. Ask which portion of the spirit is leading and purposefully yield to him or her. Observe how you are thinking, feeling and acting to learn more about how your spirit follows the Trinity. For example, the Giver portion of my spirit follows Holy Spirit by flowing with His wind.

4. Each night just before you go to sleep, talk with your spirit. Ask your spirit to show you how they saw the day go and what you need to see or learn from the day. What is a problem you need help with? Ask your spirit to partner with the Trinity to work on that problem while you sleep.

5. First thing when you wake up turn to your spirit. Ask your spirit what happened during the night. Personally, when I am first waking up in that in-between-awake-and-asleep state, my spirit often shows me what happened during the night, and I come fully awake with excitement and joy.

6. Ask people you trust to have spirit-to-spirit conversations with you. I love doing that with people who have well-developed spirits and spirit worlds. It's so much fun and rewarding!

7. Work with the spirits of children who trust you to do that. I love talking with the spirits of my grandchildren. One day, Cari and I were walking near a creek. She observed, "This water is so clear, just like spirit water."

I said, "Cari, have you seen spirit water?"

She said, "Yes, it's clear and beautiful. My spirit cleans it every day."

That's the first time I had ever heard anyone say their spirits had taken on the responsibility of daily maintaining their river of life. Children have such a natural and casual way of relating to the spirit world. We adults can learn much from them.

Spirit Project 7.2
Where and How Does My Spirit Best Connect with My Soul?

Your spirit has a mind, will and emotions as does your soul. If this is surprising to you, check out these verses:

Watch and pray that you may not enter into temptation. The spirit indeed is willing, but the flesh is weak.

Matthew 26:41

And he sighed deeply in his spirit, and saith, Why doth this generation seek after a sign? verily I say unto you, There shall no sign be given unto this generation.

Mark 8:12

And my spirit hath rejoiced in God my Saviour.

Luke 1:47

For what man knoweth the things of a man, save the spirit of man which is in him? even so the things of God knoweth no man, but the Spirit of God.

1 Corinthians 2:11

The natural person does not accept the things of the Spirit of God, for they are folly to him, and he is not able to understand them because they are spiritually discerned.

1 Corinthians 2:14

For who has understood the mind of the Lord so as to instruct him? But we have the mind of Christ.

1 Corinthians 2:16

Each portion of your spirit also has his or her own design, birthright, offices and discernment. Our spirits are sensitive to both the spiritual and physical realms and connect best to our souls according to their design.

I have a granddaughter who connects to her spirit through her feet. She loves to run. It was difficult for me to connect with her spirit until I realized it had to happen through her feet. I can communicate well with her spirit when we're walking together or we're sitting on the sofa and I'm rubbing her feet. Sitting in the car driving doesn't work so well. When she wants to have a spirit-to-spirit talk with me, she asks can just the two of us walk around the block.

She honors her feet like no child I've seen. When she was dressing for her 10th birthday party, she really didn't care what she wore except she absolutely had to have the right shoes. Shoes and feet are highly esteemed in her mind.

I connect to my spirit best through my left shoulder. When I'm talking with my spirit, I happen to notice my right hand is resting on my left shoulder. If you ever see me put my right hand there, know my spirit and I are probably in conversation!

To see lists of redemptive gifts of land, search for Arthur's free articles at theSLG.com on "Redemptive Gifts of Some States" and "Redemptive Gifts of Some Nations."

To learn more about the redemptive gifts of cities, listen to Arthur's free audio album "Redemptive Gifts of Cities" at *theSLG.com.*

To discover more about your own spirit, follow these activities:

1. God created all land to hold one of the redemptive gifts. I connect well with God and my spirit when I'm on Prophet land. Find out the redemptive gifts of land in your area and observe which land and gift best resonates with your spirit.

2. Variations of motion, beauty, nature, water, fragrance, silence, instrumental music, children laughing and other aspects of creation affect our spirits positively or negatively.

3. Personally, my spirit and I connect best when in total silence, with birds singing, or to the sound of a bubbling brook or waterfall. I especially enjoy worshipping with my spirit leading when walking along the beach to the sound of ocean waves and sea gulls calling.

Explore connecting to your spirit in all kinds of environments and experiences to find out what works best for you and your spirit. Ask your spirit to tell you where he or she would like to be or have you do to better connect.

Explore what part of your body your spirit best connects to. It might be your feet, your left shoulder, your hair, your heart or some other part of your body. I know a man who connects through his hair. When I see him run his fingers through his hair, I suspect his spirit has his attention.

Spirit Project 7.3 Ask Your Spirit for a Vision

When I was trying to better connect to and relate to my spirit, I asked my spirit for help. My Exhorter portion showed me the vision in Figure 7-5. I saw myself as the finial on the hood of a magnificent luxury car.

Think of the crowning finial, called the Spirit of Ecstasy, on the hood of a Rolls-Royce. We identify a Rolls by this finial. The finial is part of the car and helps identify and represent the car, but it's not the power or effectiveness of the car.

In a similar way, you can ask your spirit these questions to discover more.

Do the following:

1. Ask your spirit for a picture of how you, as soul, relate to your spirit. You might see some type of vehicle or a totally different analogy, such as an animal or an ecosystem, to explain the spirit and soul connection.

2. Ask your spirit questions to unpack this vision. Consider your spirit might want to teach you many things through the analogy.

Figure 7-5 My soul felt like the finial on a luxury car

For example, I saw one portion of my spirit as the engine of the car, another in the driver's seat and so forth. Just as Jesus served and empowered those He led, I saw my spirit leading me by being the effective, directing force under me.

When I searched further, I saw my Exhorter gift like a luxury car that draws attention but is dependent on other gifts for the heavy lifting, similar to a tractor trailer truck or an earth-moving vehicle in the spirit. I saw the Exhorter loves to gather together other gifts and create a platform for these gifts to build the Kingdom. Lots of insight emerged when I first saw this vision. I'm still pondering.

Spirit Project 7.4
Restore the Language of the Spirit in Community

We end the book with the following story. I hope it challenges us all to restore the leadership and language of the spirit back into our Christ-centered communities.

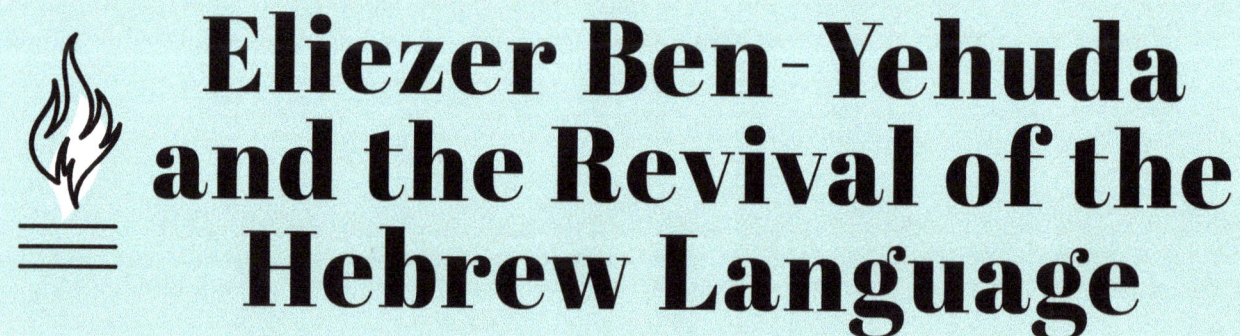

Eliezer Ben-Yehuda and the Revival of the Hebrew Language

Eliezer Ben-Yehuda, born in 1858 in Lithuania, mastered Hebrew as part of his Jewish upbringing. At that time, Hebrew was a written language but not spoken. Ben-Yehuda birthed a dream of the Jewish people returning to Palestine and reviving their language, literature and culture.

At first, his dream was nothing but a pretty little cloud. Then he had his first conversation in Hebrew with a Jewish friend in a café in Paris. The pretty little cloud grew tiny little feet. He decided his next steps would be to move to Palestine and promote Hebrew as the spoken language in every Jewish home.

When he and his wife Deborah first arrived in Jaffa, he experienced his first Hebrew conversations on his homeland with a Jewish moneychanger and a Jewish innkeeper. Then he and his wife Deborah decided to speak only Hebrew in their home so that their child, Ben-Zion Ben-Yehuda, born in 1882, would be the first child in modern history to speak only Hebrew.

And so his dream of restoring Hebrew as the native spoken language in the Hebrew culture became a reality.

For thought and discussion:

1. Children learn language naturally, and our spirits use a different language than our souls. When we train our children to communicate with their spirits when they are young, they grow up with a native spirit language that we as adults will never have. I am passionate about teaching our children to communicate with their spirits. Why is this important to bring the culture of the Kingdom to earth?

2. My passion is for the entire Body of Christ to begin working with their human spirits and for this to become mainstream in every home. What are some next steps you can take to teach yourself and your children the language and ways of the spirit?

by JEAN ANDREWS, PhD